To the God who makes Himself known

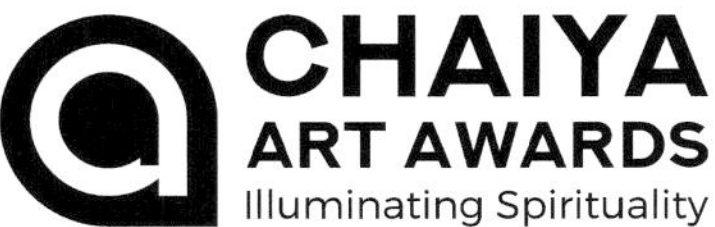

First published in Great Britain in 2023

Instant Apostle,
104A The Drive
Rickmansworth
Herts
WD3 4DU

Other books by the author:
Time to Live: The Beginner's Guide to Saying Goodbye
Where Is God in Our 21st Century World?
God Is...

British Library Cataloguing-in-Publication Data

A catalogue record for this book is available from the British Library.

This book and all other Instant Apostle books are available from Instant Apostle:
www.instantapostle.com
E-mail: info@instantapostle.com

Chaiya Art Awards
www.chaiyaartawards.co.uk
E-mail: info@chaiyaartawards.co.uk
Registered charity: Chaiya Trust 1176237.

ISBN 978-1-912726-70-7
Printed in Great Britain

Awe + Wonder

Ann Clifford

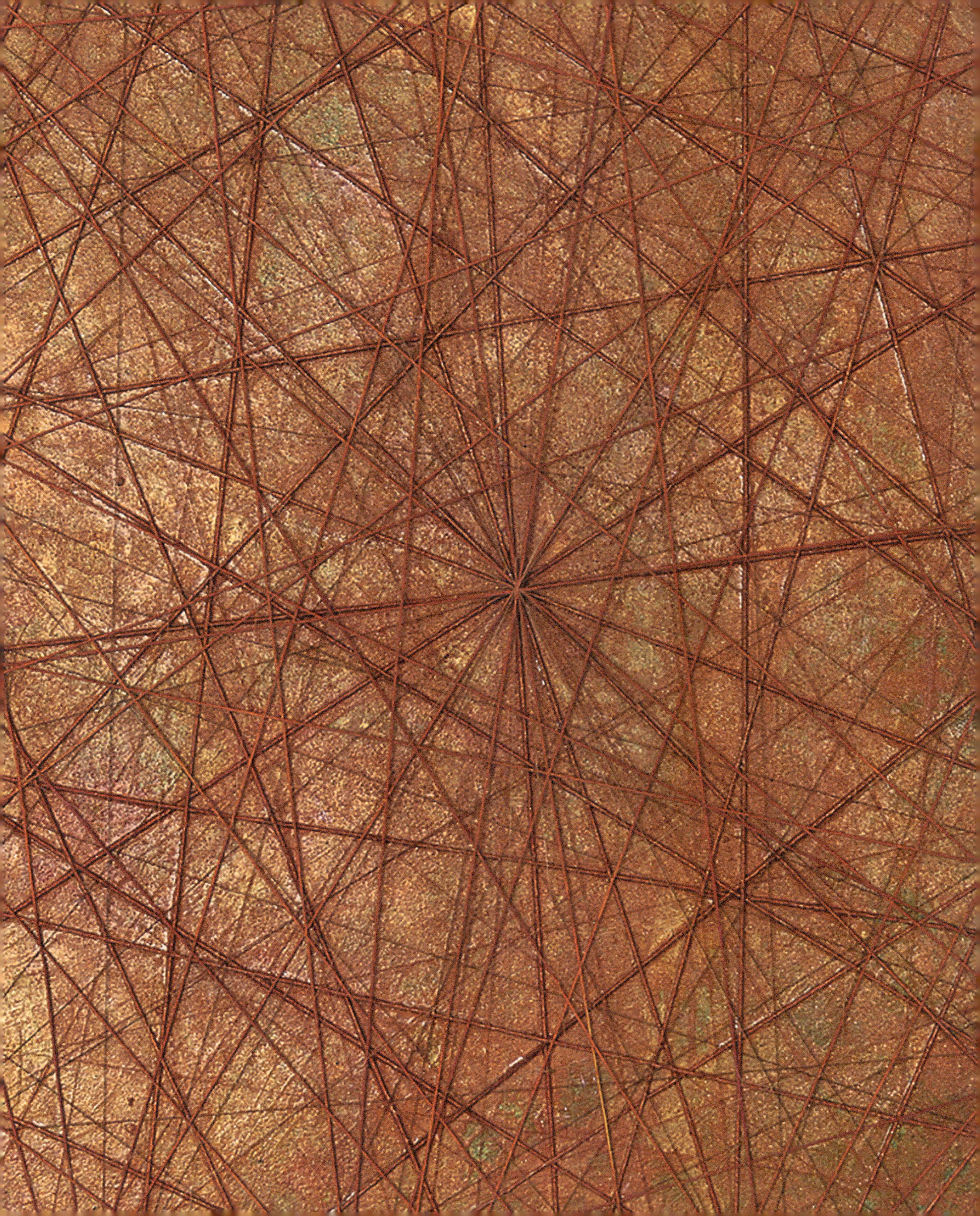

contents

« **Detail** – See page 63

‘In a world of turmoil, art matters more than ever.

Art can bring about political action, even social revolution, art reminds us of the things that really matter.

It lifts our eyes to eternity and shows us the importance of the here and now.’

JAMES KA SMITH[1]

foreword

WE ARE PRIVILEGED to present this collection of *Awe+Wonder* inspired creativity. Since our last awards, exhibition and book in 2021 (*God Is...*), we continue to deal with the impact of the Covid-19 pandemic. Add to this the death of Queen Elizabeth II (one of the longest-reigning monarchs in history), our support of Ukraine in its war with Russia, the refugee crisis, and the fuel poverty affecting most of us, it is easy to look at the circumstances in the UK and the world through negative filters.

The work of the short-listed artists displayed mined their expression of *Awe+Wonder* from many different areas: creation and the natural world; relationships; life's pain and suffering; human ingenuity and faith and spirituality.

Whatever our life experience, my prayer is that the wonderful creativity of these artists, from diverse backgrounds, alongside the illuminating prose, poems and quotes, will uplift, inspire, provoke thought and encourage us as we navigate our life's journey.

May you be blessed as this multifaceted expression of *Awe+Wonder* reveals the extraordinary breadth of the theme and brings fresh encouragement and hope.

CHAIYA TRUST

Katrina Moss, Founder, Chaiya Art Awards

« **Detail** – See page 111

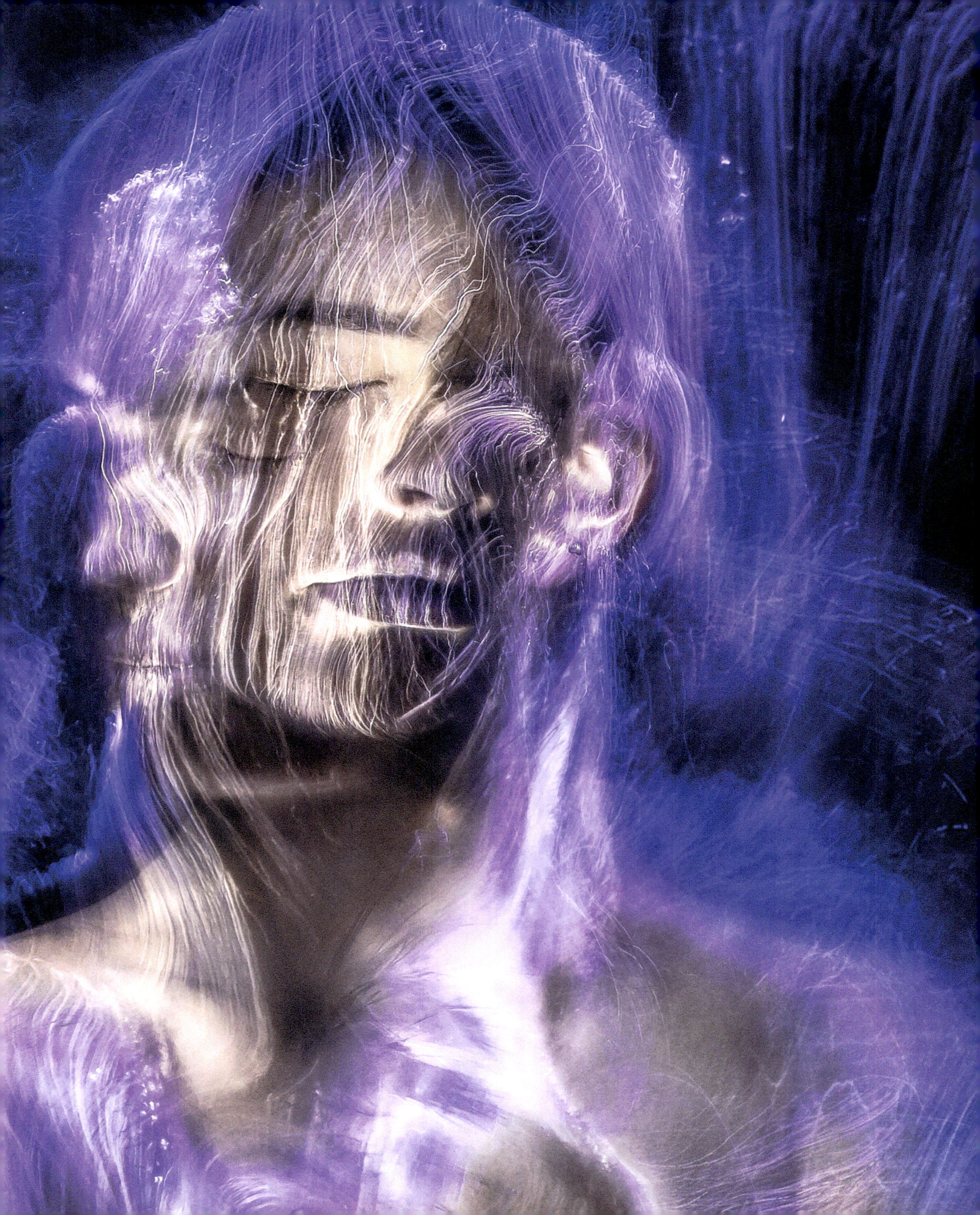

wonder's kiss

Let turmoil cease –
Stand in view-filled
space –
Alone.

Allow muscles to gentle,
And breathe.

When the mind
tumbles
and grumbles
with things undone

Press Stop.

When time
nips at the ankles –
brays its passage,
demands its entrance,
remember childhood's
deaf ears.

For wonder waits to
Kiss your space
with tenderness.

« **Detail** – See page 79
Following spread: Detail – See page 52

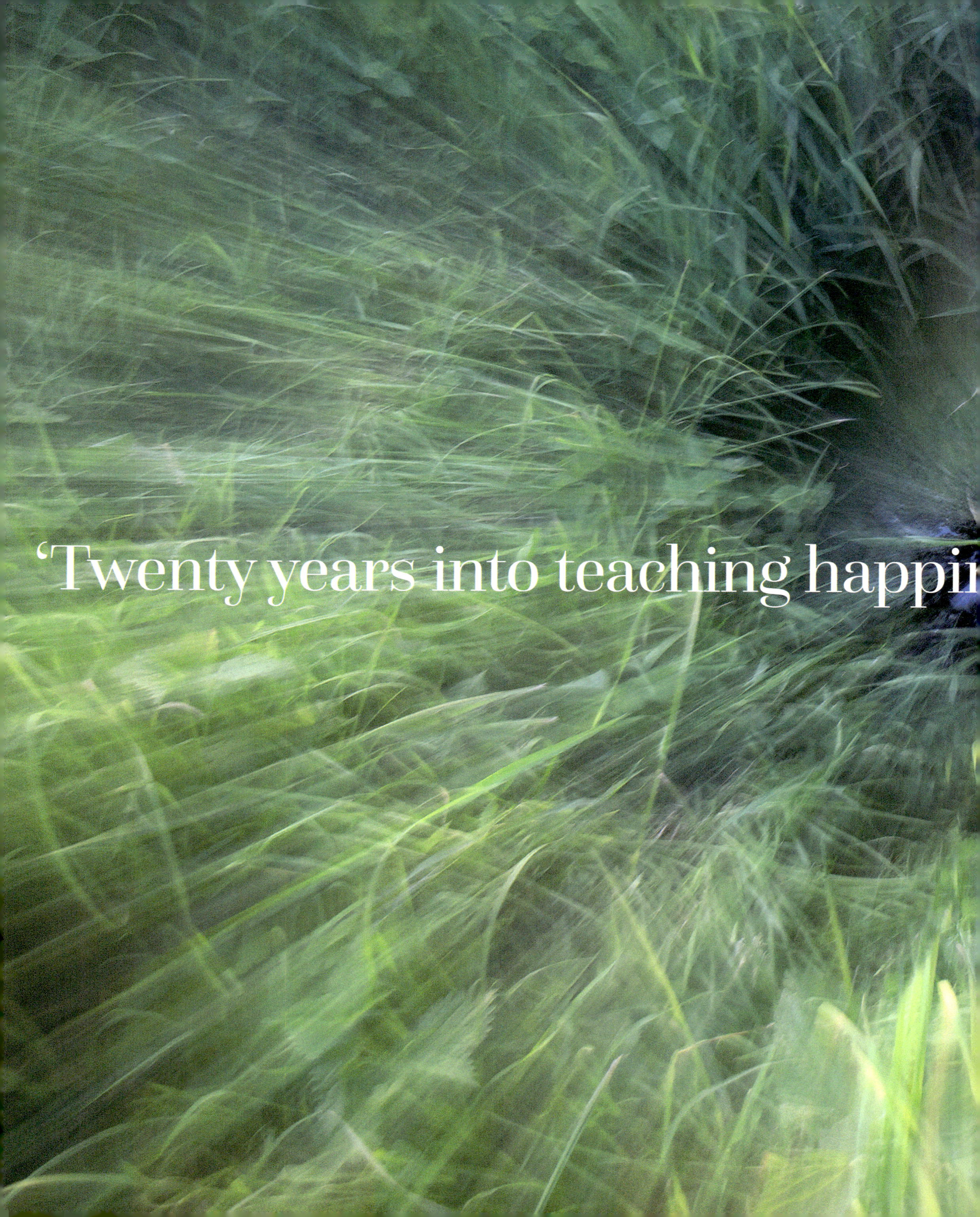
‘Twenty years into teaching happi

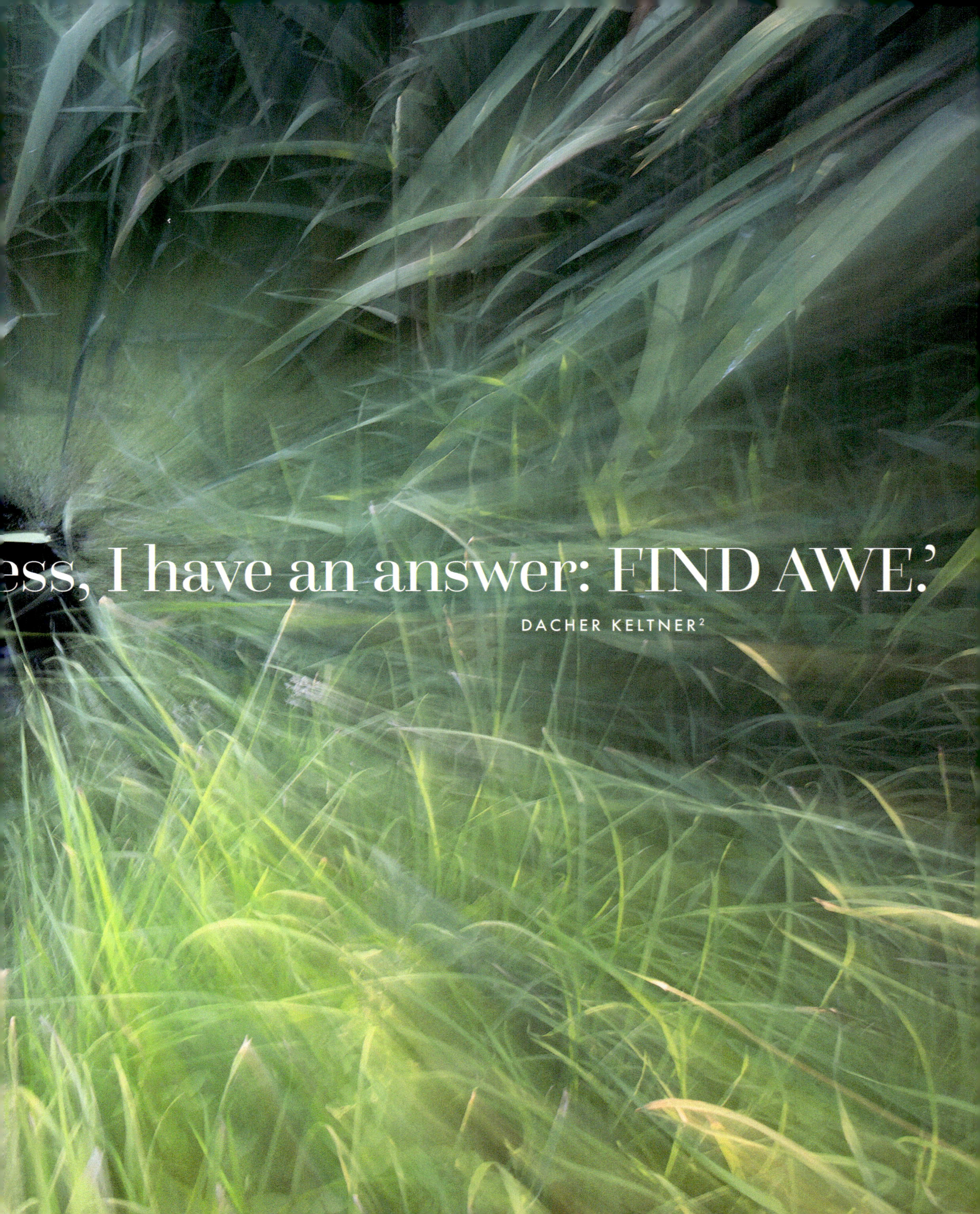
ess, I have an answer: FIND AWE.'
DACHER KELTNER[2]

introduction

An invitation to silence to create space

Space is where miracles happen

'Soon silence will have passed into legend.

Man has turned his back on silence.

Day after day, he invents machines and devices that increase noise and distract humanity from the essence of life, contemplation, meditation.'

JEAN ARP[3]

THERE IS NOISE for every moment of our lives. The more technology, the less silent the world. The TV in the background for company; music in our ear – something to suit our mood, to remove us from a present we don't want to engage with; the song from a phone never on silent, ready for someone to make contact, to press the 'like' button. The instant gratification of the dopamine hit to feel good, to feel of worth, to feel present in this world. There is nothing instant in silence, so we ignore its existence. If we encounter it, we want to break it.

Years ago, visiting a retreat centre with a friend, it shocked us to discover mealtimes were silent. Diners were permitted to bring a book to read, but if we spoke, it meant instant ejection.

She and I sat across from each other in what was, for us, an expression of madness. We could not look at each other because when we did, bubbles of laughter sprang into our mouths. It took all our self-control to contain ourselves. Dutifully, we looked at our books and read not a word. I remember no mouthful of that meal, but I do remember, when released, our swift exit, which turned into a run for our room. Shutting the door, we flung ourselves on our beds, our bodies heaving with uncontrolled hilarity.

The effect of silence.

We couldn't handle it.

What did we fail to understand?

Do we live in a state of perpetual fight or flight, with raised heart rate and elevated blood pressure terrified by silence? How will our bodies react if we remove the stress of noise, moving from a constant state of alertness to rest?

If we allow silence into our space, we can expect in our enforced relaxation a sense of battle to de-clutter our mind and heart. Working purposefully on stilling the constant bombardment of outside noise and stimuli beckons the revealing space inhabited by silence, which allows reflection and magical possibility.

Are there decisions to be made? Letting go of the constant churning of our minds allows a thoughtfulness which can bring meaningful revelation. Eschewing the barrage of outside information grants fresh insights of self-awareness. As our minds calm, we can reach for a peaceful quietude and embrace fresh creative thinking. It can turn our existence from living reactively into thought-through response. It allows questions to emerge. Taking time to think before speaking or acting permits assessment of potential outcomes and summons wisdom.

Silence is a place that is pregnant with purpose. It is a place of unreconstructed creativity. The more it is experienced, the vaster it grows. A place of exploration, delight, mystery and spirituality.

What if miracles wait to event in our lives but our 'silence avoidance' halts their passage?

There is a sensation called Autonomic Sensory Meridian Response (ASMR) which is a pleasurable tingling sensation that starts all the way up on our scalp, creeps down our neck and then through the backbone. As if someone gently traced a finger down our spine inducing a feeling of euphoria and release of anxiety. One thing that can induce it is whispering, another silence.

Sit with this book and allow the silence to fall. Journey with the artists, allowing their creativity to enliven and enrich. Some of their works will resonate more than others. May the 'still small voice'[4] of God whisper tenderly and distinctly, dear reader, as you enjoy this book, beckon the silence and allow a growing sense of awe to goosebump your body.

'Silence is not the absence of something, but the presence of everything.'

GORDON HEMPTON[5]

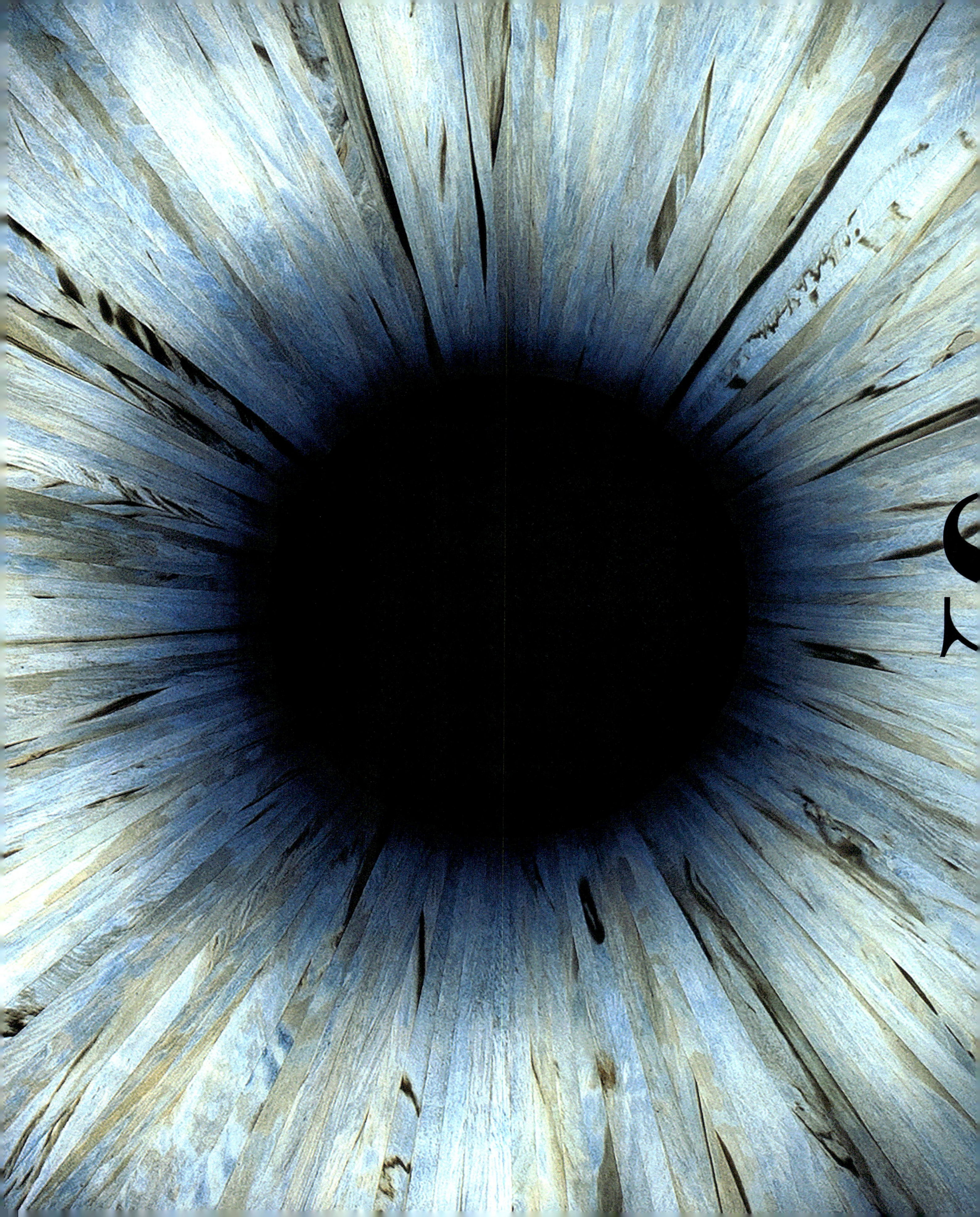

i see you

WATER-WALKERS

For a while a mother
held her newborn,
but she left her
crying so long
the babe forgot
she was loved.

For a while her father
held her
but, distracted,
he opened his hands
and babe fell apart,
fell through.

Older, still falling,
she looked at the water –
out-of-her-depth
water.

Could she, would she...
float or
swim
or drown?

How long, she thought, before
I sink,
unseen
forever?

The Water-walker beckoned,
To her?
Again, He summoned.
His hand gestured
for her to step
to Him.

What if –
once,
she water-walked?

She stretched out and
...stood

luminous peace –
awash with
effervescent awe –
soothed,
expanded
and renewed
her soul.

« **Detail** — See page 63

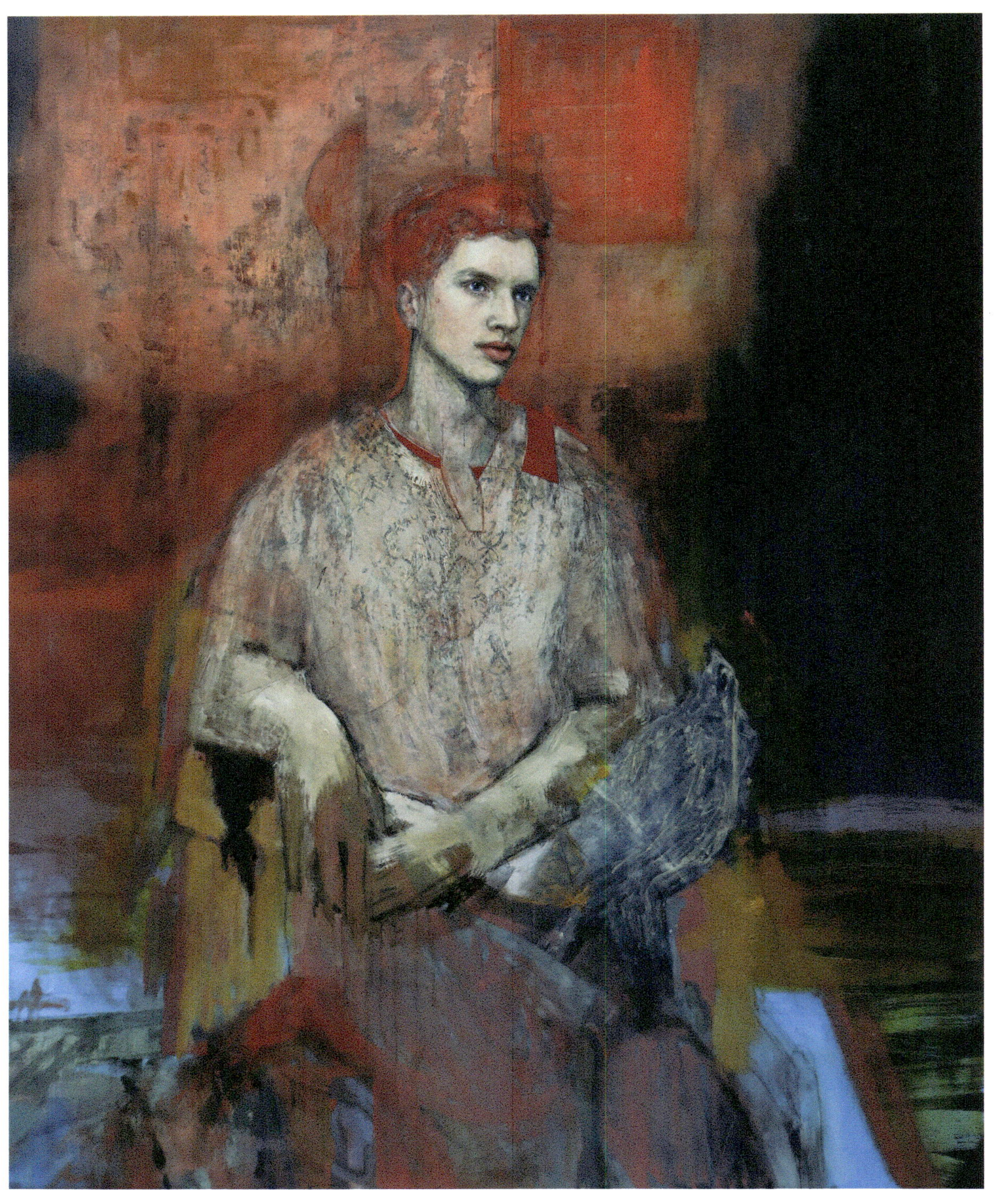

JULIA POLONSKI

Observer of Dreams

Oil on canvas

H: 152cm W: 122cm

The painting sits between two worlds. The precarious place of recalling and reframing our fragile dreams from sleep into conscious life. The time we sit with such dreams can sustain and enrich our existence and perhaps enable us to experience, briefly, the mystery of the sublime.

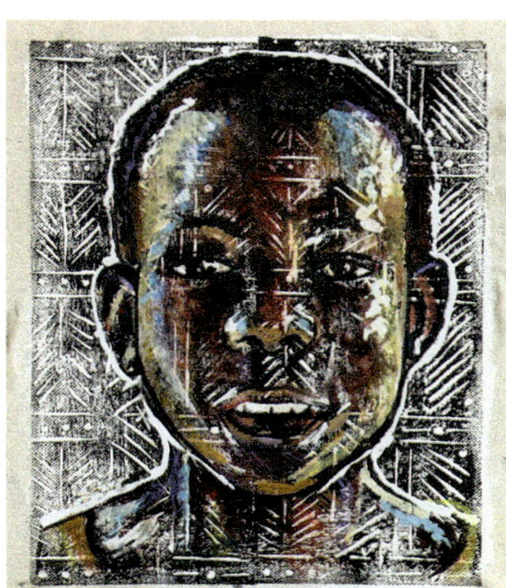

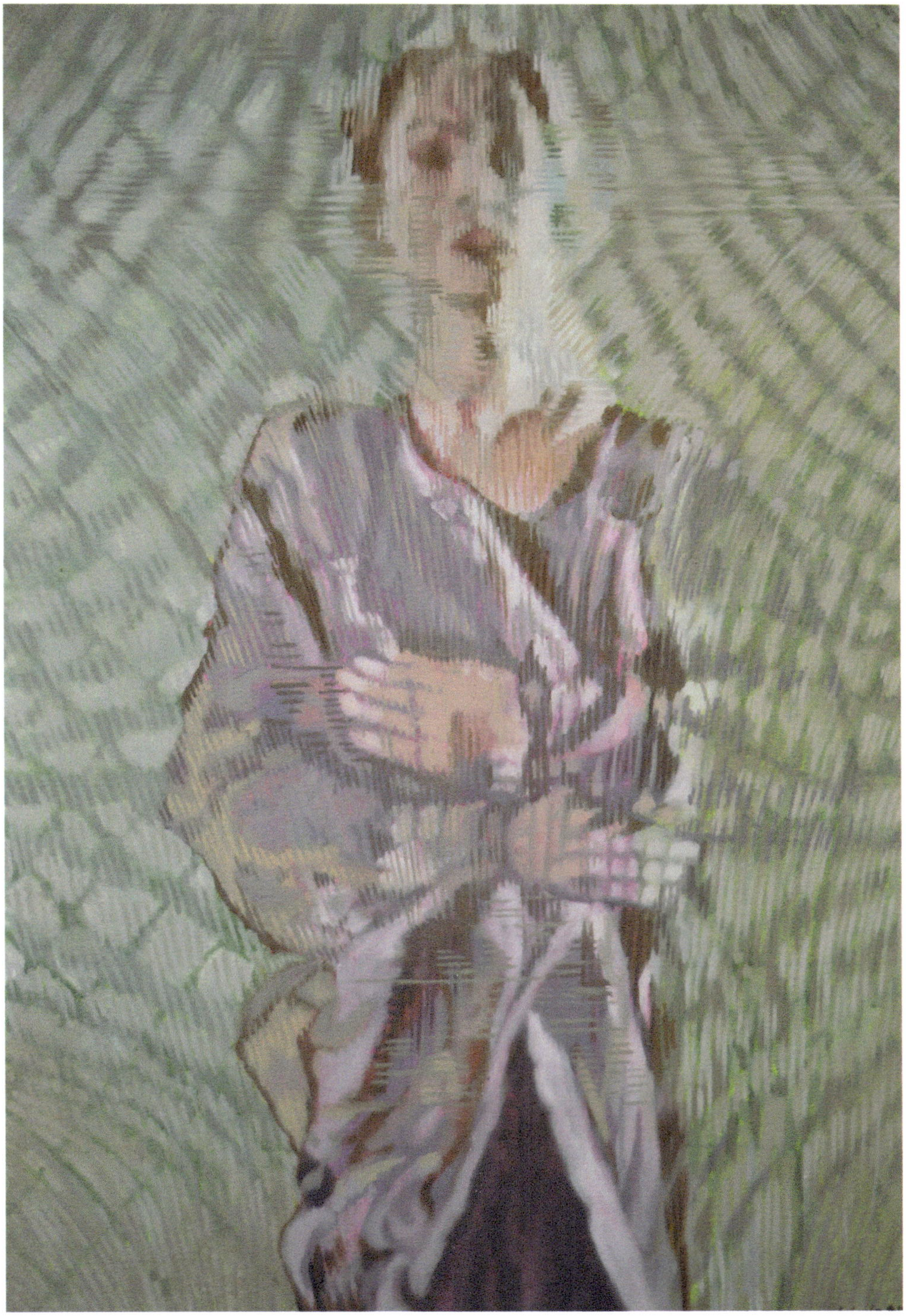

JESSICA KERRIDGE

The Joy of Simplicity

Mixed media – lino print, acrylic, pen and pencil on canvas

H: 29cm W: 25cm

I befriended a boy named Highest from Zambia while working with the charity Hands at Work. His face reflected the joy and incredible faith of those living in the most challenging circumstances. I wanted to capture in his face the simple pleasures he enjoyed and the West forgets.

LUCY CADE

Beyond the Veil

Oil on canvas

H: 76cm W: 51cm

My inspiration was photos of an old film playing on a cathode-ray tube TV. The figure is the 'ghost in the machine'. The 'Veil of Maya' is a Hindu idea that no perfect world exists. Beyond the veil lies the numinous: perfect harmony, balance and peace.

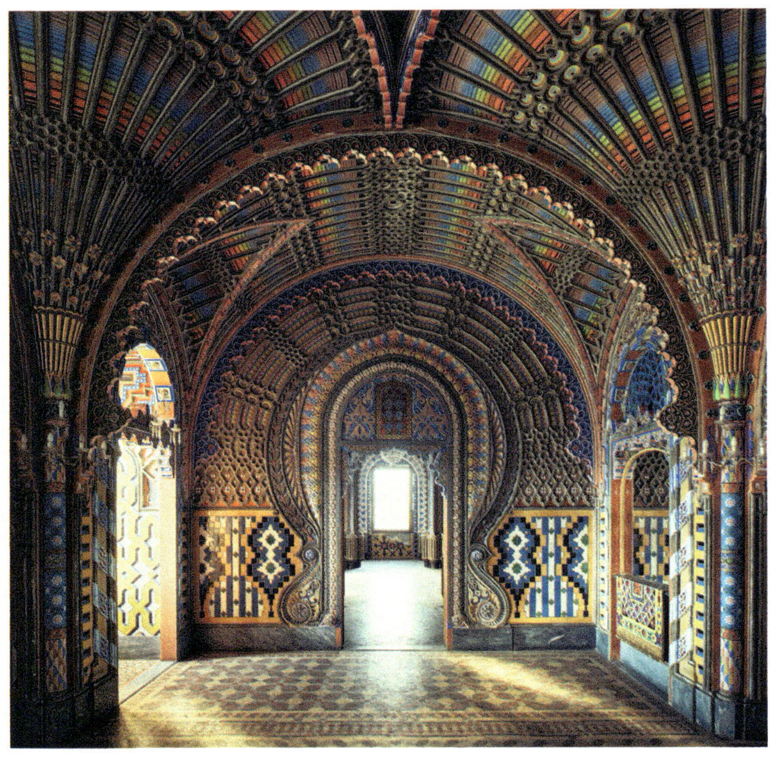

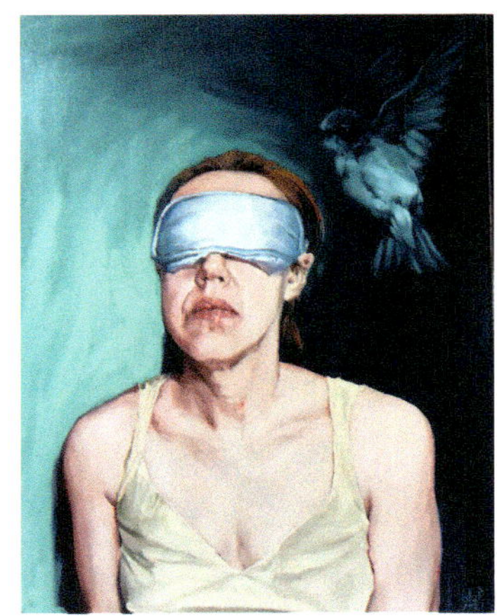

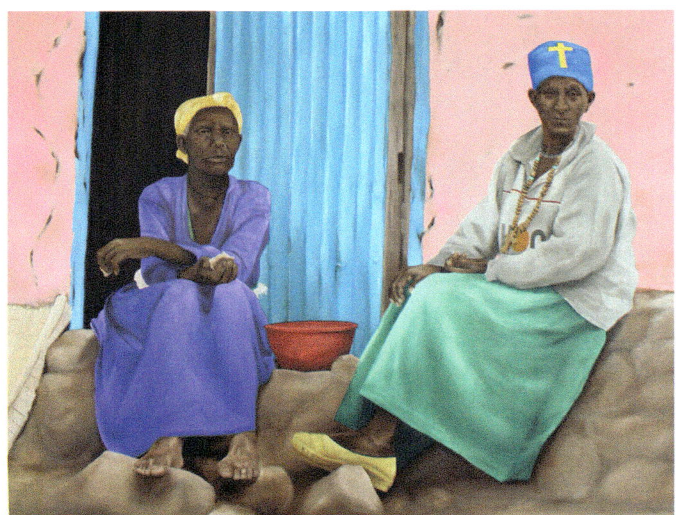

GINA SODEN

Peacock

Digital image on Baryta paper, Giclée

H: 94cm W: 94cm

An incredible abandoned castle in Italy. I was full of awe and wonder as soon as I walked into this room. The detail of the tiling, plasterwork and the colour just blew me away.

INGE DU PLESSIS

Blue Bird

Oil on canvas

H: 40cm W: 30cm

Blue bird – a dream awakening me to perceive the Holy Spirit as a small bird, flying into my heart through a metal fence where I was captive, releasing me into a warm, fertile farmland after rains. A celebration of a growing, changing, humbled yet liberated, and increasingly grateful, identity.

CATHERINE CHAMBERS

Zewday and Mantagoshe

Oil on canvas

H: 120cm W: 150cm

This double portrait of two dear friends represents the curiosity and interest in 'people watching'. Sharing stories, from a book or observation and experience, is a journey of interpretation, explanation, translation and individual perspectives with an enlivening curiosity that diminishes age.

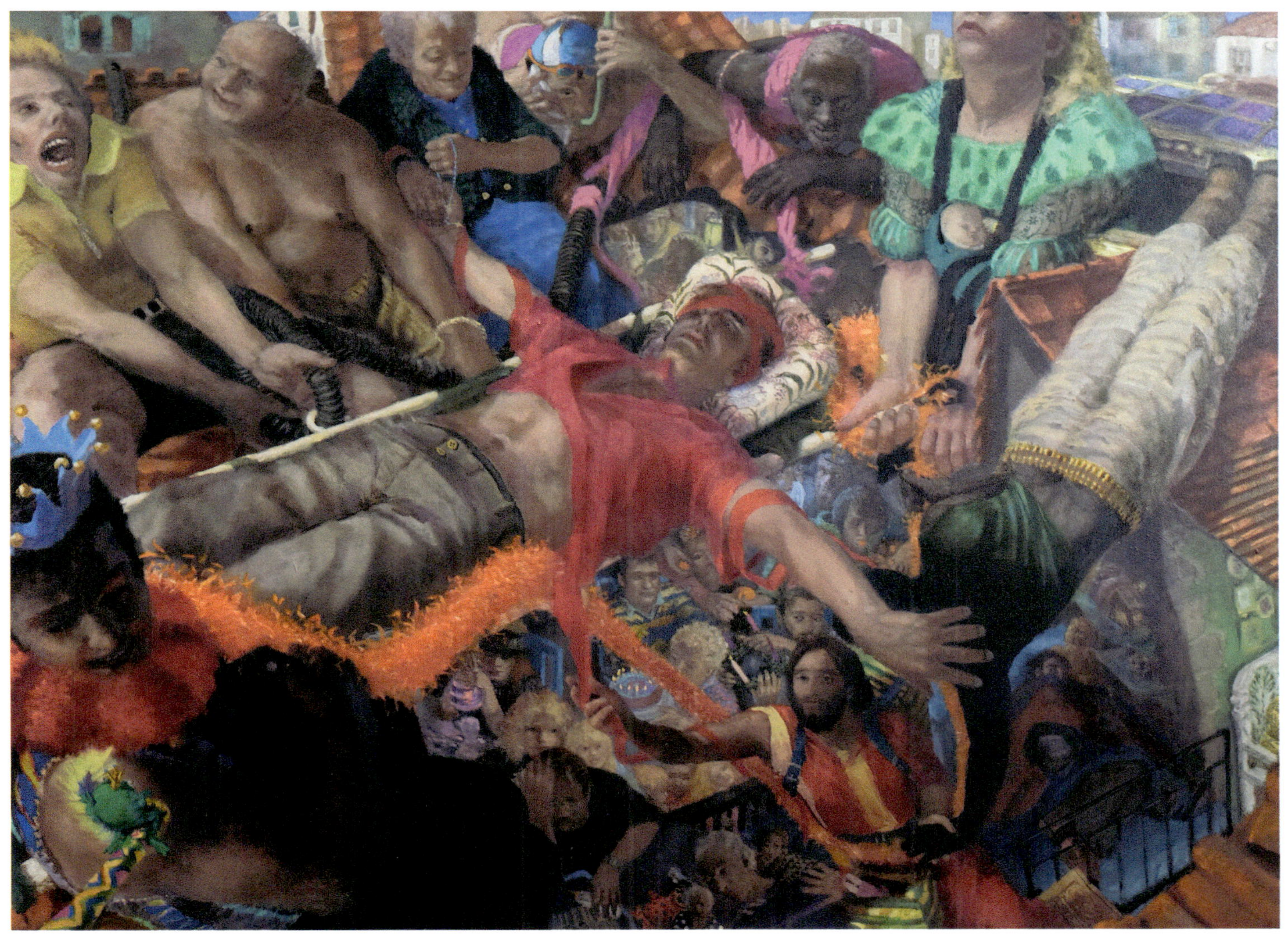

ROBERT SENIOR

Lowering the Paralytic through the Roof

Oil on canvas

H: 105cm W: 135cm

An intuitive painter, I draw on memory and imagination to encourage unexpected imagery and meaning to emerge. The spiritual appears hidden in everyday life, but occasionally is startlingly exposed. This depicts an incident from St Luke's Gospel where the suspended paralytic, in a state of fear and wonder, is welcomed by Jesus.

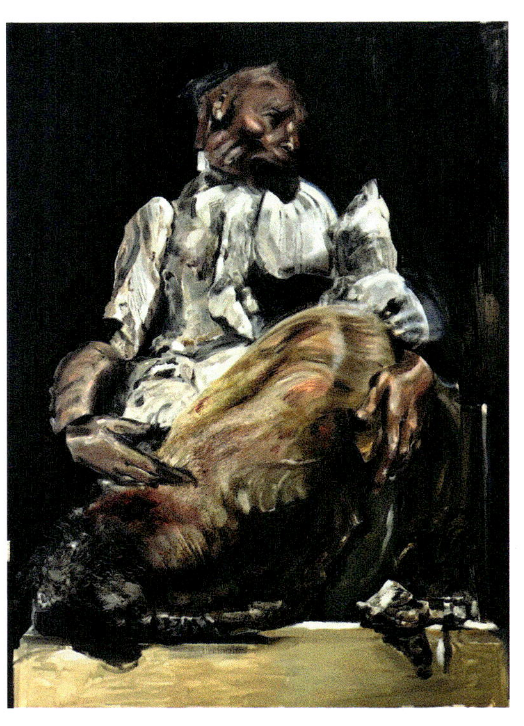

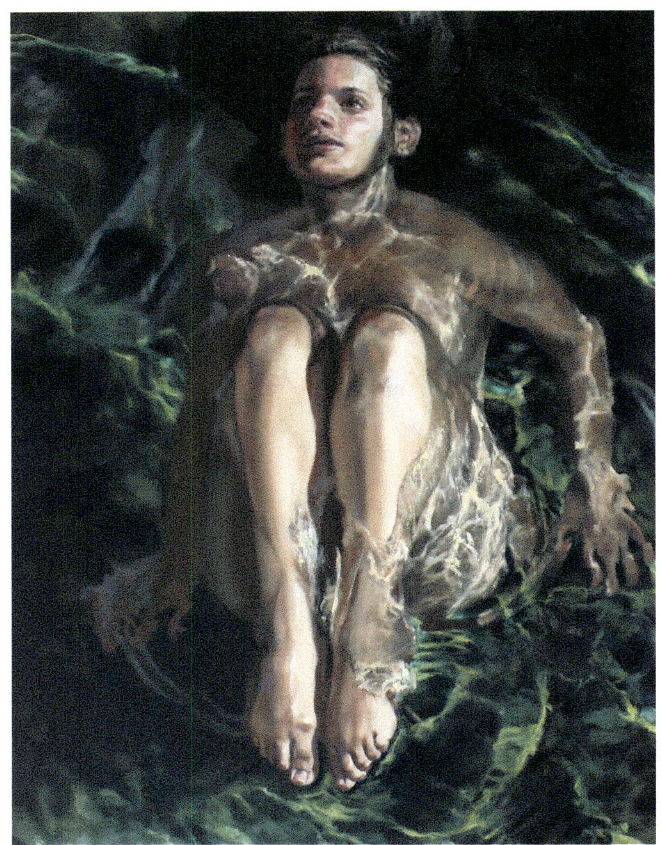

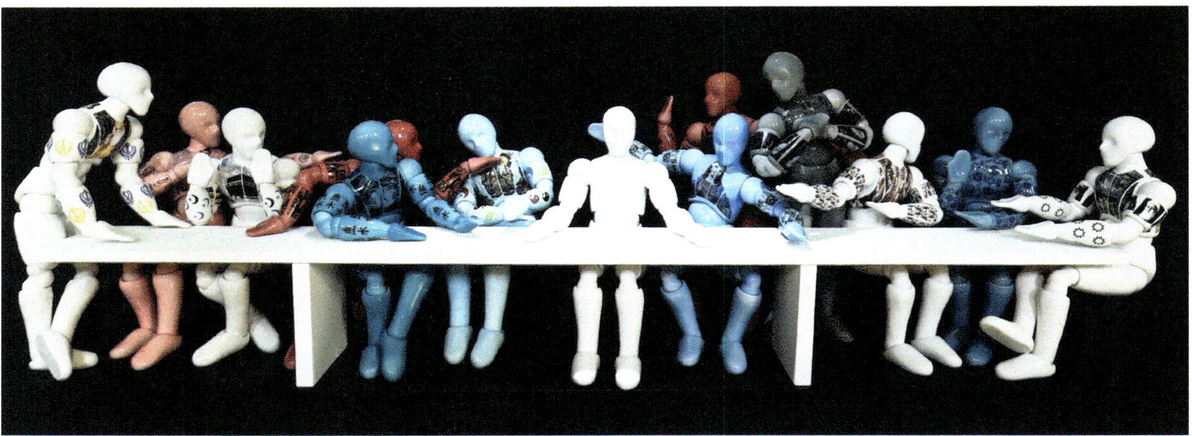

W K LYHNE

Stabat Mater La Pieta

Oil on canvas

H: 160cm W: 120cm

What if the image of the pieta, the Stabat Mater, depicts not a figure of silent, accepting grief, but one that is angry, torn apart with grief? Europe is at war again, the loss to all of every man, woman and animal is relevant. One planet, one collective loss, we are all animals.

JUDY CLARKSON

But Now I See

Oil on canvas

H: 120cm W: 90cm

A woman drifts in sunlit water, a rapt expression upon her face. She gazes upward. A blue sky? Revelation of deeper knowledge? The biblical title of the painting, spoken by a blind man who regains sight, can, as metaphor, describe the finding of new meaning and spiritual understanding.

DAVID MILLIDGE

The Last Supper

Ceramic sculpture. Slip cast earthenware

H: 50cm W: 200cm D: 40cm

Inspired by the iconic Christian masterpiece of Leonardo Da Vinci, this is not about Judas or betrayal, but rather religious tolerance. Each figure is decorated with the symbols and images of different faiths, thereby depicting a wondrous and optimistic vision of religious and ideological co-existence.

ANGELA JACKSON

Listen to the Bees and They Will Tell You Who Rules

Oil and cold wax medium on linen

H: 95cm W: 65cm

This self-portrait is an acknowledgement of the power of nature during a time of meditation. It portrays an acknowledgement that ultimately humanity, as part of nature, is under nature's rule. Here it is portrayed an acceptance and wonder of forces beyond us and recognition of the importance of listening.

SILVIE CRISTOFOLI

The Coming of Spring

Hand-painted and glazed stoneware

H: 32cm W: 15cm D: 15cm

Inspired by the feelings of hopefulness and excitement when, after the long months of darkness and bitter cold, there is a new world blooming. Natural rebirth always reminds me of the sensation of spiritual rebirth – invigorating, freshening and spirit-lifting.

DEBORAH HARRISON

Foetus

Sculpture in champagne alabaster

H: 25cm W: 16cm D: 19cm

The intricacy, fragility and detail of the human body is wondrous. Such complexity is perfectly expressed in the vulnerability of the unborn child. I saw veins and tissue-like formations in the stone. As a mother, biologist and artist, this reminds me of the birth of my children. I have no agenda with the piece – it

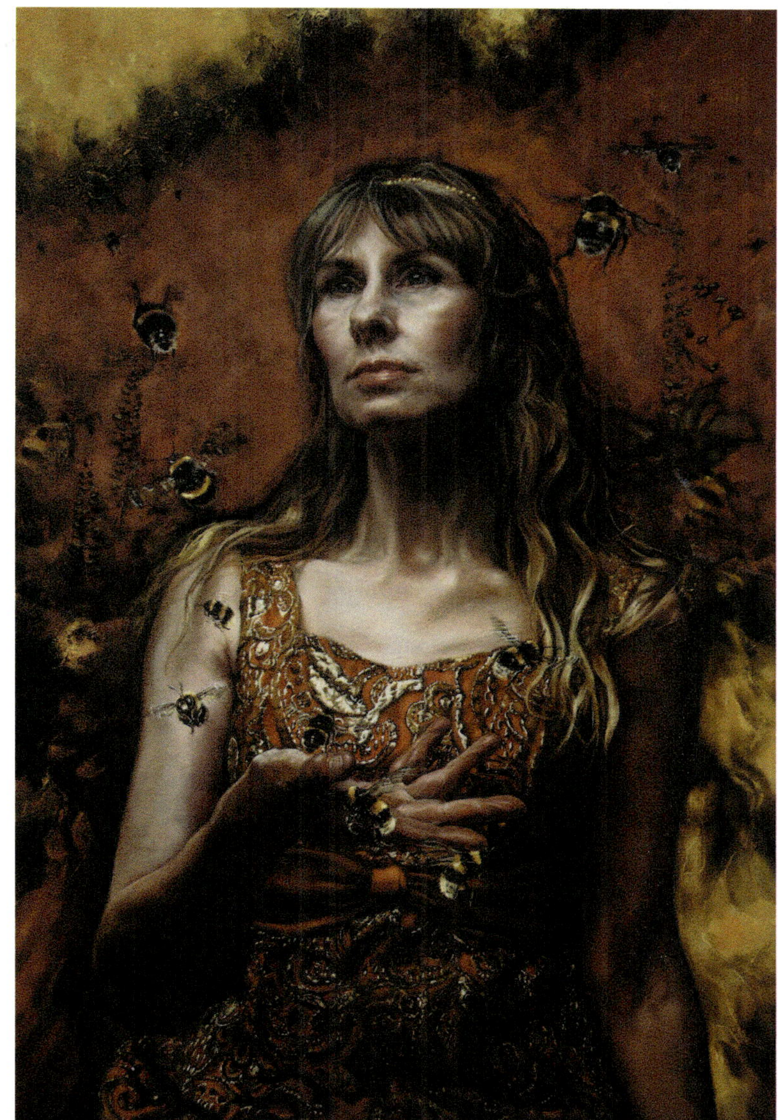

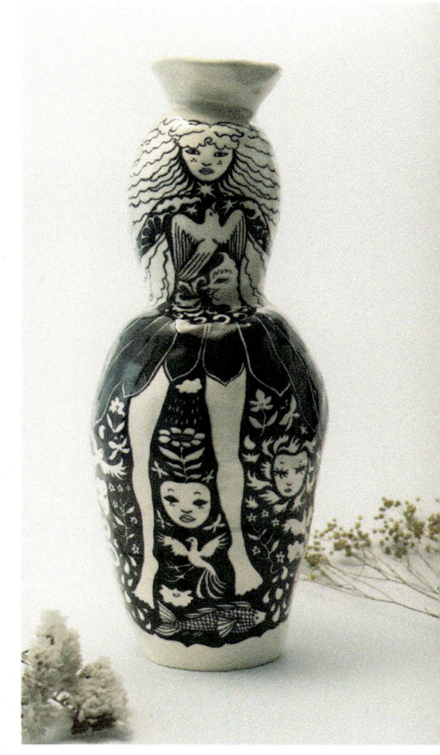

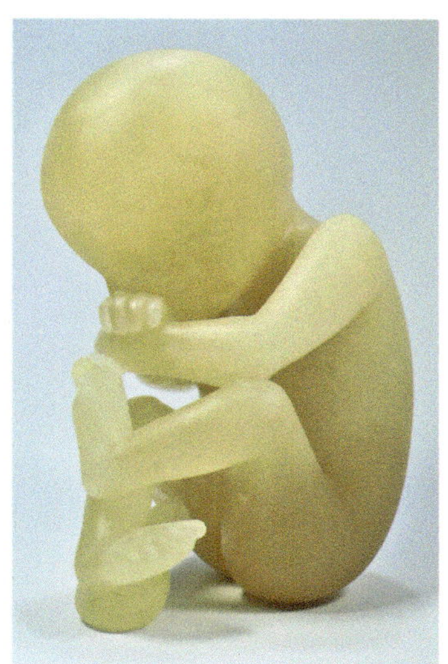

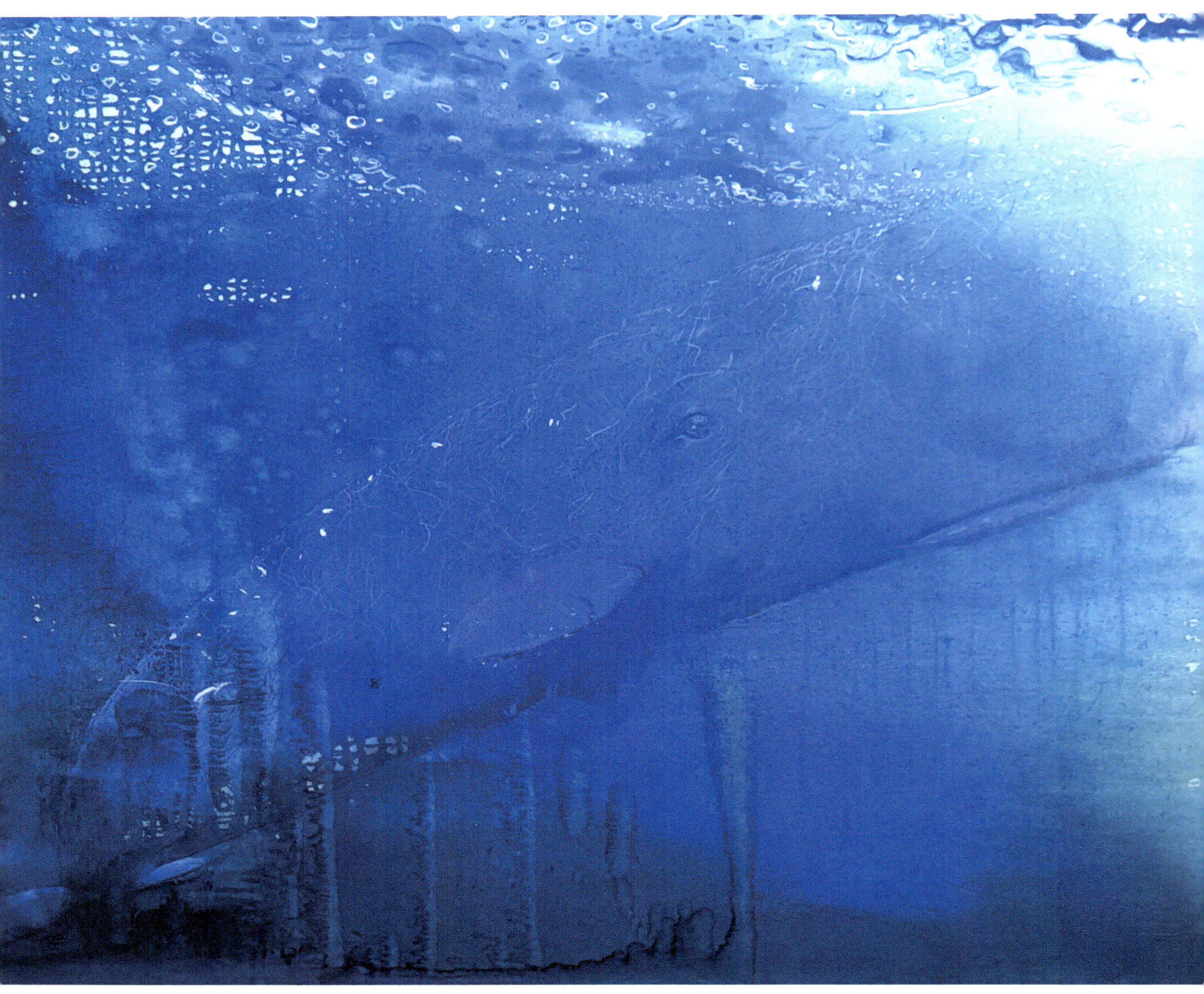

KARL NEWMAN

Deep Blue

Oil on canvas

H: 92cm W: 122cm

My inspiration to explore these magnificent and mysterious creatures was *Fathoms: The World in the Whale* by Rebecca Giggs. These majestic yet vulnerable animals captivated me. I allowed the image to emerge at the surface of the canvas, to mimic a whale surfacing for oxygen.

EMMA HAWORTH

In the morning, long before sunrise

Oil on canvas

H: 150cm W: 130cm

Rising early before sunrise and slipping out of the house before anyone is awake, full of hope for the new day. Starting an adventure or journey walking through the quiet darkness of the woods and noticing all the activity and magic of the nocturnal world.

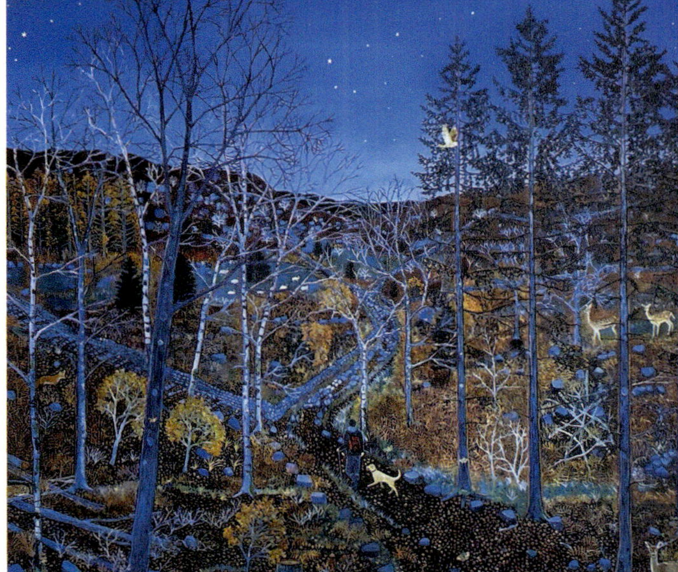

SCAPA JOE

Giants

Acrylic and spray paint on canvas

H: 80cm W: 80cm

Hope, wearing the diving helmet, greets a humpback whale and her calf. The beauty of the whales contrasts with the urban decay – a graffiti-covered train; a begging, endangered pangolin. I love our planet. Art can make people think about conserving the world and thereby the future of everyone.

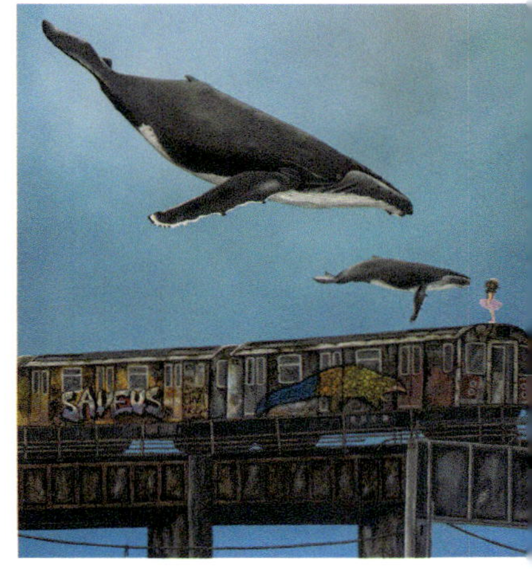

AMY TIFFANY HEMINGWAY

Yirah & Kemopath

Oil on canvas

H: 150cm W: 300cm

Adam, stunned by something new and beautiful, stares with awe at Eve. She, innocent and oblivious to him but captured, in wonder, by a bird. Here are portrayed Awe (*yirah* – Hebrew) and Wonder (*kemopath* – Hebrew). Adam, in love, holds flowers pondering his next move.

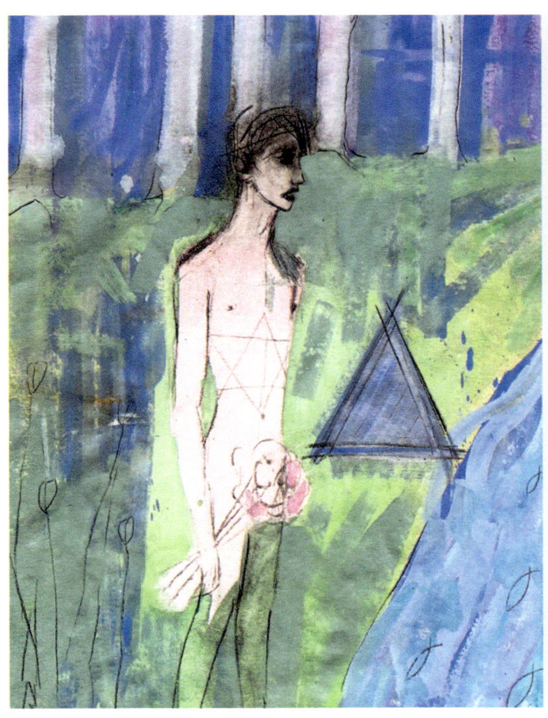

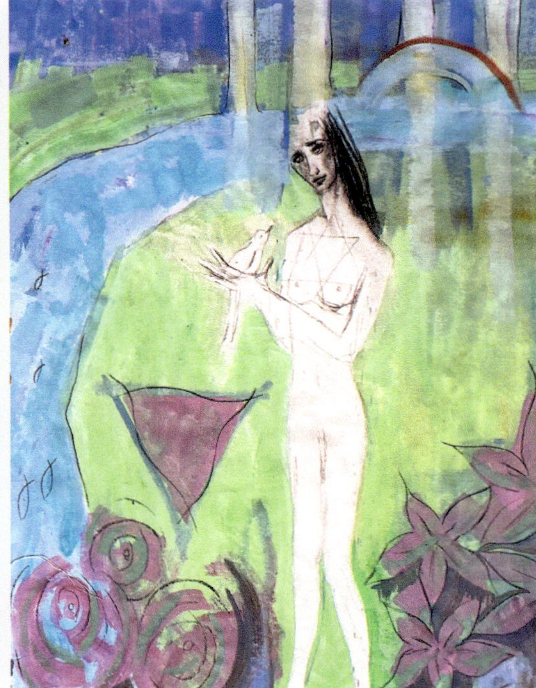

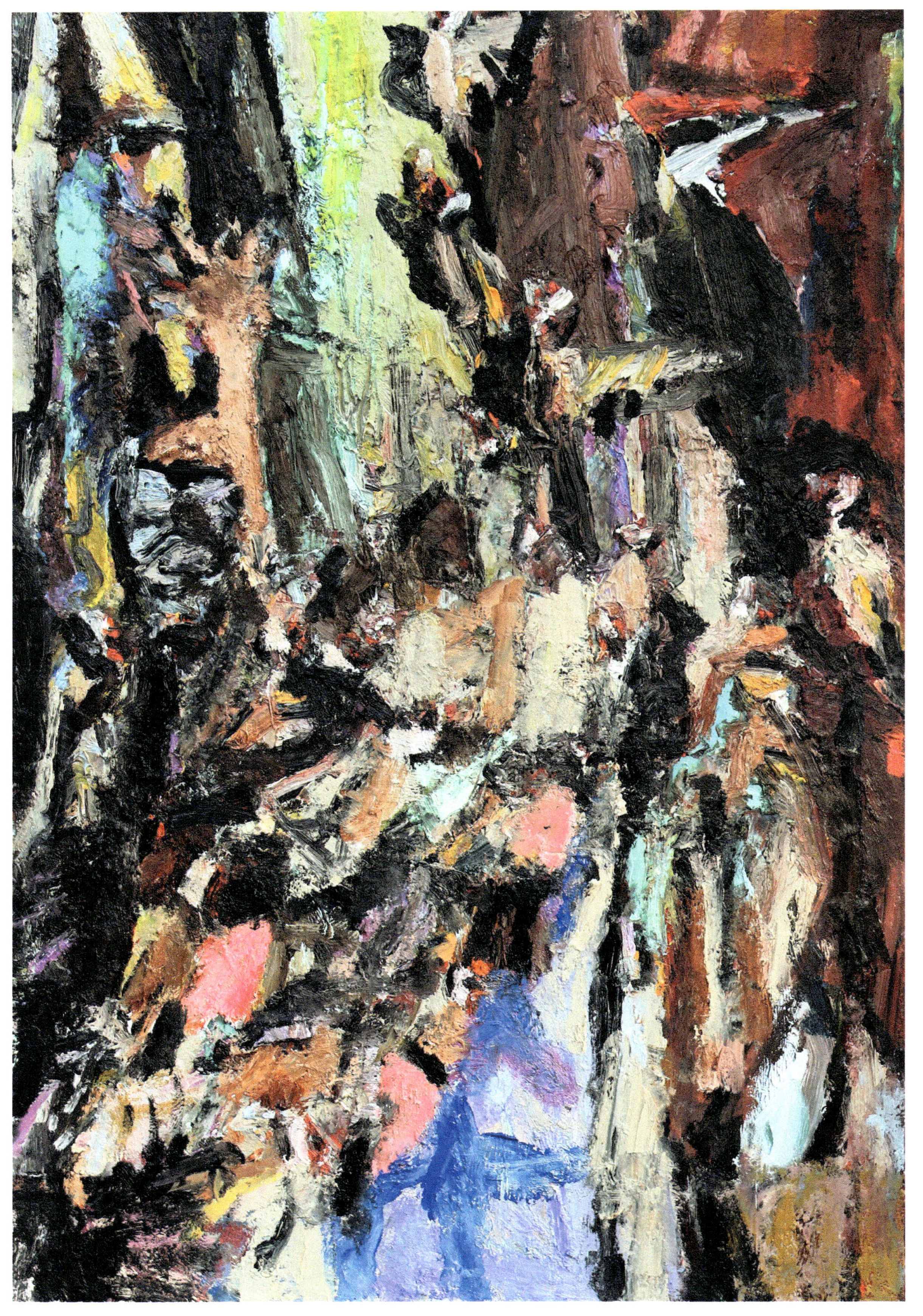

CRAIG JEFFERSON

Gold Finches and Other Birds

Oil on panel

H: 91cm W: 61cm

In the oasis of trees surrounded by three-bed semis, I walk daily, often seeing goldfinches. Taught from childhood to appreciate birds, to me God's fingerprints are unmistakable on these exquisitely painted creatures. They lift one's affections heavenward, their beauty transcending what we see with our eyes.

GEORGIA ELLIOTT

Unforgiving Elements

Original acrylic and mixed media

H: 150cm W: 200cm

Inspired by the feeling the sea engenders on the brink of a storm. The ocean's power and overwhelming force is a reminder of how small we are and our incapacity to control our environment. Alongside the appreciation of the water's awesome depth, mass and force runs a thread of fear.

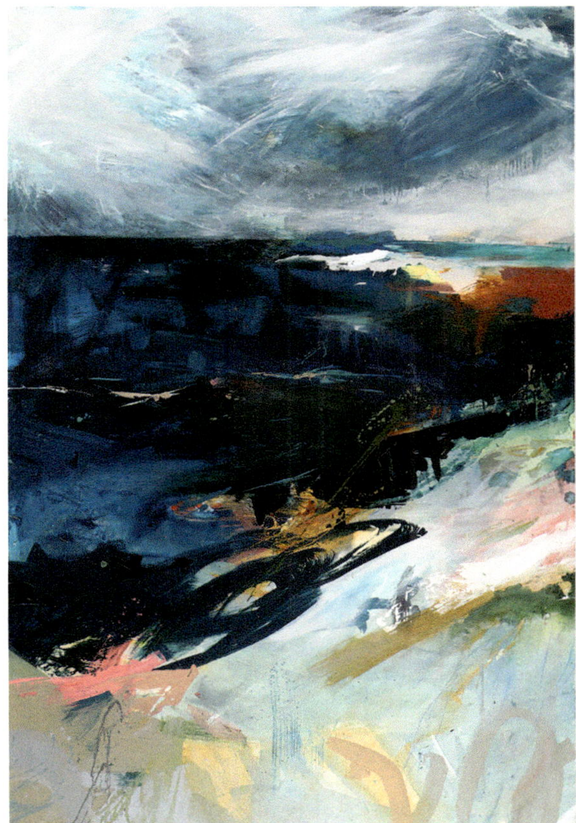

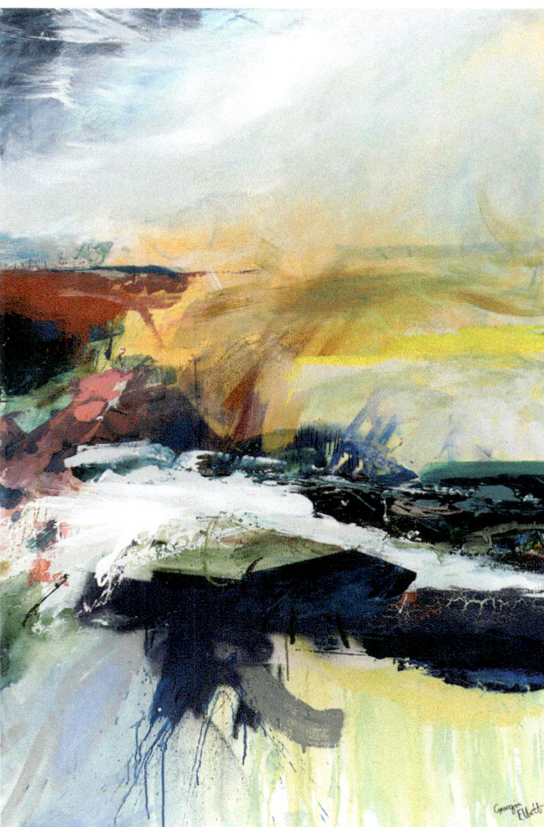

AMY POWELL

Simultaneously Sublime

Oil on canvas, blue card and yellow card

H: 120cm W: 160cm

By depositing glossy images from online sources and commercial magazines into painting, I reflect the current preoccupation of positing one's identity with continuous input of media images and aesthetics. I aim to disrupt how we assess pictures with new ways of image-making as well as subverting the meaning of the term 'sublime'.

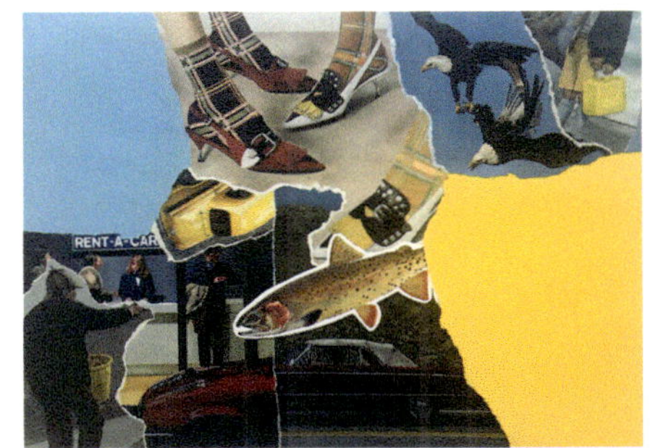

KOSTYANTIN MALGINOV

A Brave New World

Silk painting combining the author's graphics, using silk, polyester, binding base and high-quality silk thread

H: 83cm W: 130cm

Love of life in all its manifestations. The properties and structure of silk, the movement of lines, new forms, colour transition, execution, I search for innovative solutions. All devoted to a creative development expressing dreams of fantasy and reality creating space for dialogue outworked in perfect execution.

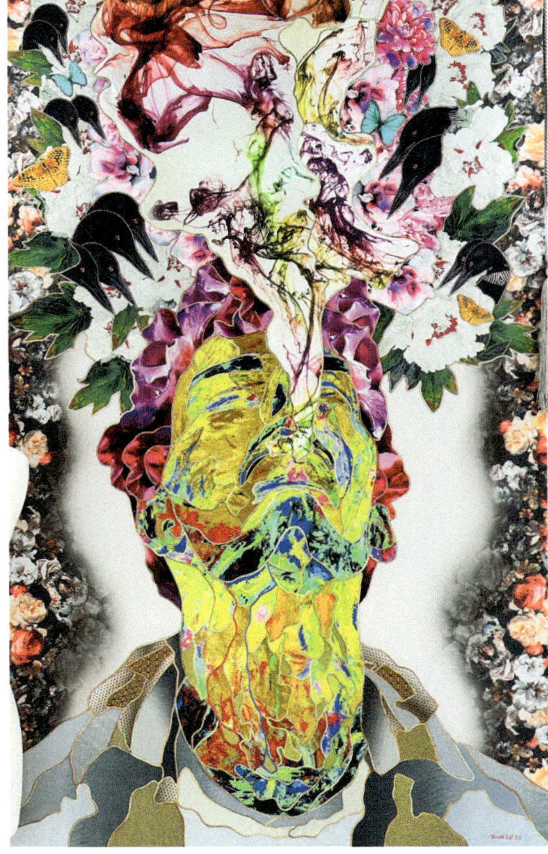

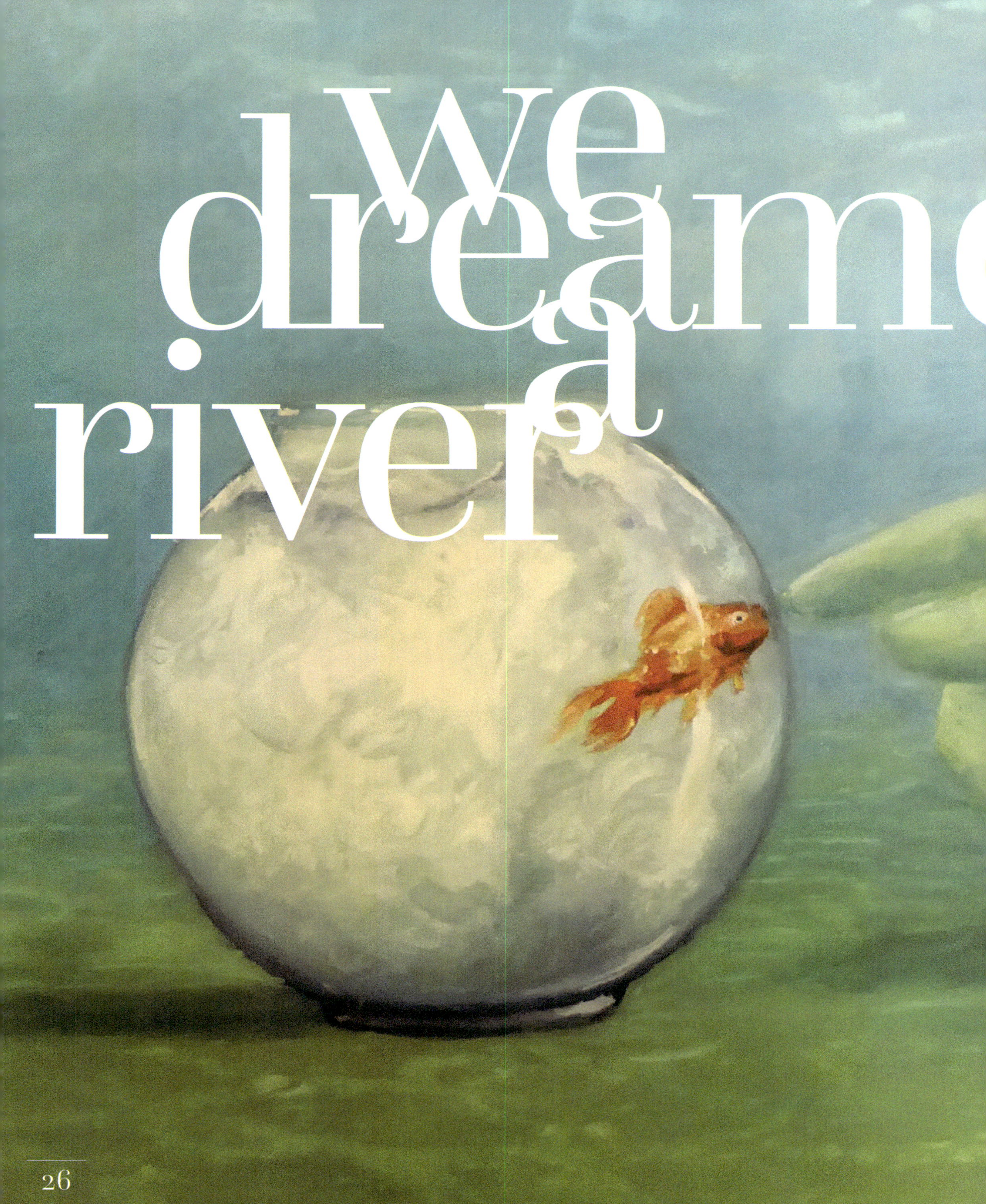

we dreame a river

SEEING IS BELIEVING

WONDERS HAPPEN. Do they? Can they? What are they?

Imagine the young woman, penniless, on her phone to her friend, anxiety pouring out of her. She has no means to travel home. What should she do? A passing stranger hears her and before she realises it, £10 is thrust into her hand with no thought of repayment.

A teenager places her travelcard to the scanner to journey home from school. It fails to work. No money, no ticket and the driver orders her to step off the bus. A woman, behind the girl, waiting to pay, stops her leaving and tells her she'll pay. And she does. The young girl is incredulous. She runs up the steps to the upper floor excitedly to tell her friends.

The middle-aged woman who prays for healing for her back, the pain excruciating. She goes to the osteopath; she exercises lightly, she moves, she lives, but every so often she grunts with deep discomfort. Night and day she prays, then, a week later, waking in the morning, feels the tiniest click and knows she's healed. She gets up sore but restored.

A couple arrive at a UK airport with nothing at the end of their holiday, everything stolen from them. They have no way of returning home. An older woman, prompted by her husband who had seen the younger woman's distress and tears, watches. The man leaves so she walks across the concourse to ask if she may help. The story pours out. Without hesitation, the older woman opens her purse and gives all she has. They can go home. Fresh tears, but different, as the man returns to enfold her. The older couple, now reunited, receive a heartfelt nod of thanks from the man across the airport void.

Coincidences?

The kindness of strangers?

Paying things forward?

Miracles?

It's possible to be present at the same event and yet interpret what happens or is said quite differently. A miracle is only so to the eye of faith.

Misinterpretation was wonderfully illustrated in *The Life of Brian* by Monty Python. In the film audience members at the back of the vast crowd, misheard Jesus as He delivered His Sermon on the Mount, concluding the intended blessing was for the 'cheesemakers' rather than the 'peacemakers'.[6]

What do we miss?

« **Detail** – See page 108

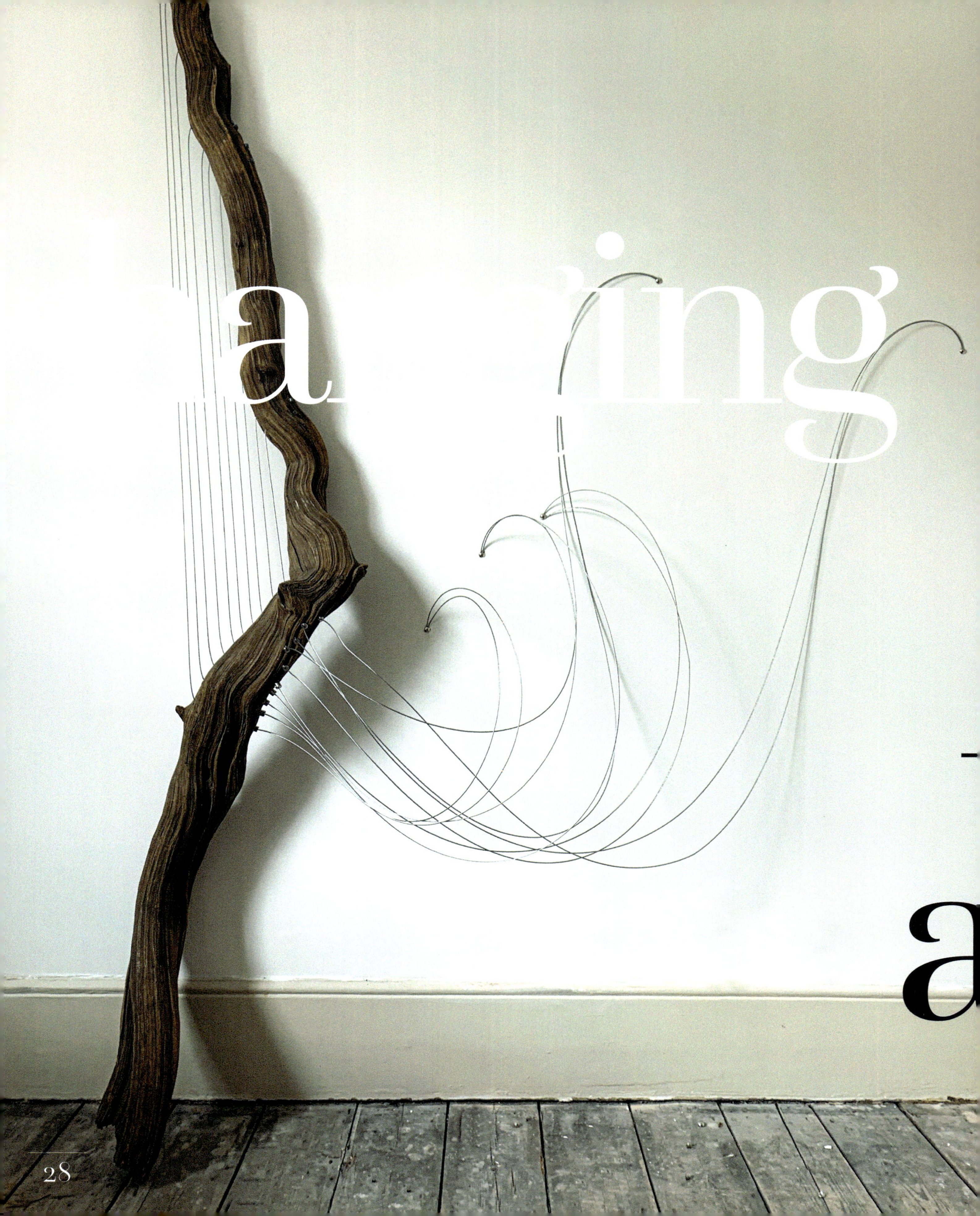

‘When you reach the end of your rope, tie a knot in it and hang on.’

FRANKLIN D ROOSEVELT[7]

THERE WAS A KING who had a courtier called Damocles from whom flowed unending flattery. The man obviously relished his status as a courtier to a king, but his eyes, surrounded by the trappings of royalty, grew larger and larger. The king, watching the worm of envy grow into a snake, offered Damocles the opportunity of spending one day as king of all he surveyed. The man accepted eagerly.

The following day Damocles, dressed in the king's finery, entered the court where spread before him lay a royal banquet, with golden goblets alongside golden plates and utensils. The seating the plushest, the entertainment unequalled, the servants numerous and, above all else, stood the royal seat. The king gestured for him to take the highest place. With great ceremony he seated himself, his eyes registering everything now under his command.

The king, in attendance, pointed to one other thing he had arranged. High above the royal seat, unnoticed by most, hung a large sword shaped like a Japanese katana, its blade sharpened with surgical precision, hanging by a single horse's hair. This represented, said the king, the knife edge of life and death under which a monarch ruled.

This fresh perspective on the vagaries of kingly rule greatly unsettled Damocles, colouring every moment with such foreboding and he failed to last the day as temporary king.

The story of Damocles is a precise representation of the situation under which every human being exists. We live on earth for a span until we die; however, death is not something we talk about in our society. Millions are spent by some, determined to overcome this ‘final frontier’.

We live in a painful world, filled with suffering, much of it undeserved.

There is a biblical story of a man called Job written about 2,500 years ago. It's a vibrant and superbly written piece that wrestles with the problem of suffering.

by thread

« Detail — See page 110

Job is presented as a good and upright man who loved and followed God. He was rich in family, goods and land.

God knew he was a good man, but was challenged by a figure, a fallen angel, Satan, in heaven who declared Job only loved God because of all he had accrued in his life.

God agreed that everything might be taken from Job to disprove his accuser. Satan stripped Job of everything, including his health, but he refused to curse God. What Job did pursue was God Himself. He wanted God to answer for his terrible suffering. Surely all his anguish meant God was not a just God.

Three friends debated with Job. Their summation of Job's situation was that the fault was his because of wrongs committed and his failure to ask for forgiveness.

Refusing to be cowed, Job, knowing full well his innocence, determined God must answer for the injustices visited upon him. When God finally answered him, it was not as Job expected.

Why, demanded God, responding in great power, did Job have the temerity to question Him?

Could Job create the enormity of earth, sky, space? Could Job oversee the universe and keep it functioning?

Could Job oversee the minutiae of life on earth?

This dangerous world was beset by terrible suffering alongside abundant, extraordinary life. Each state visits all humanity – the best of us and the worst of us. Job's God revealed Himself as both transcendent and immanent, and beyond human comprehension.

God did not answer Job's question, but Job discovered something that changed him profoundly. He gained perspective on the smallness and fragility of a single human being. God was God, Job's life was in His hands, and all God asked was for Job to follow Him and trust Him. Job's response in the face of God's magisterial greatness was unabashed humility:

Surely I spoke of things I did not understand,
things too wonderful for me to know.

You said, 'Listen now, and I will speak;
I will question you
And you shall answer me.'

My ears had heard of you,
But now my eyes have seen you.
Therefore I despise myself
and repent in dust and ashes.

Job 42:3-6

There are many ways to hang by a thread.

'All our knowledge brings us nearer to our ignorance,

All our ignorance brings us nearer to death,

But nearness to death no nearer to God.

Where is the life we have lost in living?

Where is the wisdom we have lost in knowledge?

Where is the knowledge we have lost in information?'

TS ELIOT[8]

» **Detail** – See page 23

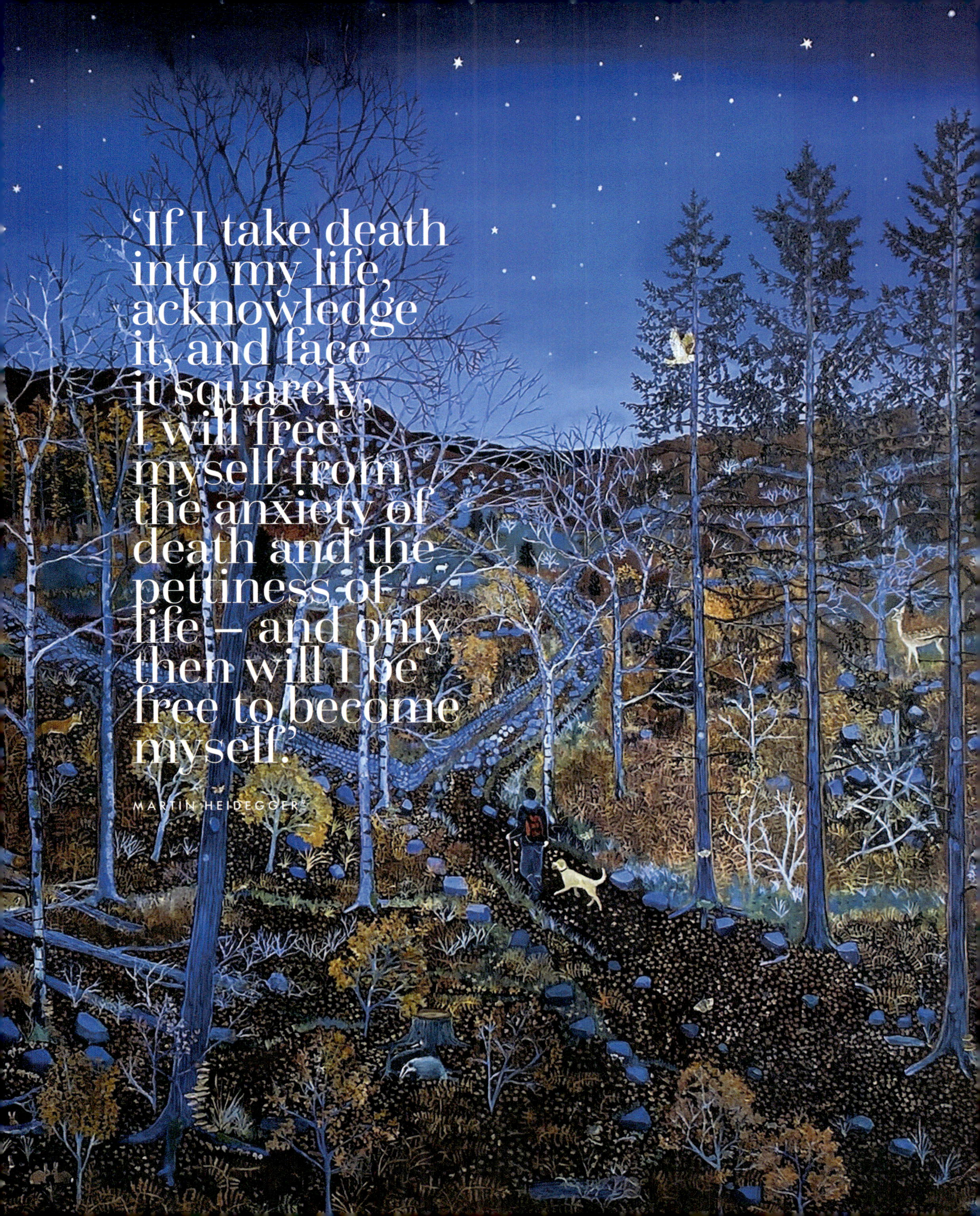
'If I take death into my life, acknowledge it, and face it squarely, I will free myself from the anxiety of death and the pettiness of life – and only then will I be free to become myself.'
MARTIN HEIDEGGER

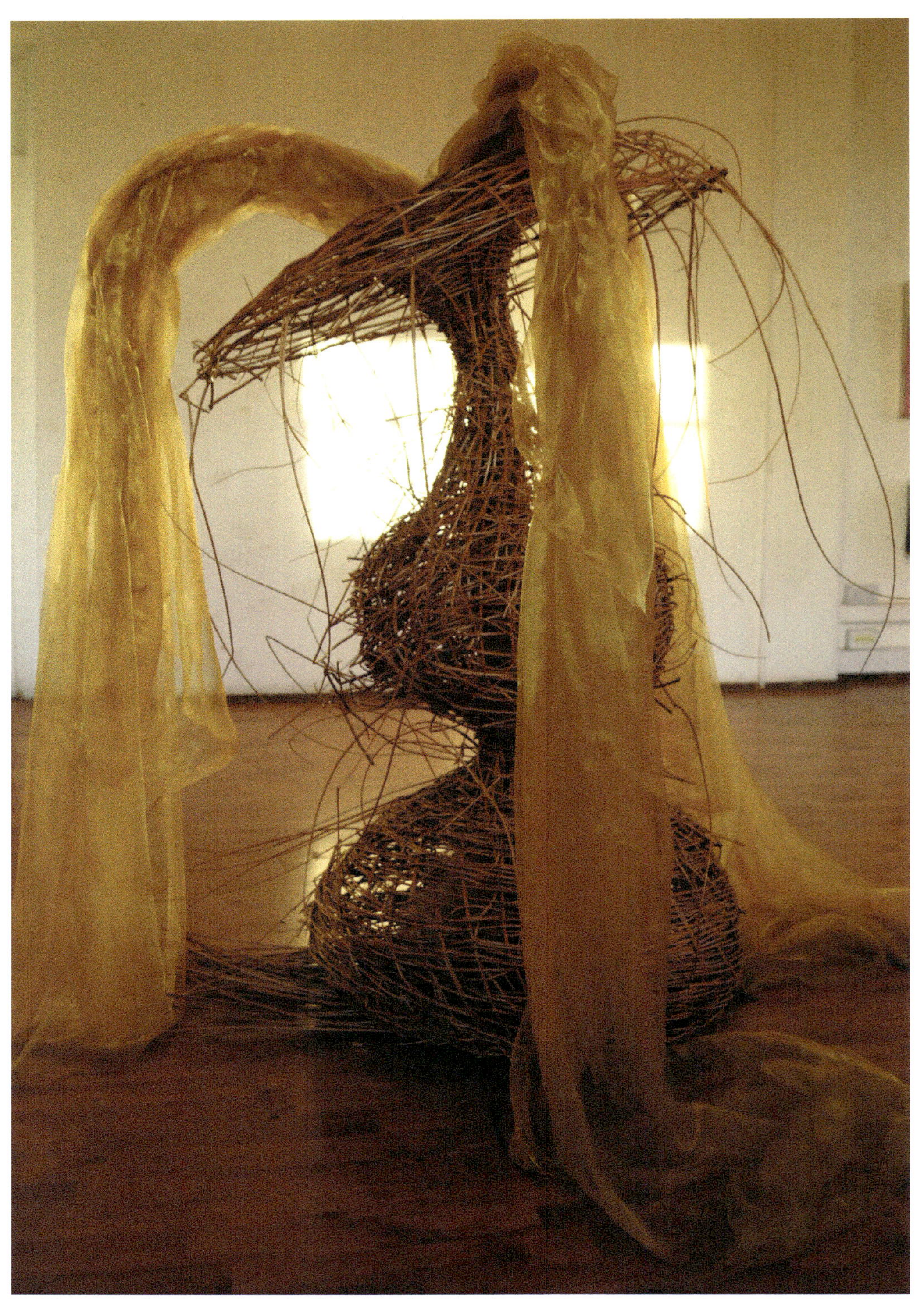

KATE CRUMPLER

Everlasting Joy

Sculpture made of willow, steel, organza and Perspex

H: 160cm W: 125cm D: 150cm

An expression of the unconditional joy lavished upon us by God, and a reflection on the wonder of this mysterious spiritual reality. To make the unseen seen in dramatic material form aiming to speak of things we struggle to articulate. Willow symbolises loss, and the hope of future retrieval.

SAROJ PATEL

Mandala

Steel, cotton, acrylic paint, Indian block-printed fabric, old clothes, glass beads, Indian temple bells and ceramic beans

H: 200cm W: 200cm D: 150cm

Mandala is a Sanskrit word meaning 'circle'. It is symbolic in Hinduism, representing different aspects of the universe. The circular designs symbolise balance, transformation and interconnection of all things. It explores the nature of being, of existence, systems of reality, metaphysics and Indian astrology.

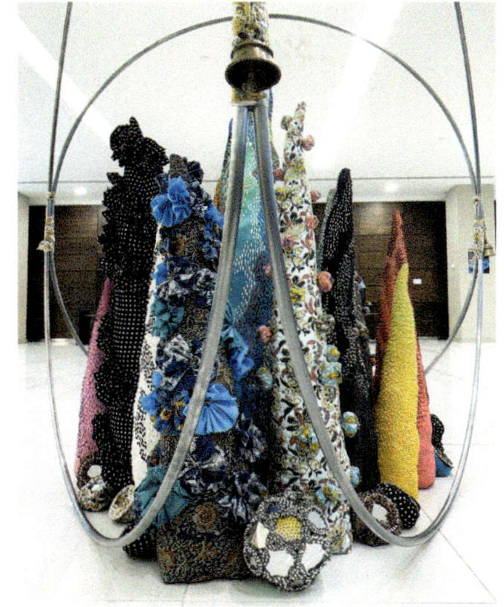

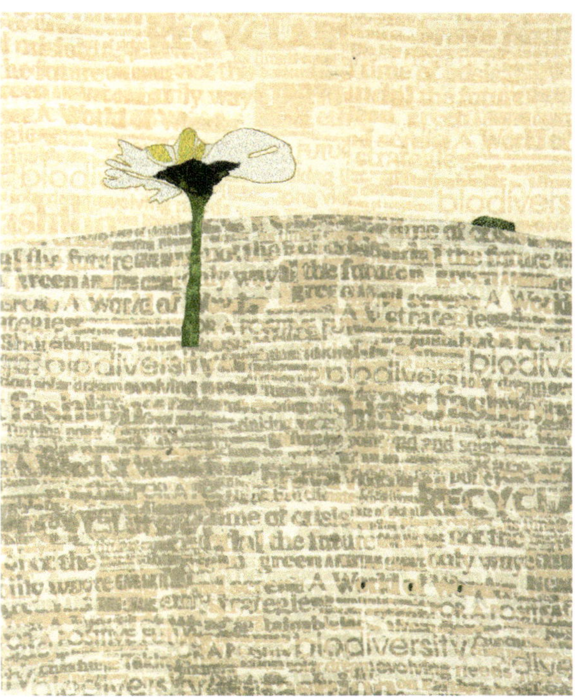

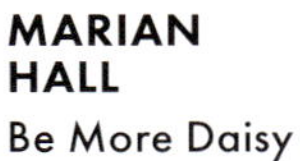

MARIAN HALL

Be More Daisy

Fabric, dyes and stitch

H: 53cm W: 43cm

A daisy created from discarded things. Rather than being one single flower, a daisy head contains lots of individual flowers which work together for their greater good, and astonishingly, adjust their position so they always face the light. The daisy seemed a fitting symbol for the focal piece of the work. Be more daisy.

CINDY MORENO

Huitral

Sculptural lighted textile piece, made of natural cotton and pure Merino wool, mahogany wood, brass and LED flex

H: 210cm W: 70cm D: 20cm

'Huitral' is inspired by the crafts of a Patagonian traditional community. Mapuches weave histories on their looms. They weave about the sky, nature, identity, but overall they use their looms as a healer. 'Huitral' is the desire to have a mindful society where we, fully sensed individuals, all beat by the rhythm of nature.

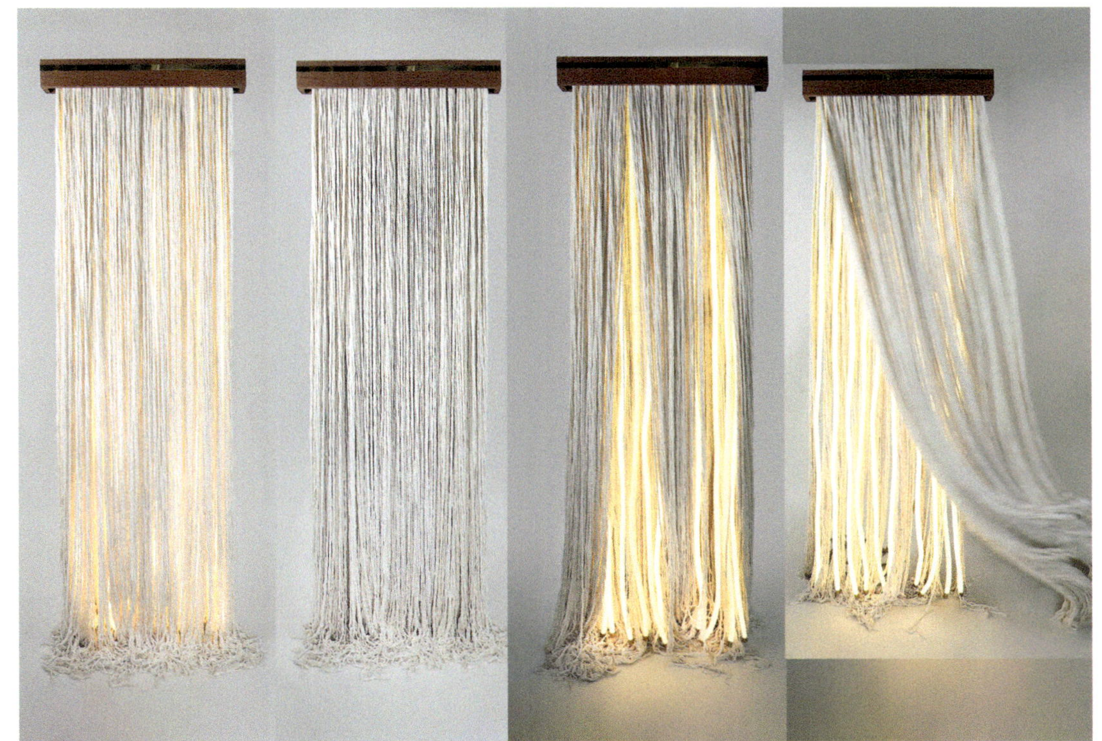

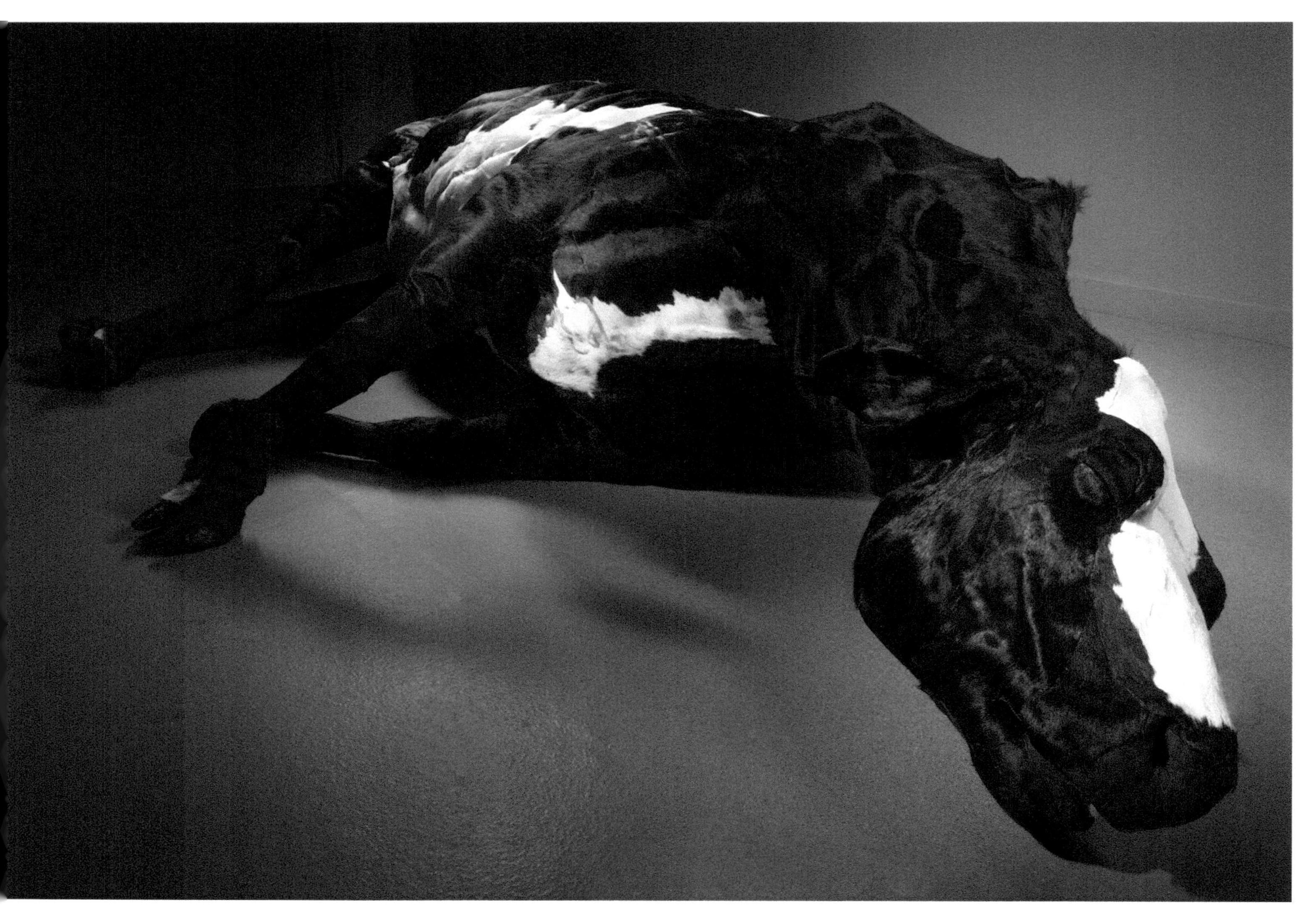

ABIGAIL NORRIS

Awaiting the Soul's Return

A large-scale musculoskeletal sculpture of a cow, made from four reclaimed cowhide floor rugs and domestic materials

H: 68cm W: 295cm D: 200cm

The body of a cow is symbolic of the severing of relations between humans and other living beings. Perhaps a contemporary version of the Palaeolithic bison, an act of re-pairing, re-membering, re-valuing and re-connecting. Interested in investigating 'absences' within Western culture, my intention is to create opportunities to contemplate the 'nature of being'.

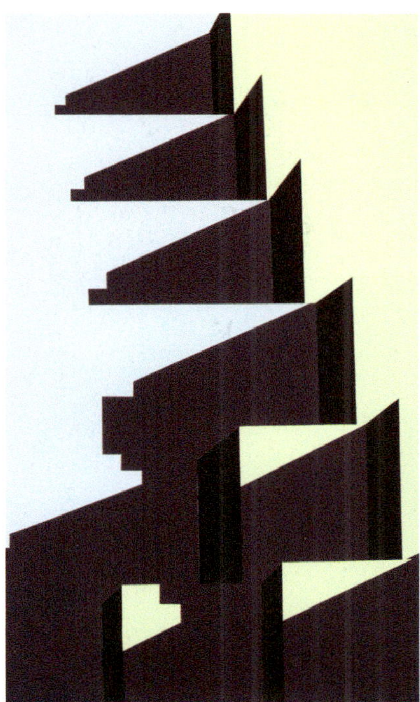

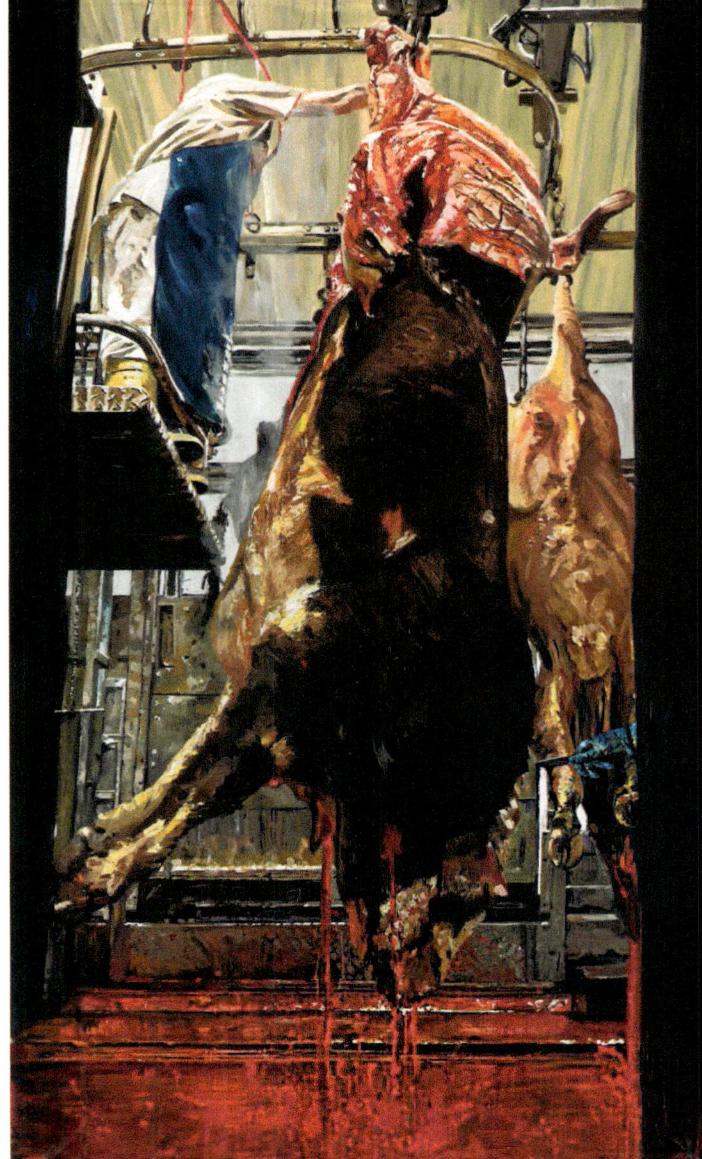

KATHERINE LUBAR

Ziggurat II

Acrylic on canvas

H: 100cm W: 60cm

Ziggurats were a type of building in ancient Mesopotamia used by Sumerians and Babylonians as temples, built on raised ground, with receding levels of steps leading to a flat roof, believed by some to connect heaven and earth. Perhaps the contemporary yearning to build ever higher buildings, if not exactly ziggurats, points to the same longing for transcendence.

W K LYHNE

The Flayed Ox

Oil on canvas

H: 330cm W: 200cm

Throughout the history of art, the dead ox represented a direct allusion to the homecoming of the prodigal son and Christ's redemptive death. The ox's patience and obedience in the face of certain death resonates, and an anthropocentric interpretation allows the animal's death to become a metaphor for the inevitable death of all living creatures, including all humans.

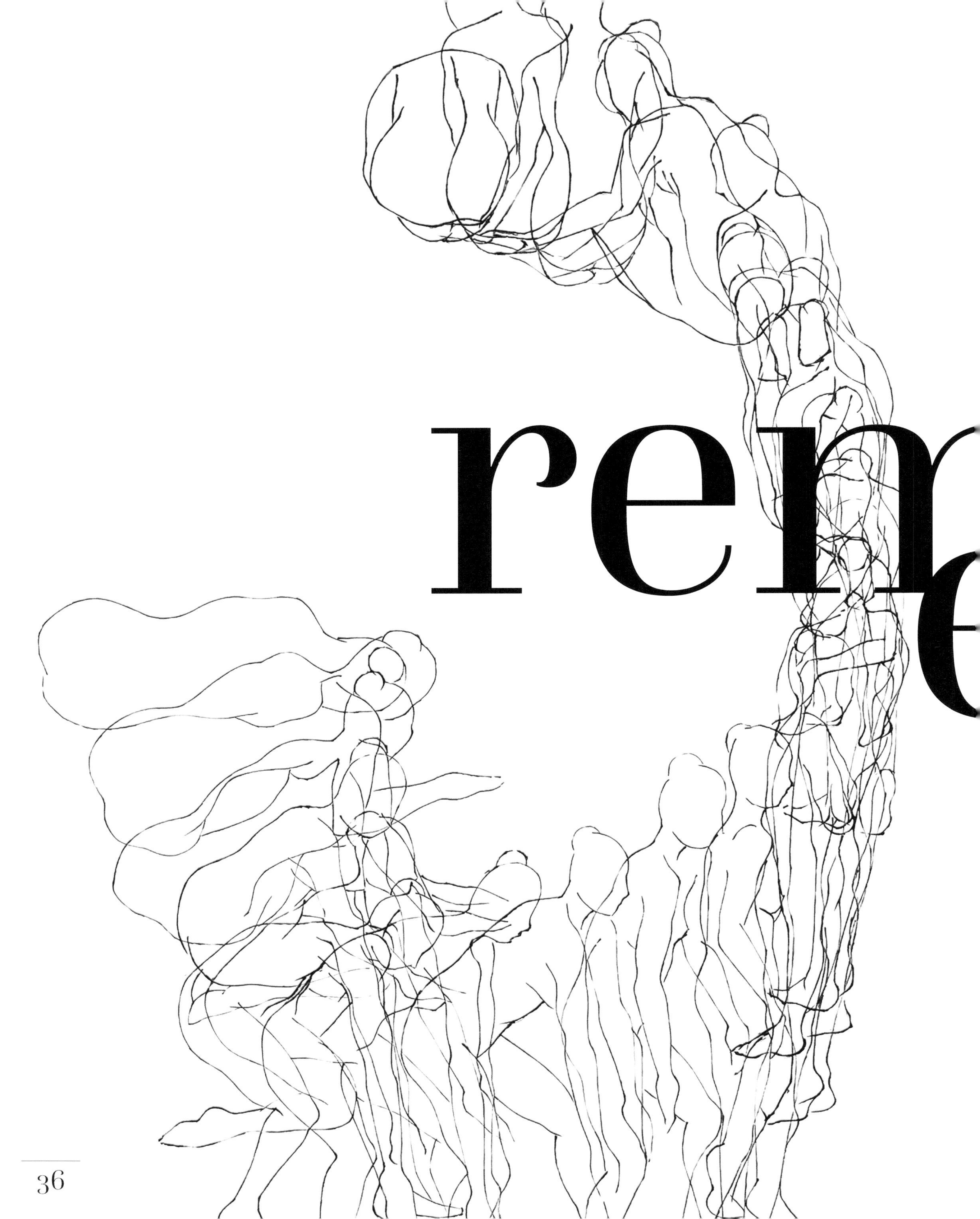

What do you see?
Now,
Today?
Does it make you smile,
Groan,
Weep?

Whatever it is
Catch it in the now
And know
You are alive.

If your heart
Rises like the sun
Resplendent over your life,
Dance,
Rejoice,
Remember oh remember life.

ember

If your heart
Hurts so it fails a beat
Life's random part
Grief's hollowing,
bellowing pain
deafens living,
Remember oh remember life.

Can anyone stop time?
Can anyone stop
The dying of the light?
Who can control
The randomness of existence?
All posturing,
All purpose,
All attempts at meaning?

Can we compare with the
mountaintop?
The watery depths?
The clouds of galaxies?

We grasp at the vapour of control
Suspended cloudlike
Before us
Leaving us always
Empty-handed.

Each a pinprick in time
Remember oh remember life.

There is equality –
It exists
Within our birth and death
From which
no one escapes.

« **Detail** – See page 64
Following spread: Detail – See page 76

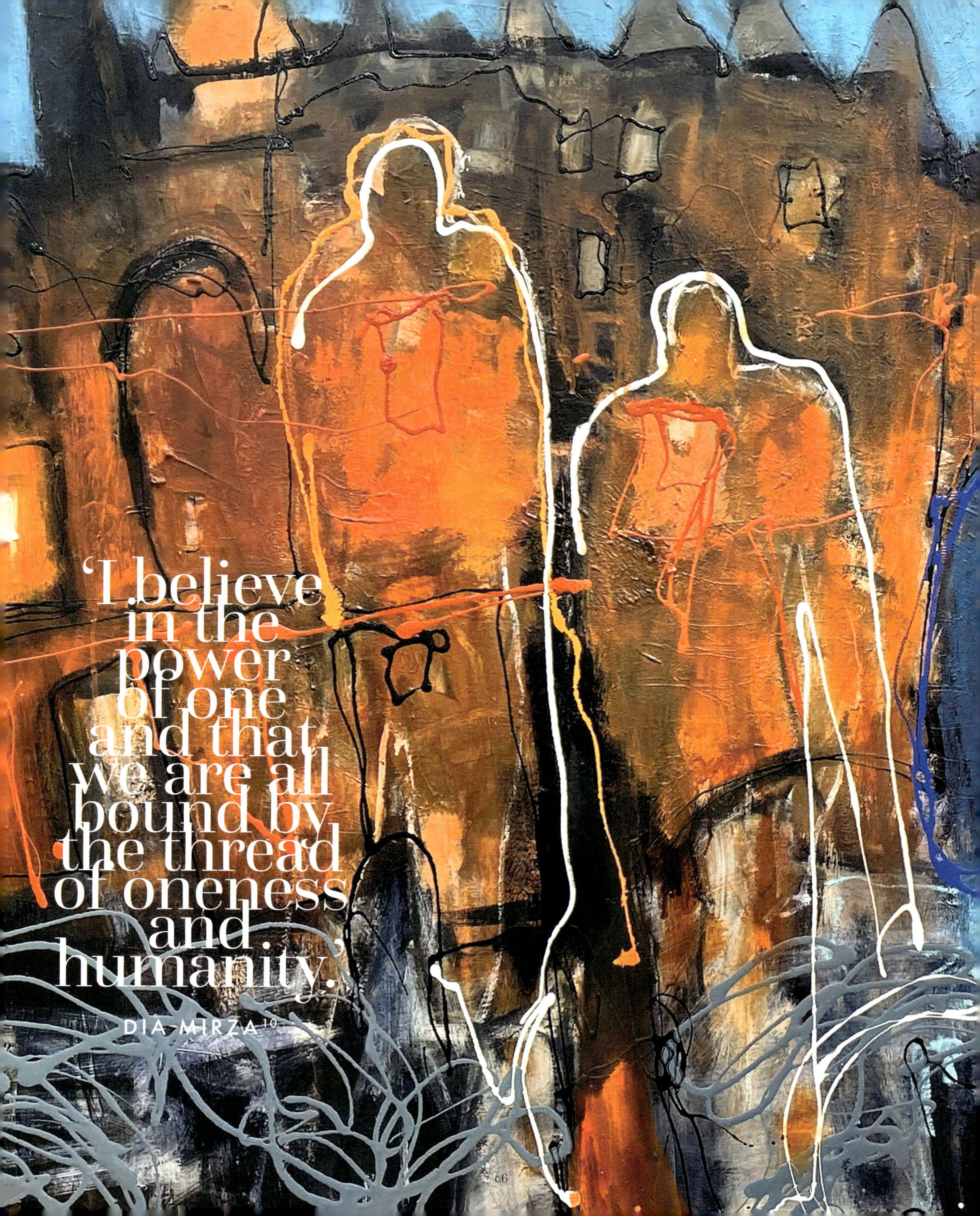

'I believe in the power of one and that we are all bound by the thread of oneness and humanity.'

DIA MIRZA[10]

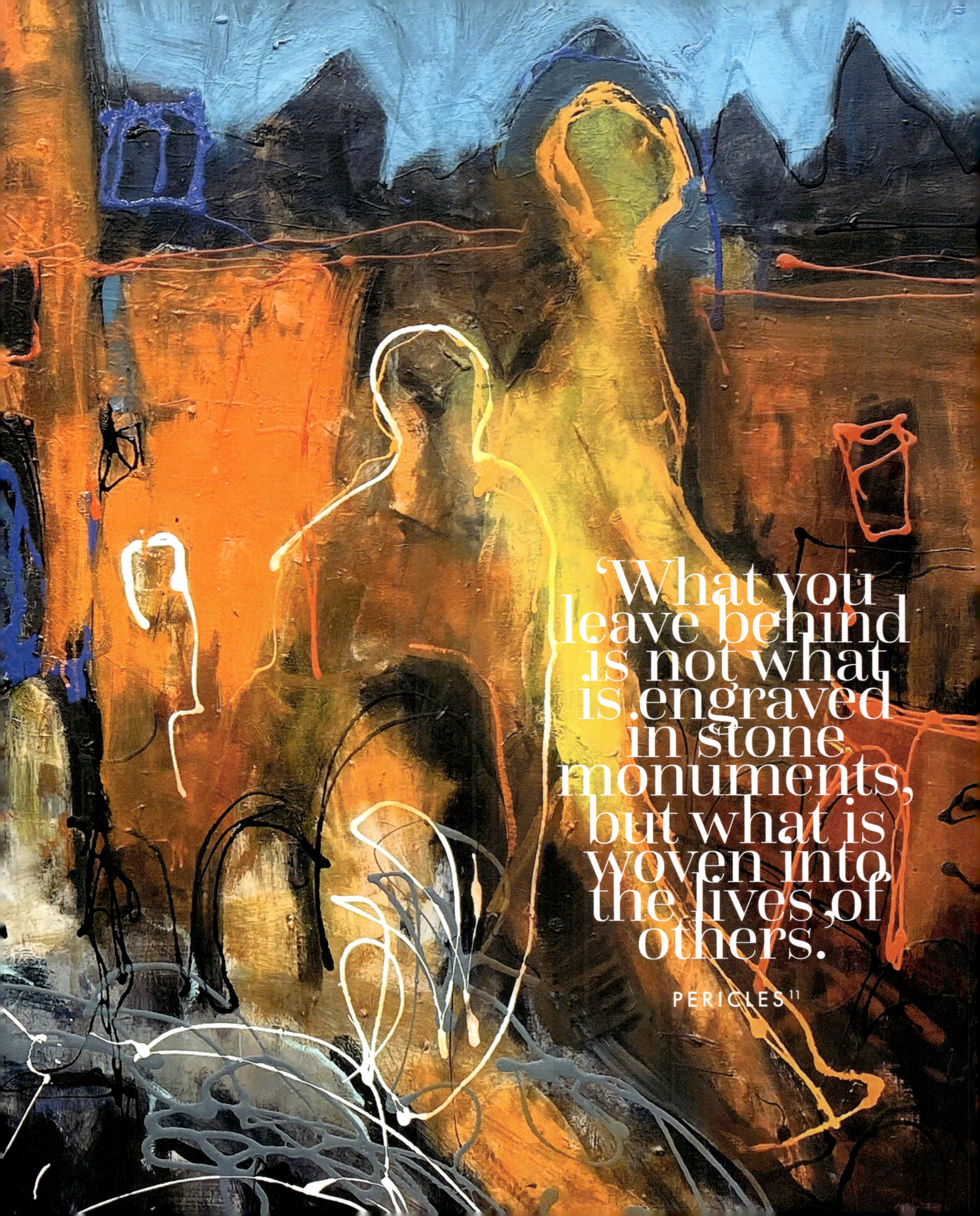

'What you leave behind is not what is engraved in stone monuments, but what is woven into the lives of others.'

PERICLES[11]

paradi

'Hope is like a bird that senses the dawn And carefully starts to sing while it is still dark.'

ANONYMOUS[12]

GLUE-SEEKERS[13]

DO THE CULTURES in which we live leave us in mental and emotional chaos, bereft of purpose and disorientated? Unsurprisingly, it may result in a gnawing anxiety and/or depression – a 'heart and soul' sickness. Cultures where we lose confidence and hope, which dispirit and corrupt our moral compass – any notion of 'right' and 'wrong' – must disrupt our sense of how to live. Without shared notions or 'morals', how can we live well together?

How can our 'society' work?

Our Christian heritage in the UK might be ebbing away, but it has instilled a sense of right and wrong; expectations of how to treat each other; endorsed law and order.

Our society is materialistic, debt-ridden, increasingly demanding of busyness, and self-oriented, encouraging us to develop 'My Truth' which trumps all others.

Isn't a life about 'self' too small, too ineffective? Isn't there something more substantial?

As human beings we have very distinct needs. We know these are not found in 'things', but in genuine connection with fellow human beings. Social interaction and growing relationships bring a sense of identity and belonging. Social media can't hug you, smile, welcome you, enjoy you. We lose our ability to connect with others face to face at our peril.

'We need joy as we need air. We need love as we need water. We need each other as we need the earth we share.'

MAYA ANGELOU[14]

What is the glue that helps us bind together rich and fulfilling lives? It must include intimacy,

se
lost

Demoralization: to lose confidence or hope; dispirit; corrupt the morals of[15]

genuine friendship and trust; their erosion from everyday living leaves us poorer, ailing in boredom, discontent and disappointment. Life is challenging and brings many things to throw us off balance. If we can build on something firm, then we can grow much-needed resilience.

Resilience helps us process and overcome hardship – we can learn to ride the wave rather than be doused and drowned by it. Problems can be faced, thought through and resolved as networks grow, enhancing our mental and emotional strength. We gain confidence as coping skills develop when we journey alongside others.

How do we build resilience?

Anywhere you look for ideas on how to build resilience, the primary tip is about connection. Building positive relationships is not easy. It requires thought, intention, an ability and resolve to personally learn and change, and courage to open oneself up to others. It encourages us to grow emotionally, mentally and spiritually not only to receive, but also to give. The fruit of the Spirit (Galatians 5:22-23) talks about love, joy, peace, patience, kindness, integrity, loyalty, gentleness, and self-control. These are truly challenging things to grow in our lives. However, people who exhibit some or all of these qualities are usually the people we want as friends.

We need each other, and more, we need community. Being among others we see displayed a kaleidoscope of ways to live differently.

This is the precious glue – a waterproof, anti-clog, strong, all-purpose, long-lasting, extra-strength, shock-and-temperature resistant, good-for-repair and reuseable glue.

Learning to love others is the journey that will rebuild our 'cognitive map', and hope, meaning and joy will visit us. This is the real, glued-together 'normal' life.

How brave are we? Are we prepared to look at ourselves in the cold light of day? To explore our inner and outer landscape, to choose well, to find and use the right glue and build well?

Does your core whisper – there must be more to life than this? Believe it.

We are physical, mental, emotional and spiritual beings and the whisperings of our soul and conscience testify to this.

Be a glue-seeker.

'A life of compassion is the expansion of our hearts into a world-embracing space of healing from which no one is excluded.'

HENRI NOUWEN[16]

« **Detail** – See page 105

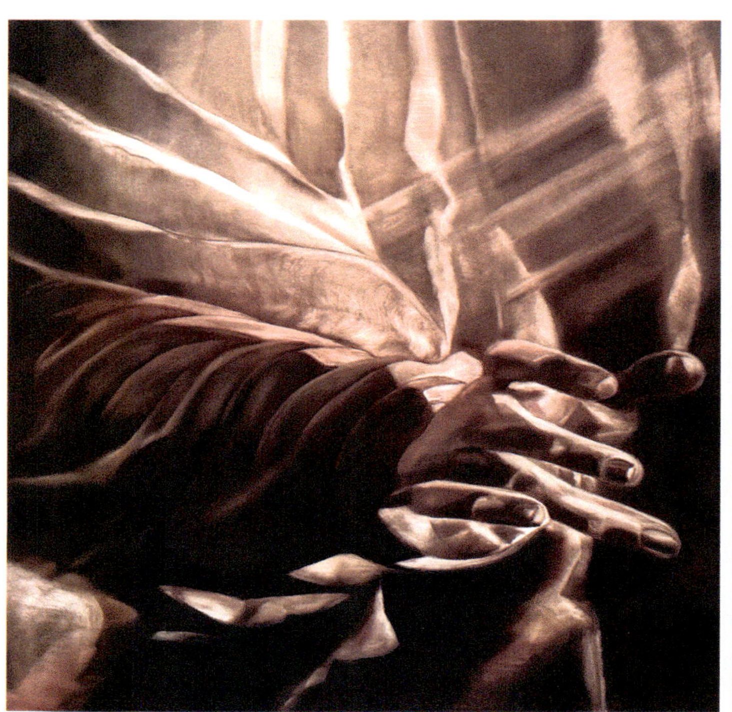

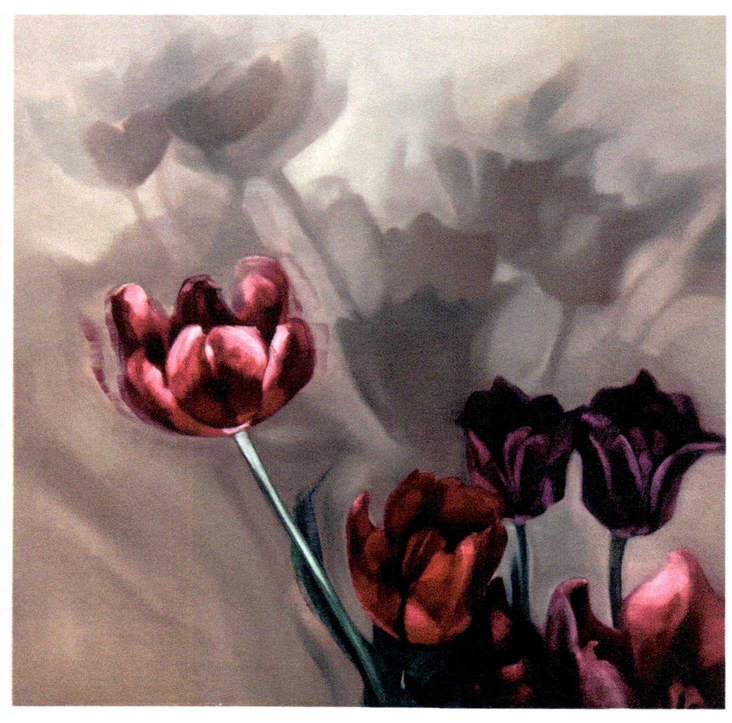

DEBORAH PEARSE

The Temptation of St. Eve

Oil on canvas

H: 100cm W: 200cm

Eve, since biblical times, has been assigned the role of transgressor. Here she becomes deified, yet the cost is to be cast in stone. Her re-imagined dilemma continues to explore the apparent paradoxes within Western spirituality, embodiment and knowledge. The shadows of the surrounding tulips appear as a heralding chorus in this exploration of the first temptation.

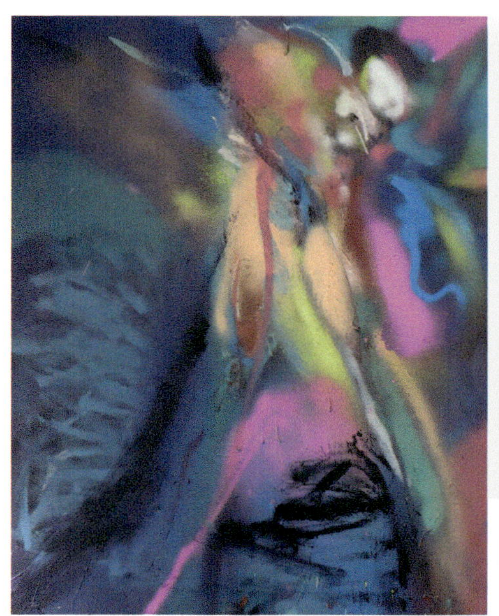
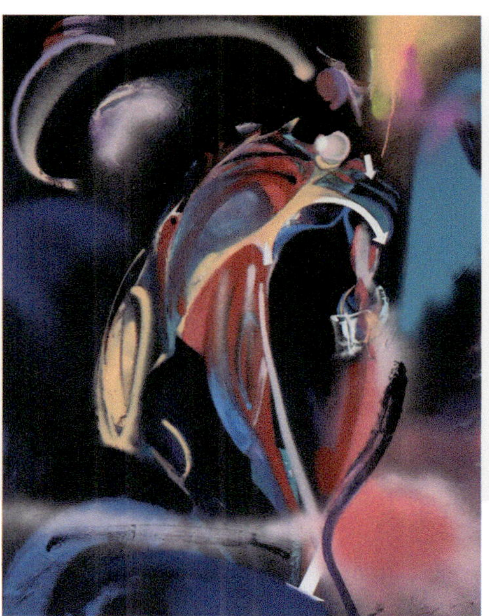
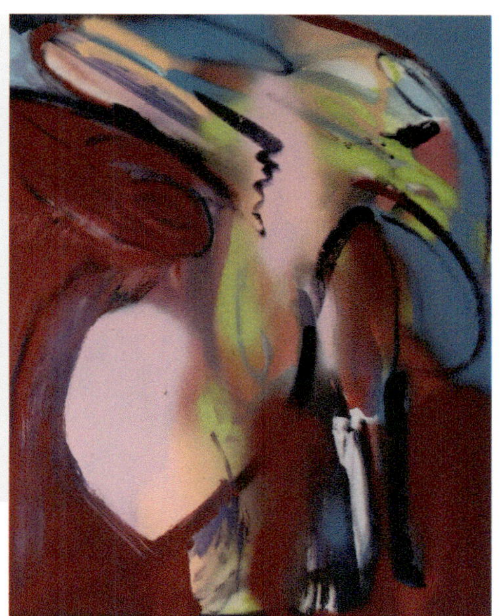

MATTHEW PRIOR

Manifestation!

Acrylic on linen

H: 200cm W: 460cm

A triptych of self-portraits portraying the acute feeling of awe at living, plucked in an instant from the silence of oblivion back to inescapable, incomprehensible, deafening reality producing violent postures wracked in tension.

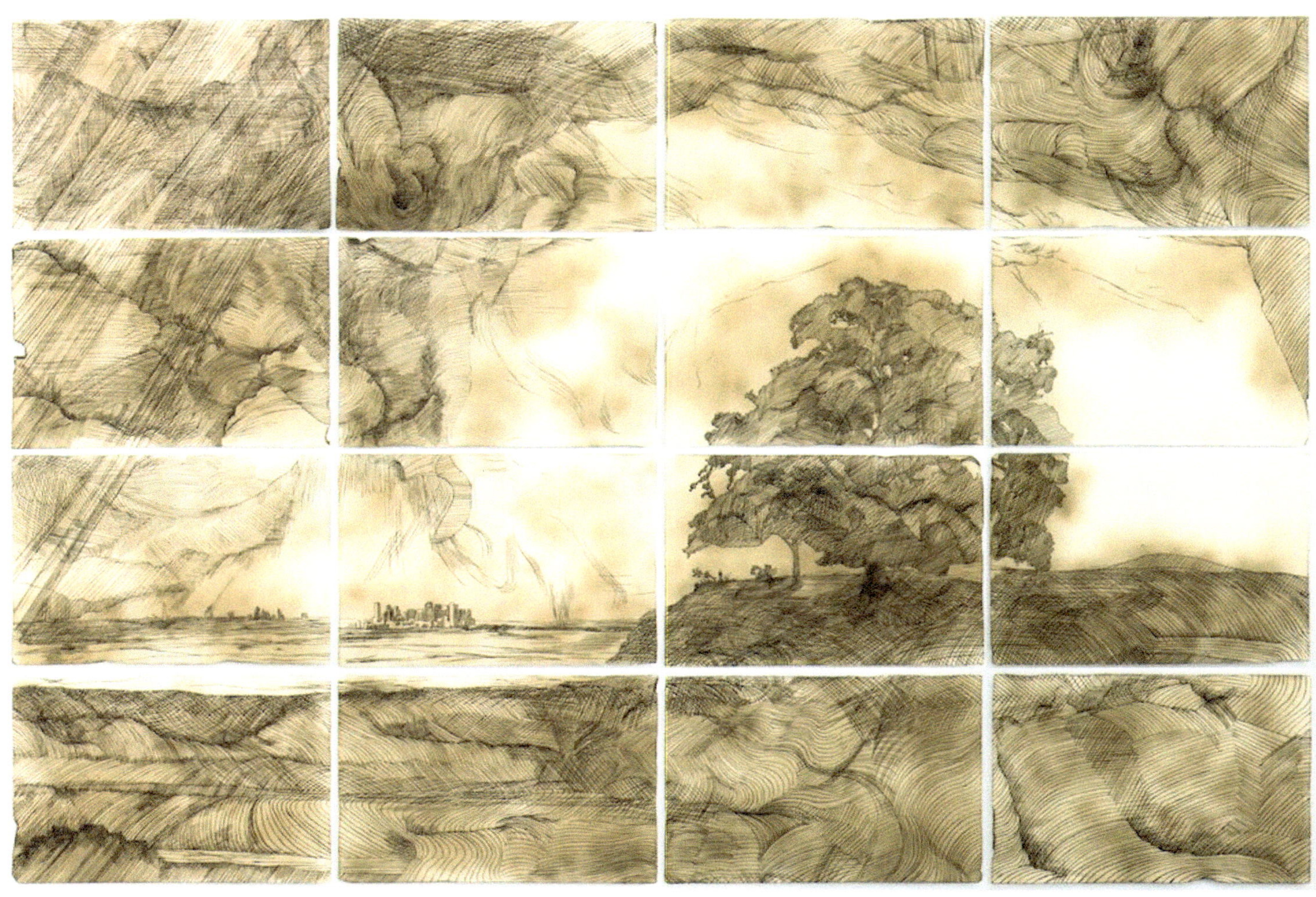

KAORI HOMMA

Lament Over a City

Aburidashi fire etching on paper

H: 200cm W: 250cm

A London cityscape produced during lockdown, referencing the uneasy stillness of the halting of human activity. Perhaps a lament of Christ over the city, a yearning. Our twenty-first-century technology and knowledge have not absolved us from ourselves.

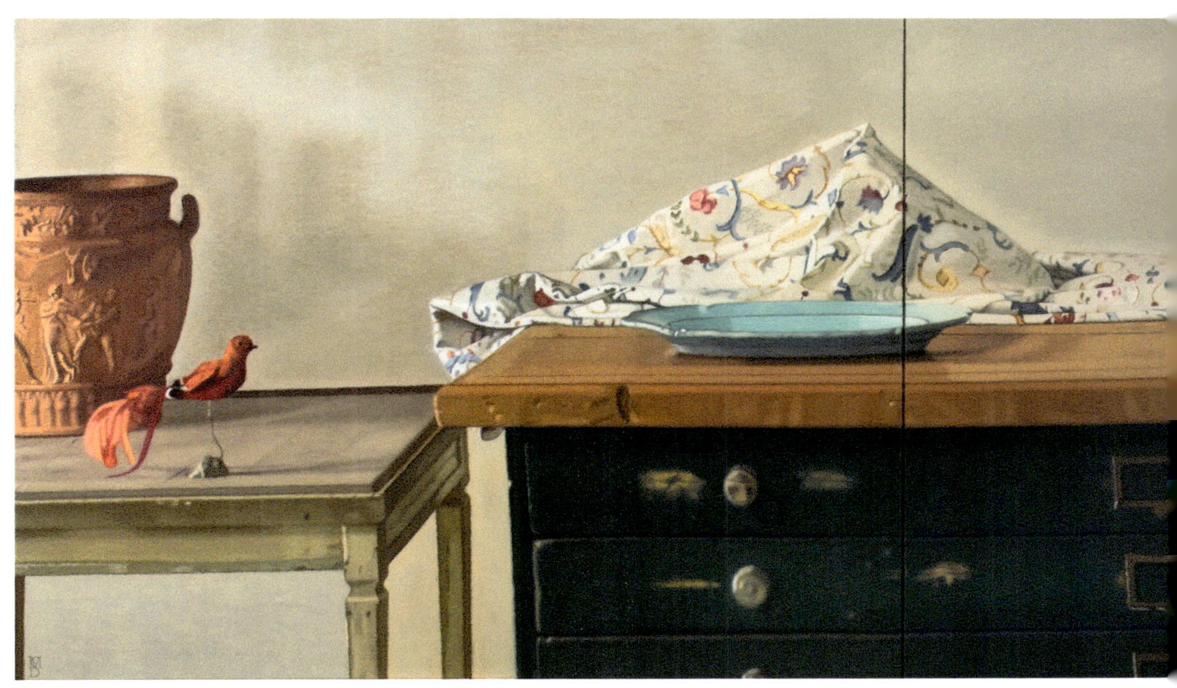

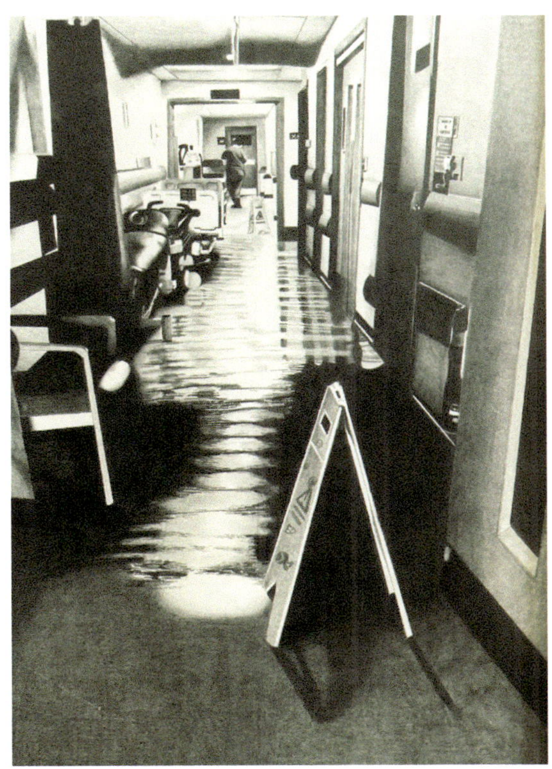

MICHAEL SANGSTER

The Red Bird and the Mountain of Paradise

Oil on linen

H: 88cm W: 153cm

A Preface to Paradise Lost by C S Lewis, where he acknowledges a land with ancient cities but the Mountain of Paradise shining exponentially, is the catalyst of meaning captured in the mountain-shaped cloth. A consummation of ancient symbol meeting with individual contemporary perception.

LAURA MERCHANT-MARTIN

Numbed

Pencil drawing

H: 42cm W: 32cm

Beauty can be found in the bleakest of places, provoking awe and wonder from the mundane. Hospitals can carry oppressive connotations, numbing us to how remarkable they are: technology, the understanding of medicine, the resilience of the human body, the compassion of many.

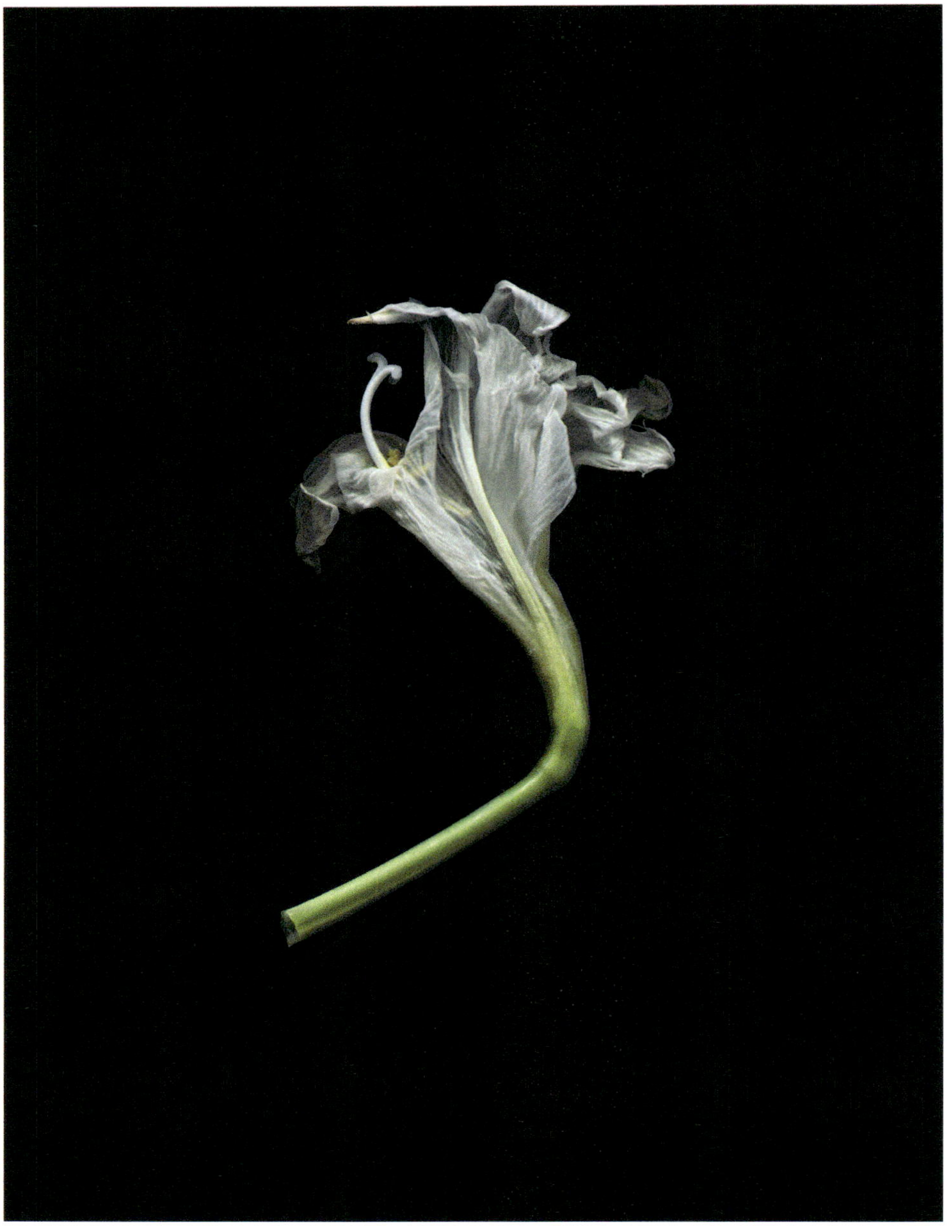

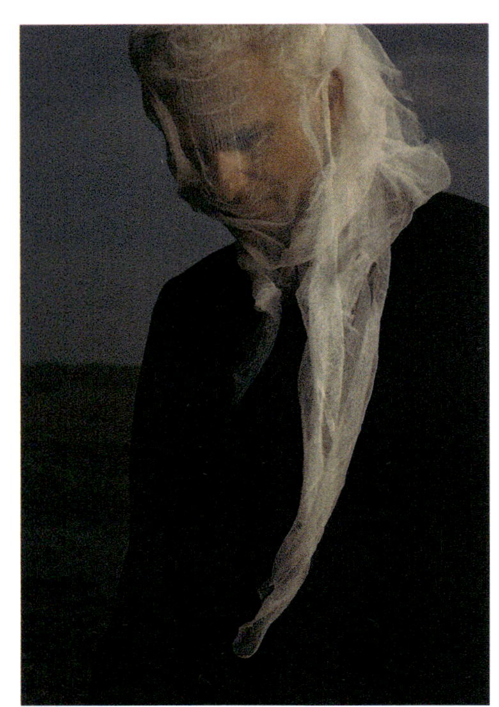

CESCA DIEBSCHLAG

White Amaryllis Ageing

Giclée print of digital photograph

H: 40cm W: 30cm

All living things experience the process of ageing. Contrary to the superficial 'prettiness' championed by popular culture, many life forms, including human beings, are at their most beautiful as they go through this process, expressing the poignantly transient nature of existence.

STEVE PILL

Untitled (Out to Sea #70)

Photography (framed C-type print)

H: 40cm W: 29cm

From a project exploring the water's edge along the shoreline of England's Blackwater Estuary finding back roads and pathways that connect across this somewhat desolate, mysterious and spiritual location. The subject, an old friend, his spirit and changing mood owing to his personal transformative experience.

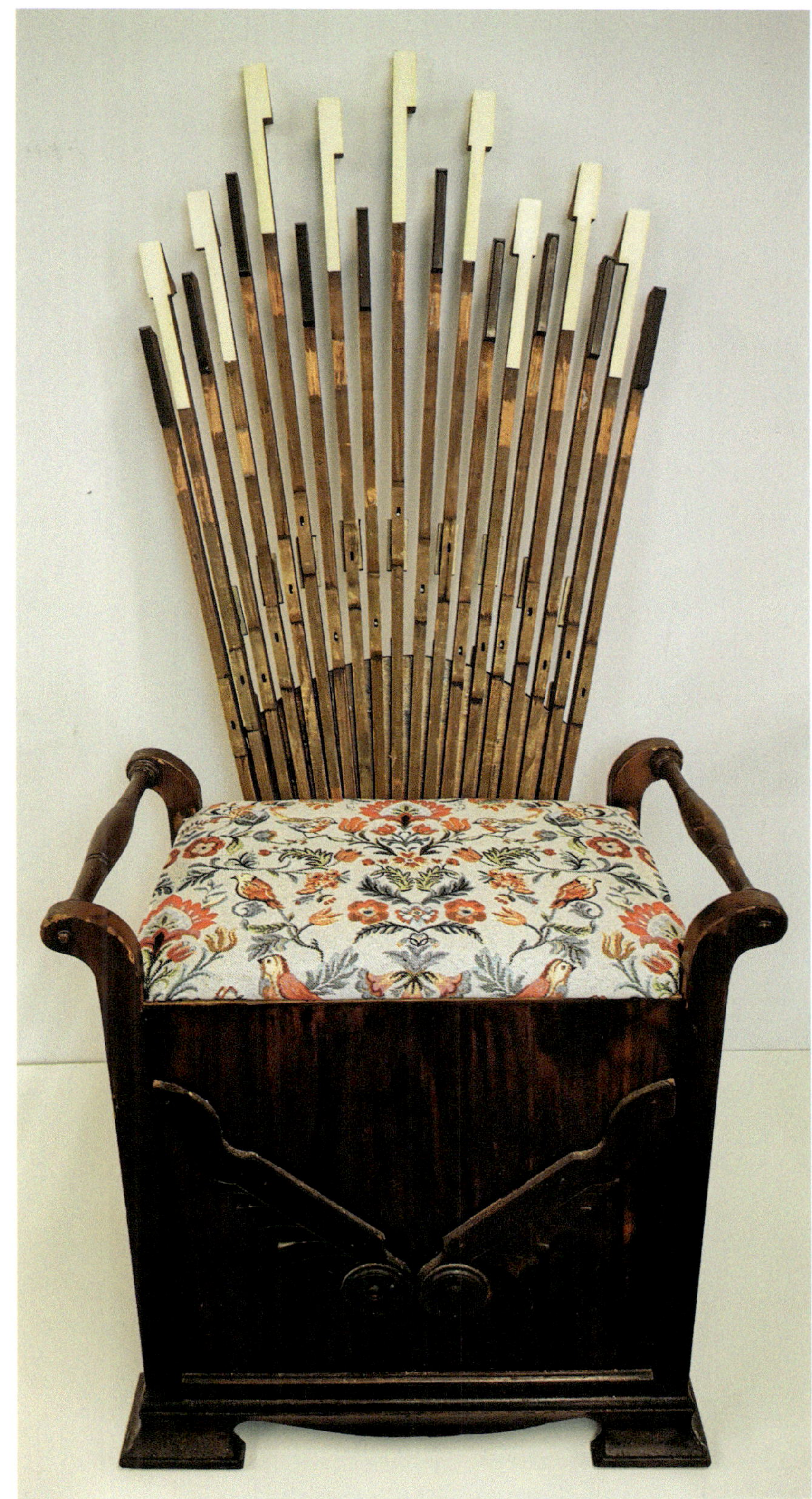

MAUREEN JORDAN

Voix Celestes (Heavenly Voices)

H: 120cm W: 53cm D: 40cm

'Voix Céleste' is an organ stop consisting of either one or two ranks of pipes slightly out of tune. It also means Heavenly Voices. Allow the world to quieten and sit and activate each of the six stools. Hear recorded birdsong or music inspired by birds – Ralph Vaughan Williams' 'The Lark Ascending' or Messiaen's 'The Blackbird'.

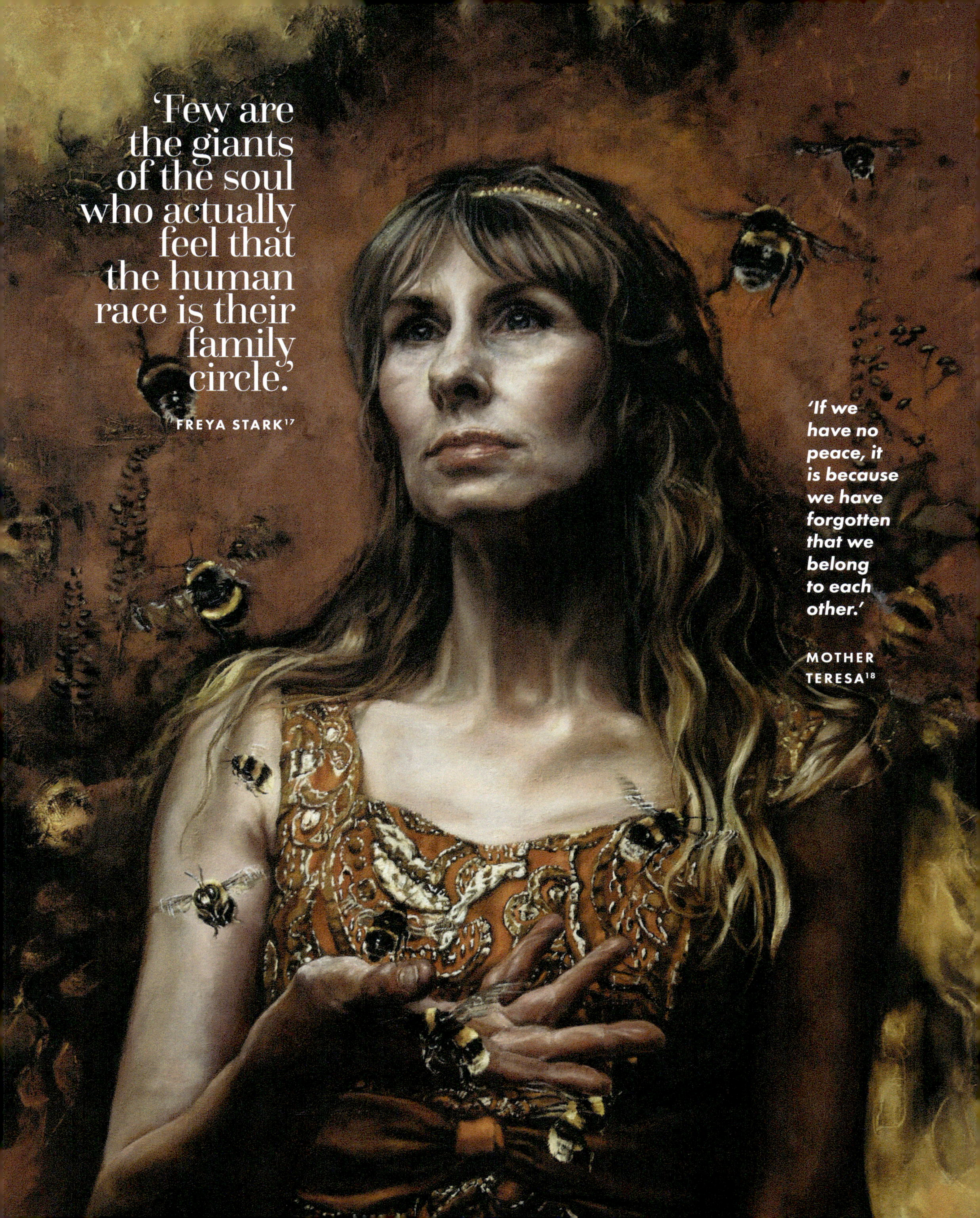
'Few are the giants of the soul who actually feel that the human race is their family circle.'
FREYA STARK[17]
'If we have no peace, it is because we have forgotten that we belong to each other.'
MOTHER TERESA[18]

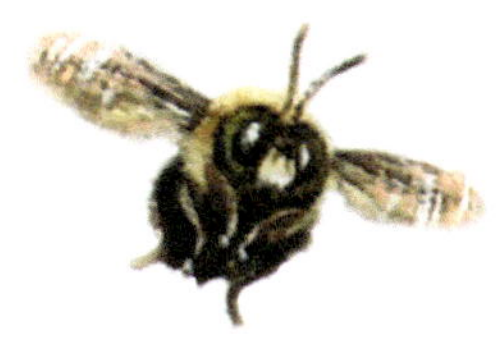

ONENESS

THE ARCHETYPAL ACCOUNT of Adam and Eve, as expressed in Genesis 1:27, makes the most extraordinary claim:

So God created mankind
in his own image,
in the image of God
he created them;
male and female,
he created them.

Whatever our thoughts on this story, or our beliefs, the philosophical idea inherent within it is remarkable.

It suggests that we are made in the image of God, not only as individuals, but as a collective. Genders together represent the likeness of God, but not simply as, for example, a marriage unit; rather the fullness of the form of God is made manifest through the oneness of all human beings together. In our divine connection with the rest of humanity, an extraordinary, many-faceted whole, we exhibit the entire image of God.

Think of a queen honeybee. She is the mother of the hive – every single bee that works within the colony will have been born from her. She doesn't control the group, other than releasing pheromones that instruct the worker bees what cells to construct in the hive. Colonies may be more than 50,000. Collectively they are one. They swarm as one; they care for the hive as one; they work together as one. All descend from one.

'If you change the way you look at things, the things you look at change.'

Wayne Dyer[19]

There is something powerful and spiritual about coexisting in a unified state with our fellow human beings. Equally important is the distinctiveness of everyone. We are not clones. The DNA of each is unique. It is beyond surprising and somewhat overwhelming that estimates are that 117 billion members of our species have lived on planet Earth. There is no average person in this. Each human being is remarkable! You, dear reader, are unique and wonderfully made.

What if we lived as a whole family of families? There wouldn't be 'Othering' with this philosophy, no 'me', 'mine' accumulation, no abject loneliness and isolation, rather family working at loving each other.

The ambition of this idea is breath-taking and humbling.

But it is not how we live.

Current armed conflicts, some of which have lasted more than fifty years:[20]

Region	Conflicts
Middle East and North Africa	**45+**
Africa	**35+**
Asia	**21**
Europe	**7**
Latin America	**6**

The estimated number of civilian casualties in Ukraine during Russia's invasion, verified by OHCHR 22nd January 2023, is 7,068, with 438 of those children; injured 11,415, children 838.[21]

« **Detail** – See page 21

first light

'Earth's crammed with heaven,
And every common bush afire with God:
But only he who sees takes off his shoes.'

ELIZABETH BARRETT BROWNING[23]

Awe: 'the feeling of being in the presence of something vast that transcends your current understanding of the world.'

DACHER KELTNER[22]

DREAM

THE MAN STOOD facing the landscape of his life. A life he had built with care, growing beauty, friendship, intimacy. He had dreamt of streams of living water, succulent and teeming, beside which would grow a tree.

This tree, begun as a seed filled with promise, had germinated and broken through the ground. He wanted it to reach the sky. Over the years, despite the storms that ripped branches from the trunk, it had stood and continued to grow. New life emerged through all the times of brokenness into fresh fruitfulness. Leafy branches spread out over the flowing water that filled it and him with soul vitality.

But now a fresh storm had turned the stream into a river behind him, flooding the rock and earth, and with its growing strength and momentum the flow had undermined the water-saturated soil, which had begun to move, sliding down a growing incline.

His strength was corroding through vulnerability, insecurity and fear. It gathered pace as his circumstances refused to abate, and the emerging slope grew steeper. His fear accelerated. His inner trembling battered his peace and sense of self, and he cried out for help.

His desperate eyes searched the landscape, but it was empty.

His soul quietened in Time's awful yearning.

A sound. Several sounds. Footsteps.

He scanned the far distance, to the horizon – nothing. Was he imagining the noises?

More footsteps – closer – behind – he turned.

Beyond the now steep gradient a tiny figure walked towards him.

It's too sheer, he worried.

The figure grew larger and larger.

He watched him put a foot onto the sheer pitch without hesitation. With each of his steps so the gradient lessened, bringing the figure closer until he stepped from flat ground onto the space behind him.

Comfort lifted his arms and embraced him from behind so both overlooked the man's landscape. The sense of being held, his isolation broken, his pain silently understood made the man weep.

'I have your back,' came the whisper.

The trembling stopped.

Fear fell from him.

The storm continued.

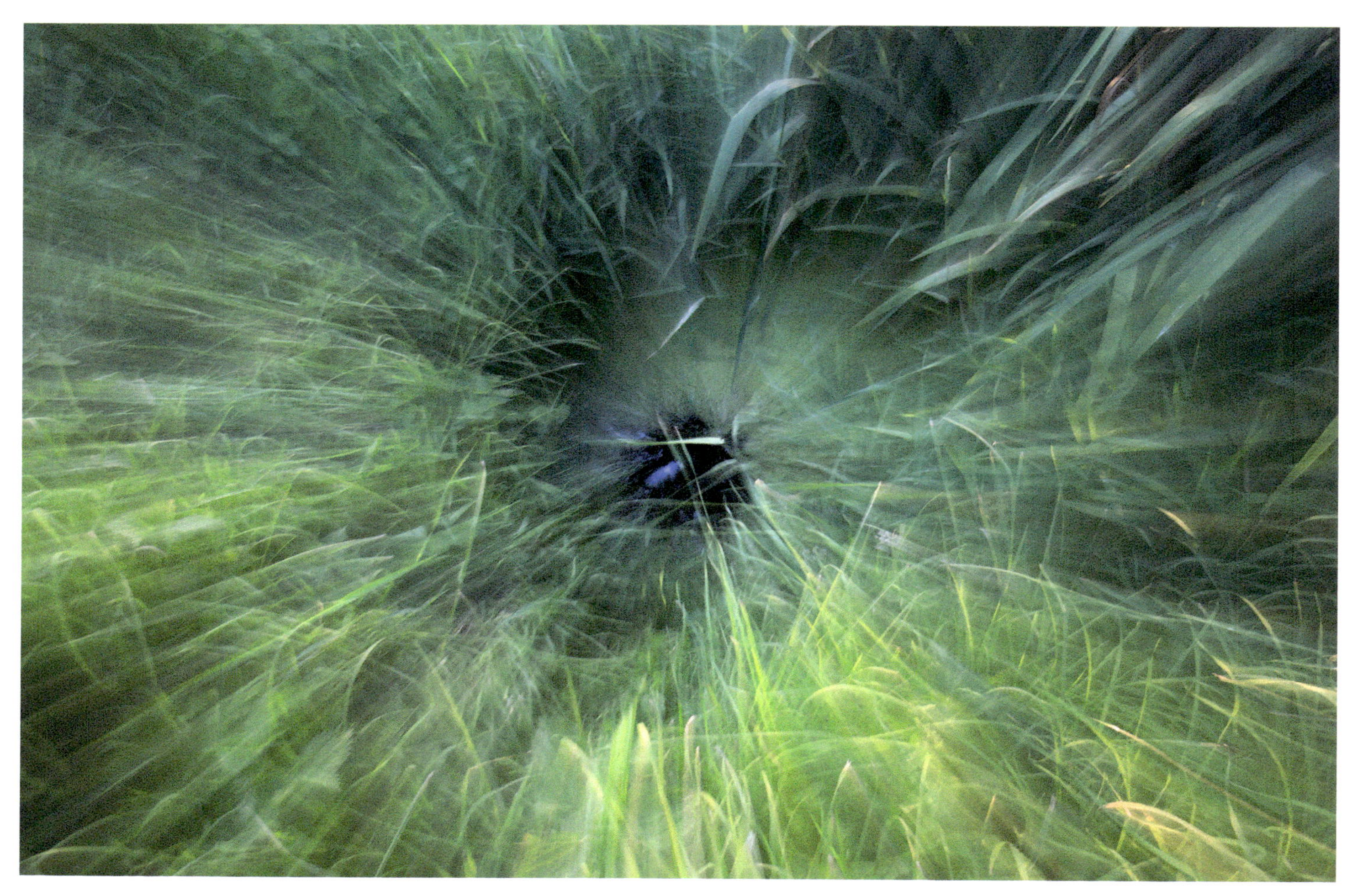

MARIA SCARD

Eye of the Well

Photograph mounted behind HD Acrylic, 1 of 10

H: 100cm W: 150cm

A spiritual journey exploring 'thin places'. A Celtic term for locations where the veil between the physical and the spiritual is almost transparent. These liminal (threshold) places include gifts of a glimmer of light, a whisper, a strength, a presence and peace. The location – the Eye of the Well of St Mary's Well, Thelnetham, Suffolk.

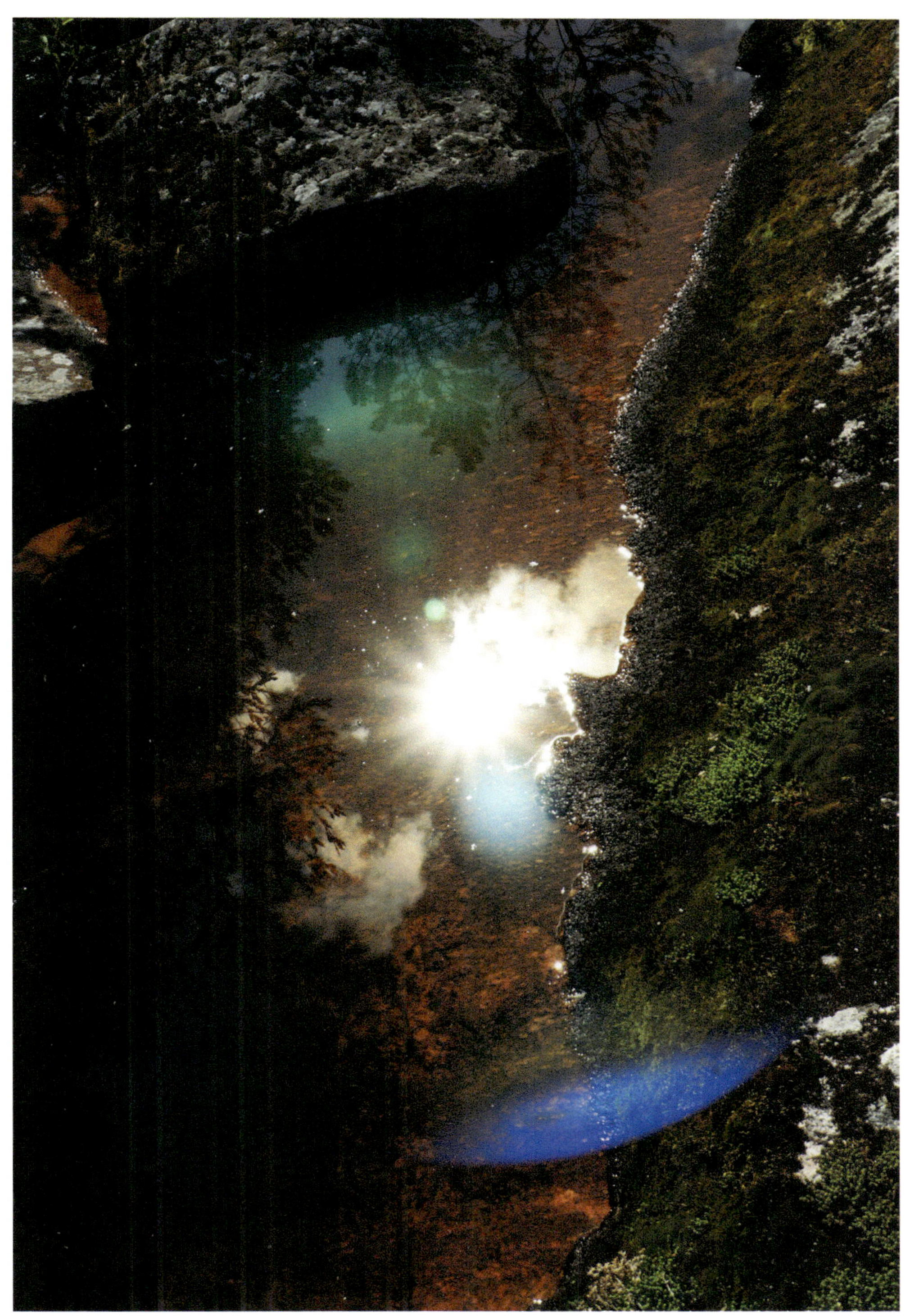

HEIDI KUIVANIEMI-SMITH

The Universe on Earth

Photograph

H: 75cm W: 55cm

Inspired by a reflection from the sun in a puddle on a small island of Lake Saimaa in Finland. I am fascinated by reflections, and immensely inspired by nature. All my visual art and music aim to present the wonder of it in a unique way.

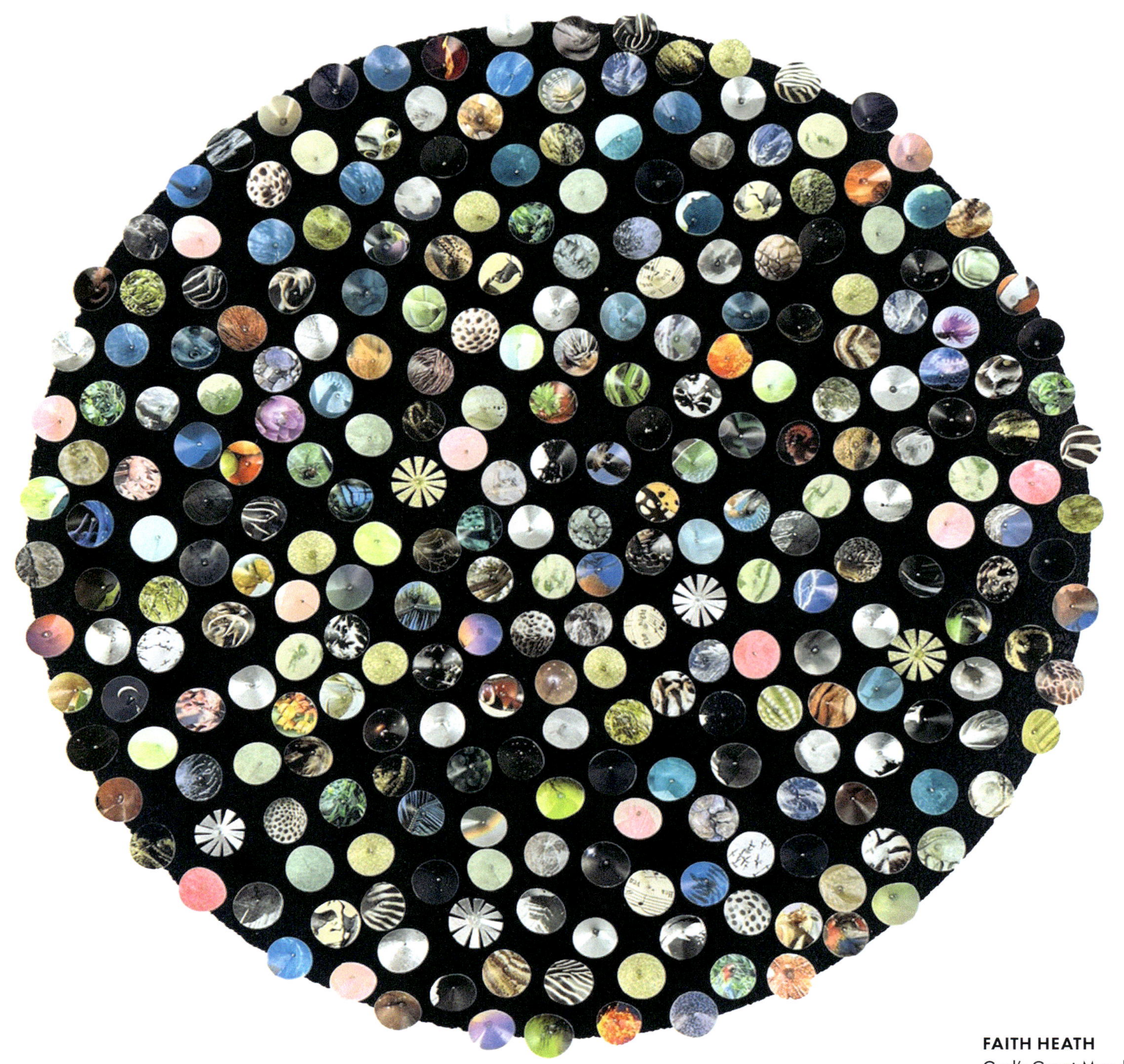

FAITH HEATH

God's Great Mood Board

Pinned paper collage on cork board

H: 50cm W: 50cm

The unfathomable supremacy of God – as if every flash of inspiration were pinned on a giant master plan. Space, time, colour, form, shape, depth, height, texture and substance. The work aims to express the great mystery at the heart of science. A magnificent simplicity underlying the astonishing complexity of the universe.

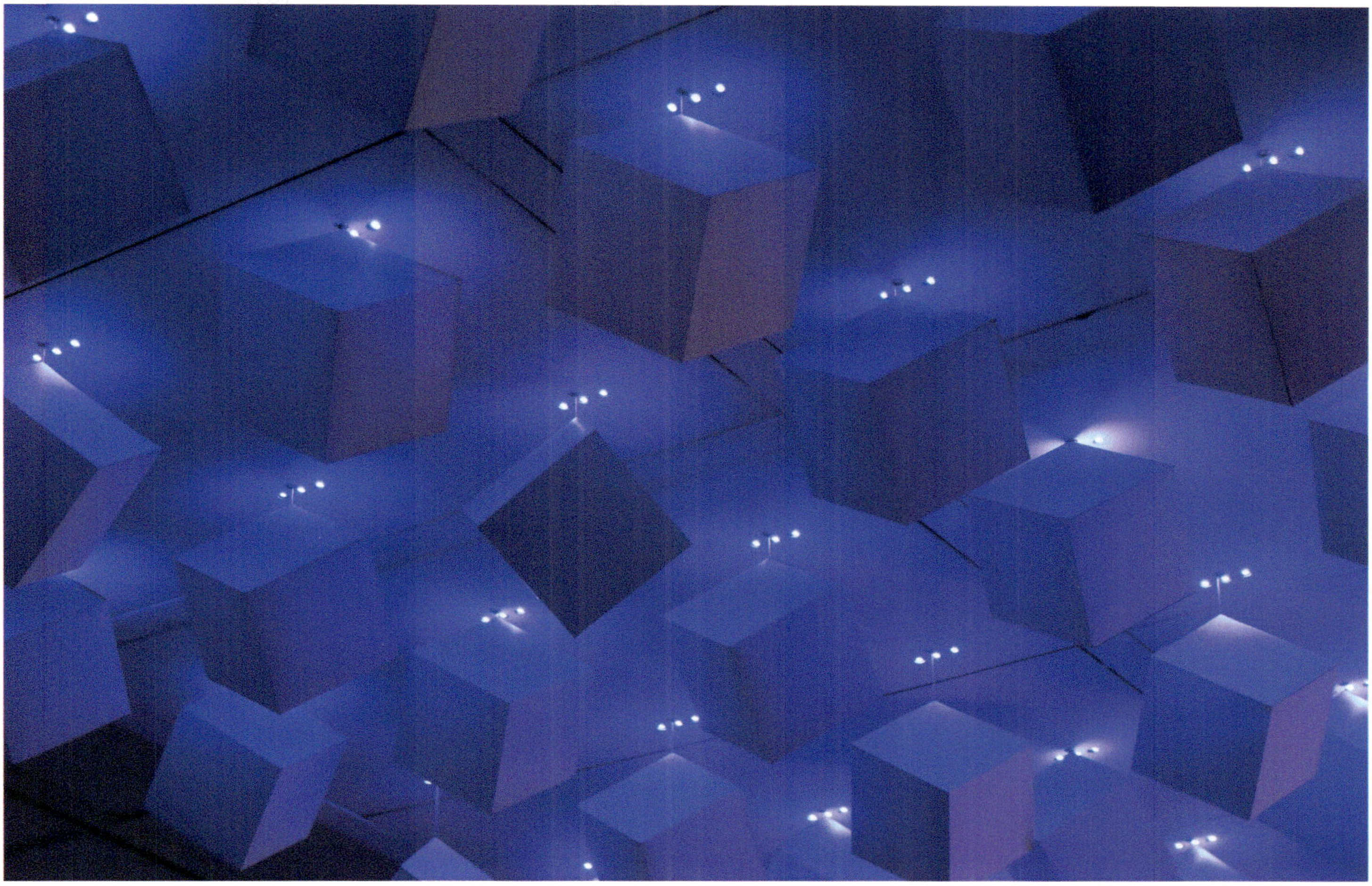

TOBY BROCKWAY

Kinetic Wonder

A kinetic wave

H: 50cm W: 260cm
D: 160cm

From the disorder of formless matter and infinite space, God illuminated every atomic particle He spoke into existence. These particles continued their mesmerising dance to bring awe-inspiring order to an ever-evolving creation. Observe the illuminated geometric shapes make organic patterns, creating the perfect sine waves replicated throughout creation, forming the building blocks of the universe.

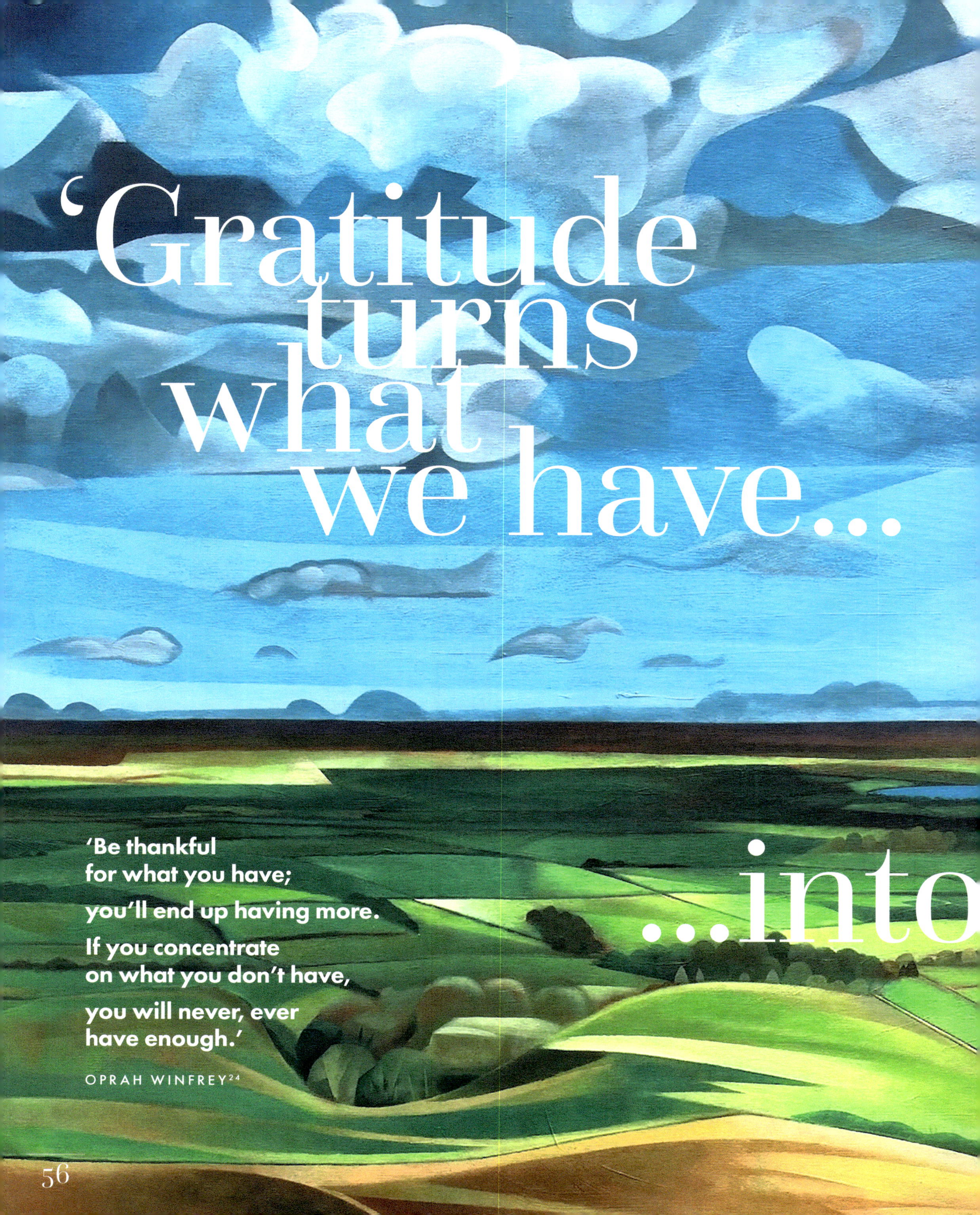
'Gratitude turns what we have...
...into
'Be thankful for what you have; you'll end up having more. If you concentrate on what you don't have, you will never, ever have enough.'
OPRAH WINFREY[24]

WONDERMENT

IT HAPPENS at different times.

When walking along a beach. Nostrils fill with the scent of salt, lungs breathe fresh wind-tossed air, eyes cast longingly over the vast expanse of grey water, taking in the equally grey clouds scudding across unending sky. The sight of windblown gulls lifting and swooping. The sand pattering on calves and back as it races along the length of shore creating a carpet of sandy rivulets upon which to trudge. Leaning forward into the spattering air, dancing around the incoming waves. The all-encompassing sounds rich with tones of bird squawks, discarded pebbled sand, alongside water thrumming onto the beach. The hoarse water's cry of return to the sea.

It happens when walking in winter sunshine among season's ending. The smell of damp leaves downed by bucketing rain, their golden auburn heightened in welly-splashing delight.

enough.'

MELODY BEATTIE[25]

Diffused light enlivens the multitude of greens displayed by the leaves still clinging to the branches rich with birdsong. Above, bright blue sky hosting a singular snow-white cloud, bursts with colour. The small lake echoes a perfect reflection of trees and foliage, of sky, of natural ornament. The patient foraging and diving of ducks. Mysterious paths littered with autumn's debris disappear into the still leafy forest, their trunks creating complex shadows through which is spied a golden sunlit space.

It happens when watching children play, their faces alive with endless possibilities. The special moment when the substance of a fresh idea for a game breaks out into improvisation. How quickly they communicate with each other! Objects transform their usage. Cushions become dens. Fabric a waterway. Mummies transform into threatened individuals involved in a critical incident who require the emergency services.

It happens when looking at a partner's face as they take over the kitchen to bake their bread. A Covid-learned skill to provide continuous soda bread. The preparation is as serious as any CEO decision made in a previous life.

What happens?

An outbreak of thankfulness. A thankfulness for life, for love and for being the recipient of both.

Thankfulness doesn't just happen; it is a learned way of seeing the world.

« Detail — See page 109

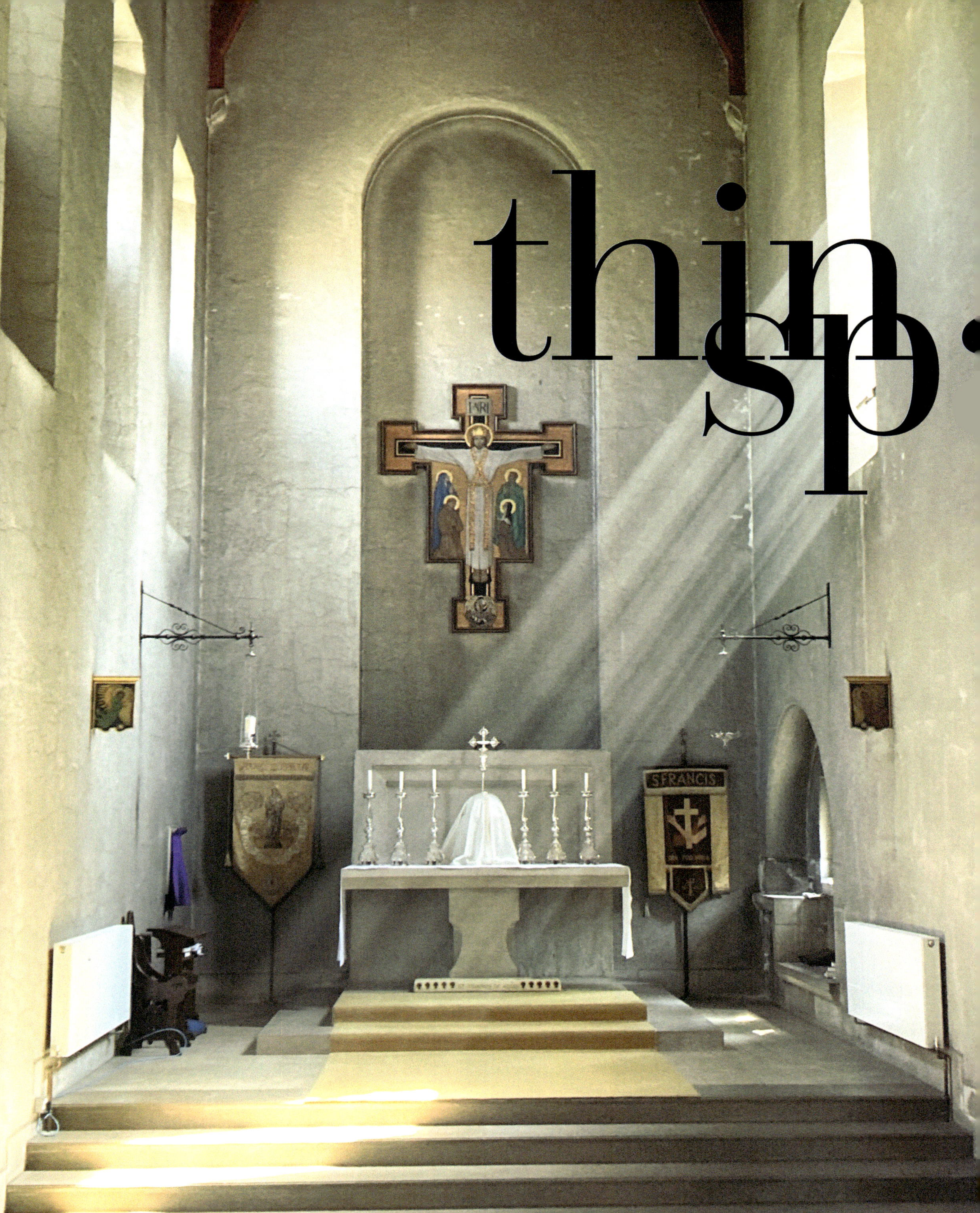

thin
sp

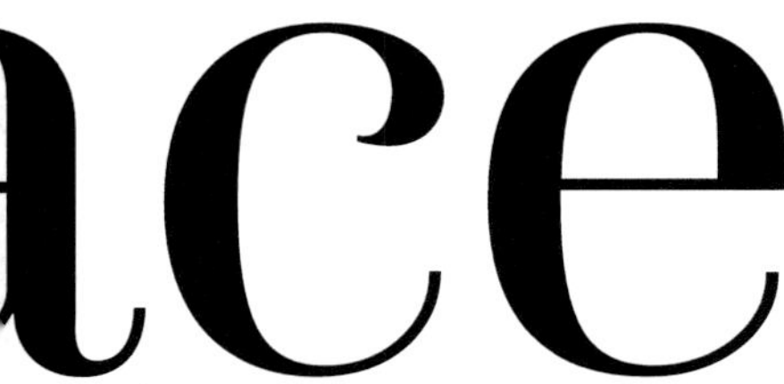

PRESENCE

Rains fall, but do not soak –
Peace descends –
Beauty unfolds –
An opening,
A scent,
A perfect hymn of praise
Sung without words.

Presence deepens,
Emotion wells,
And tears meld with thankfulness.
To be known,
Allowed to be.

Enfolding ripples of warmth
Flow in never-ending languor.
The presence of the numinous
Captured
Within and without
A simple human.

What promise awaits
When flesh departs to be
emancipated
Into spirit?

Spirit and Spirit Three shall dance
A reel
Outside time
Into all things new.

'Awe is almost always nearby, and is a pathway to healing and growing in the face of the losses and traumas that are part of life.'

Edward Posnett[26]

« **Detail** – See page 65

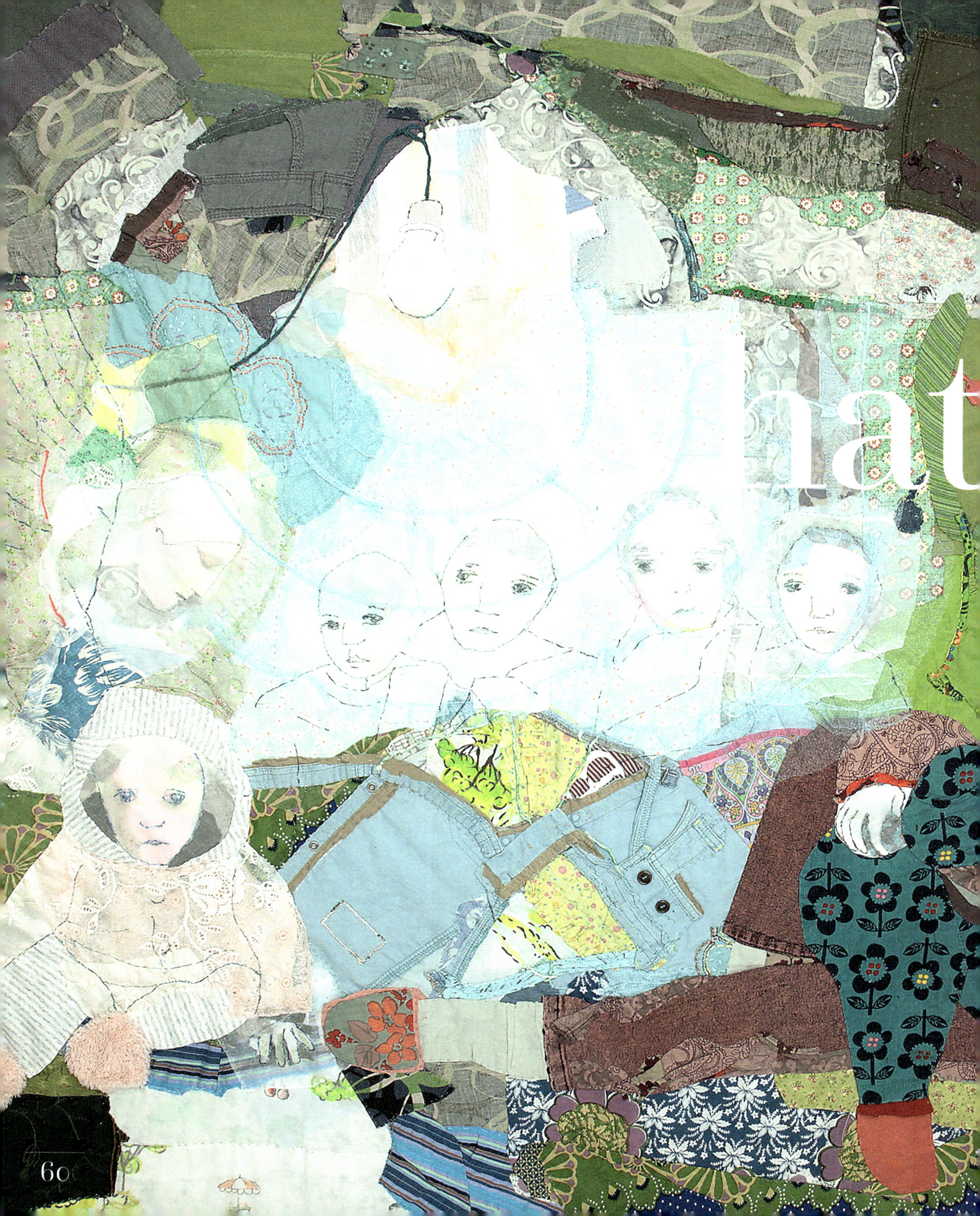
hat

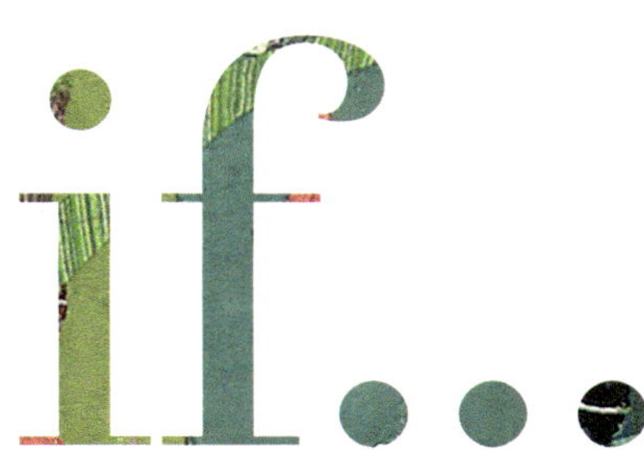

'Aim at heaven and you will get earth thrown in.

Aim at earth and you get neither.'

C S LEWIS[27]

WHAT IF it were possible to live a life without fear? Fear of anything in our past, any mistreatment, aggression, oppression, of abusing power and its relentless pressing. There is no dislike, envy, comparison or hatred. No desire to force ourselves upwards, and no accusation. The joy of being able to journey where we will, to any place, devoid of fear of attack, robbery, disfigurement, injury, rape or any disgusting diminishing of any type. No crime, no petty destruction, no alcoholism, drug-taking, nothing that reduces the human being.

WHAT IF it could be a life without stress? No having to, must do, should do. An active, purposeful life but joyful, fulfilling, doing/building/making/creating, filled with absorption, delight and sharing without comparison, without competition, without ridicule or misunderstanding. The simple life of acceptance and delight with a place for all we were made for. A usefulness coupled with appreciation. An existence empty of depression or any type of mental or physical illness.

WHAT IF it were a life without pride or ego in oneself or others? No in-fighting, out-fighting, toxic behaviour, tearing down, belittling or mockery. A place where your name is known and said with a smile.

WHAT IF we all embrace a life of humility? Individuals with a sense of who they are, their abilities, where they fit – because there is a perfect place for each – allowing rich contentment. The only agenda to give. No 'rightness', no keeping order, because people live in harmony exhibiting their best selves, enjoying each other.

WHAT IF we could love perfectly and receive perfect love? Love's infusion frees, delights, fills. Love's light allows each to dance in their own way, to bring everything together into glorious technicolour focus. It releases dreaming, thriving, motivation, connection, embracing. The intimacy of shared laughter and experience. The confidence to love ourselves, in quiet contentment with no regret, recrimination, nagging criticism, finger-pointing transgression. The constant replaying of upsetting memories of shame, selfishness, violence, our wrongdoing dismissed never to return. Each person, as themselves, is enough.

WHAT IF it were somewhere filled with learning, song and awe? Among such wonder finding some of the people we loved in a longed-for, never-to-be-separated-again, reunion.

WHAT IF we found ourselves in the actual presence of the Creator we loved, never to be parted?

WOULD WE WANT TO RETURN TO LIFE ON EARTH?

« **Detail** — See page 78

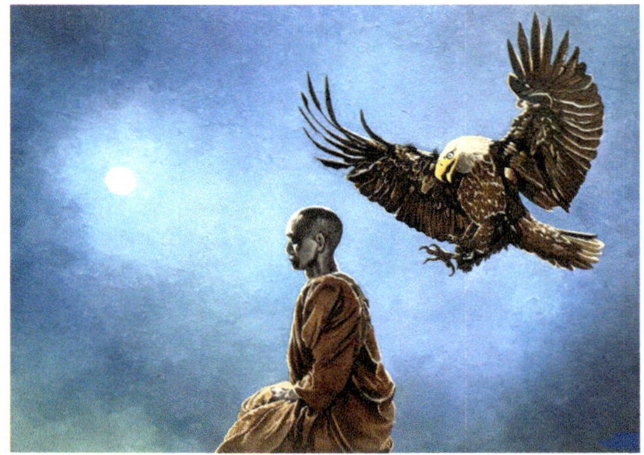

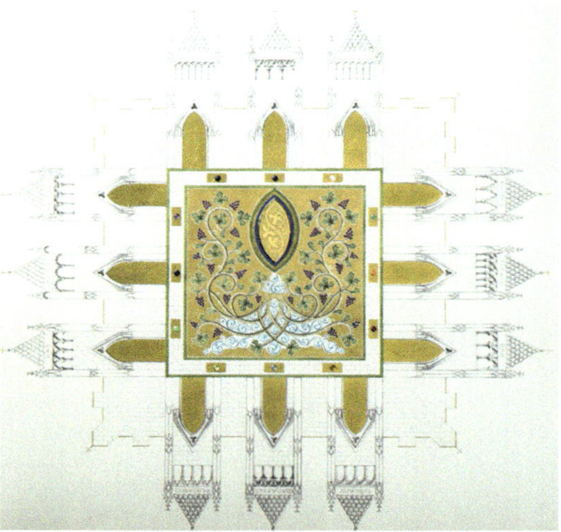

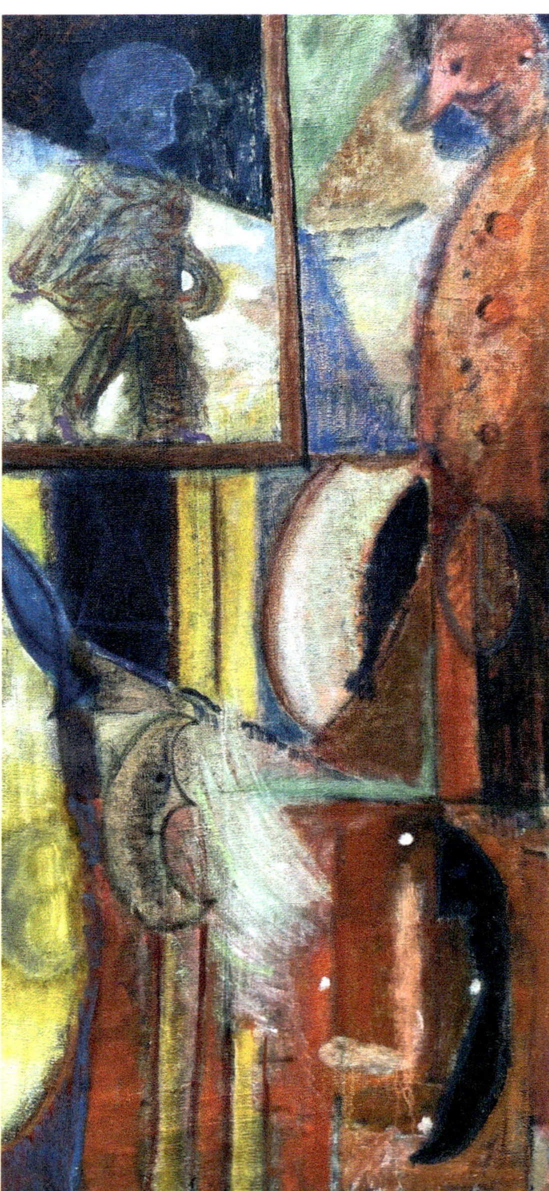

BARBARA WIELGOSZ

Dream Within a Dream

Oil on board

H: 60cm W: 86cm

Inspired by Edgar Allan Poe's eponymous poem: a conversation with God symbolised by the bird of prey overlooked by the moon, symbolic of transformation. How can atoms convert into cells, into living beings able to experience the universe? We hold on to nothing, and life never stops changing and transforming.

HELEN WHITE

The Heavenly Jerusalem

Gold leaf, shell gold and watercolour on vellum with cabochon jewels

H: 62cm W: 62cm

(photo credit Ian Fraser)

The description of the Heavenly City (Revelation 21, the Bible) is astonishing: only here will our longings for peace, security, wholeness, justice, righteousness – and much more – be satisfied. My illumination uses gold leaf to represent the glory of God. This portal between heaven and earth is personified by the fully God and fully human Christ.

SAM McGOUN

Two Moons

Oil on hessian

H: 167cm W: 76cm

All the characters are in conversation with one another: the figure on the right is all-knowing and floats above this world, spectating, admiring and closely watching his creation in wonder. The boy will start an exploration of his own into the Creator's world and walk through fun, colour, mystery and the miracle of life itself.

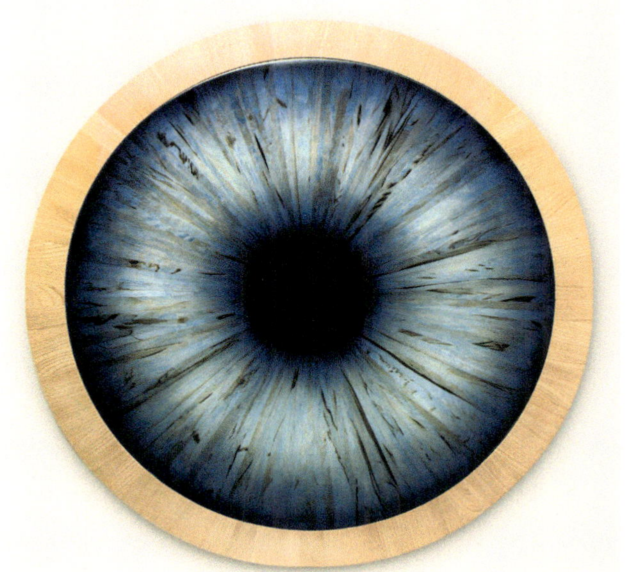

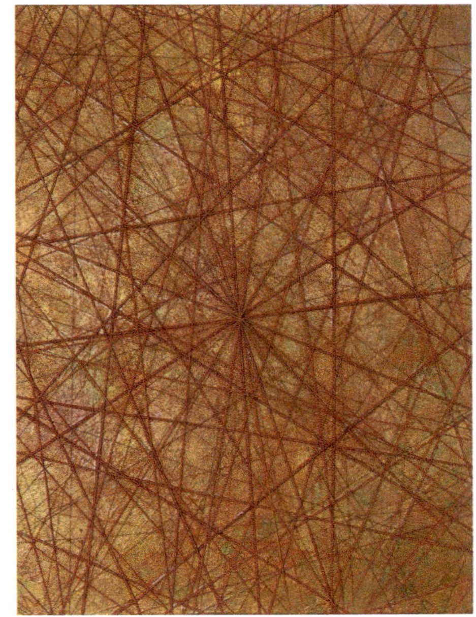

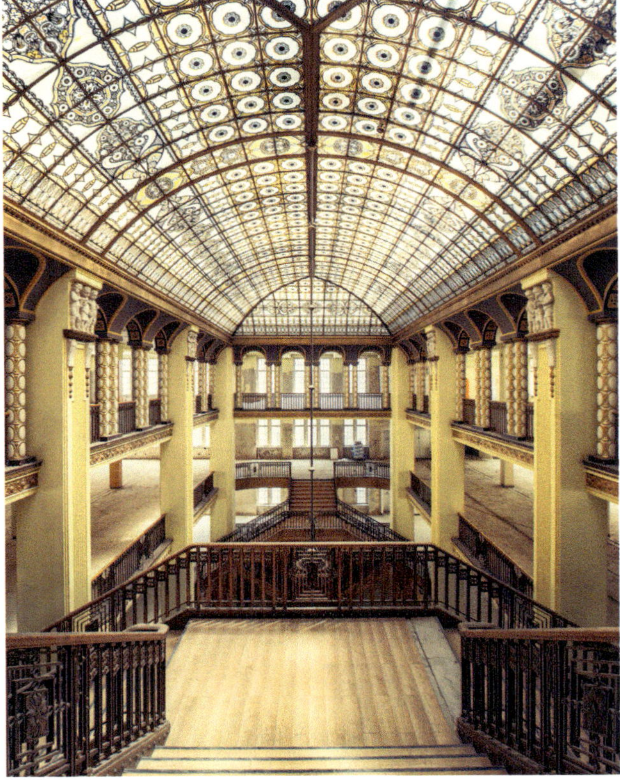

ROBERT ELSDALE

Addiction

A stylised blue eye made from spalted hornbeam wood and finished in a mirror gloss

H: 66cm W: 66cm

Out of all the colours of the eye, I find blue eyes the most compelling. Intense blue eyes radiate with depth and emotion. Here black oak, carbon-dated at more than 6,000 years old found submerged and untouched underwater in the Cambridgeshire Fens, was reclaimed to form the pupil.

LEWIS DEENEY

The Sun of Intelligence in the World of Ideas

Acrylic, spray paint, metallic pigment, thread, varnish and drawing pins on canvas

H: 81cm W: 61cm

The work is a meditation on emergence, exploring a new cosmic narrative of a self-organising universe waking up to understand itself. Simple interactions create emergent complexity. There is a purpose to the complexity as it is what allows life to exist, evolve and flourish, bringing meaning, awe and wonder into existence.

GINA SODEN

Atrium

Digital image on Hahnemuhle 326gsm

H: 105cm W: 88cm

A beautiful abandoned former department store in Germany, used by Wes Anderson on location for the filming of *The Grand Budapest Hotel*. I got permission to shoot here several years ago. It was an awe inspiring building with a huge and fragile beautiful stained glass ceiling.

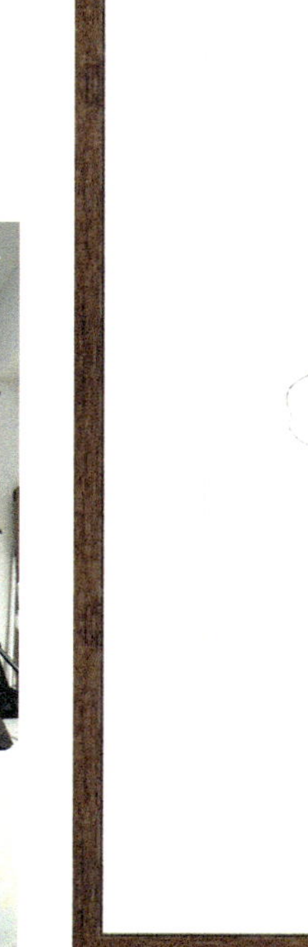

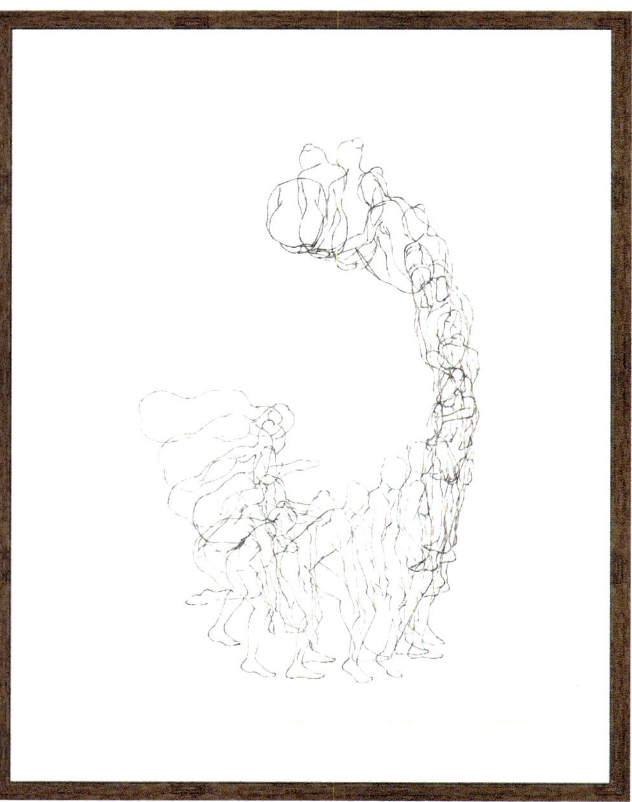

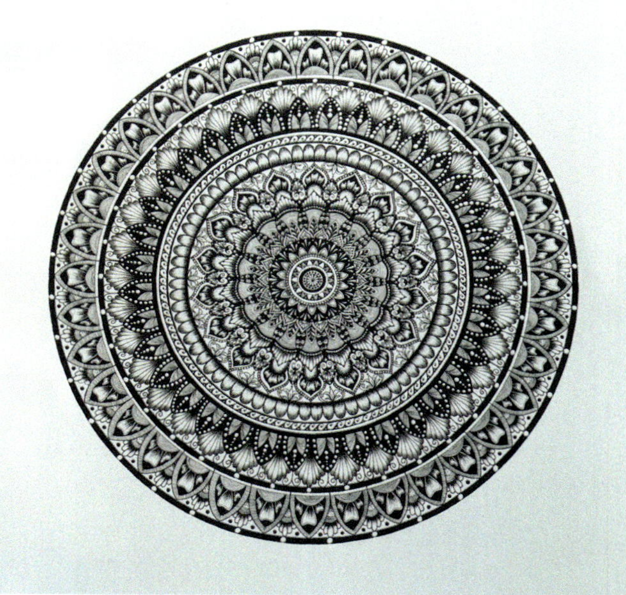

MELODY THORNTON

Melody Fights the Elders and Saves Susanna

Photograph on art paper

H: 120cm W: 85cm

I operate as a modern-day superhero and go back in time to save female protagonists from their impending fate. Inspired by the works of Artemisia Gentileschi (1593–c. 1654), I take heart from her interpretation of classic stories and address the beautification and embellishment of these allegories still pertinent today.

ROSIE WINN

Stillness

Pyrography woodburning pen on paper

H: 95cm W: 70cm

'Stillness' explores the fluidity of emotional change as we navigate through all life experiences, including trauma, to healing and acceptance. The work is drawn with a wood-burning pen, searing onto the paper, promoting an economy of line that encourages non-essentials to be stripped away, allowing purity of form to be revealed.

RACHAEL HARMAN

Transcendence

Pigment ink on illustration board

H: 60cm W: 50cm

Inspired by the reoccurring patterns (fractals) in nature, the universe and the human body, eg, a lightning strike captured in a tree branch and the structure of the human lung. Are we all connected way beyond our comprehension? Be drawn into pattern, into detail, and be transported.

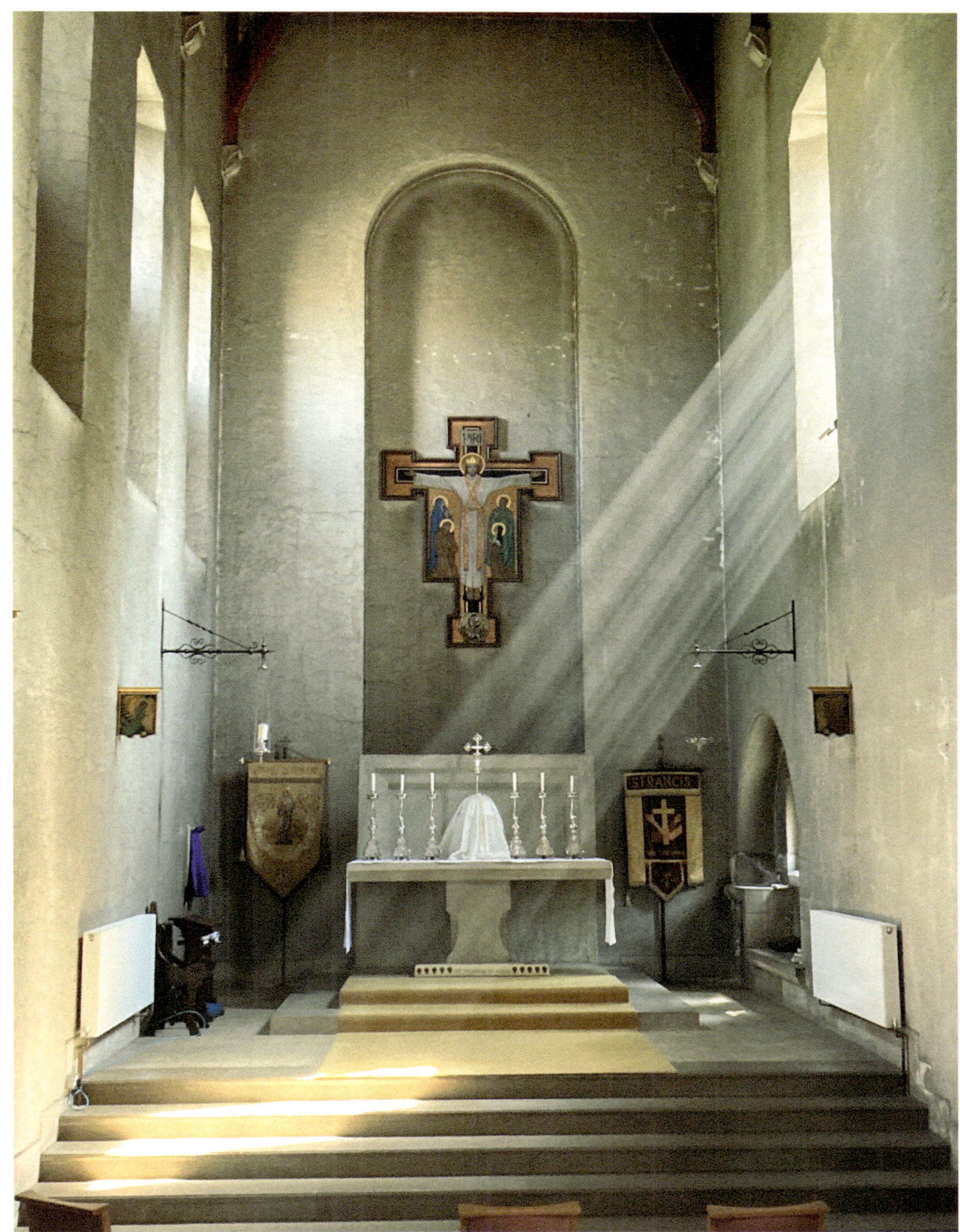

LOUISE HIGGS

A Glimpse of an Eternal World

Digital photograph

H: 121cm W: 91cm

A moment of stillness, embracing awe and wonder within the atmosphere of the church, as if time had stopped, experiencing overwhelming peace. A calmness enveloped my soul. An ephemeral, out-of-time moment with the sunlight aiding a growing awareness of Christ.

embracing the dust

'I find it hard to think of a word that is as unmoored from its root as "awesome".

It comes from the early Middle English *age*, meaning dread, or terror,

but these fail to capture awe's particular blend of fear, reverence and submission.'

EDWARD POSNETT[28]

THE OLIVE PICKER

SHE WAS HOT; she was tired. Everybody had stopped because of the heat of the day, and it was time for food. She raised her head upwards and the light of the sun winked through the trees, its mottled shadows spreading over her skin. One step higher, one further extension of her right arm, and she would reach a plump cluster of green olives.

She stepped, she stretched, she clasped and pulled, then sudden triumph. Some fell to the ground on the fabric laid out to catch the fruit, those in her hand she placed in the bag she wore on her back. As she clambered down the ancient tree, she felt the weight of her plump harvest.

Fifteen minutes ago, many other women, now gone to rest and eat, had stood on the ground, reaching up into the abundance. Others shook the branches to release the fruit. But she had always loved to climb, ever since she was a little girl, and her father taught her how to do it safely. The women would look and shake their heads at her daring, all the while chattering warning, alongside their smiles and laughter at her antics.

She loved the sound of insects vibrating around her; the welcome shade from the intense heat; the occasional brush of wind on her cheek; the smell of the harvest; the yelp of a dog, the bell of the goat. The knowledge of parents who loved her, waiting for her to lunch with them, made her heart sing.

'Thank You, God,' she said in her heart, for Mary was a carefree teenager who loved her life. A life that would soon be turned upside down when she married. A frown crossed her face. She felt excited, but nervous. At least he hailed from the same area.

She looked at her hands and laughed. Dirt lay ingrained in her fingerprints, under her fingernails. 'Farmer's hands,' she thought. Good hands, useful hands.

'Shalom.'

She turned on her heel to face the sound. It had made her jump. A man she had never seen before stood some distance from her under an adjacent tree. He started tipping the fallen olives he had collected from the cover into a container. He smiled at her. He finished his pouring, walked towards her and stopped at an appropriate distance, to face her.

She was aware of stillness. The thin air, the motionless leaves of the tree, no incessant insect sound, rather a habitation of peace, as if time itself had paused its breath.

'Be still my trembling body,' she thought as she inspected him. He wasn't a farmworker like her. His clothes were... spotless. His face had more than a smile...it...shone.

« **Detail** — See page 21

dust

'*Shalom*, beautiful lady. God is alongside you.'

Her right hand involuntarily moved and presented him with an outstretched palm. 'No further,' she thought as she stepped back, her mind puzzling over his strange words.

'Don't be fearful, Mary...'

'He knows my name?' her head screeched. 'What is this?'

'God delights in you.'

The man knelt to the ground and smiled, his gaze never leaving her face. His eyes, so searching, so kind.

'You're going to give birth to a baby, a son; you must call Him Jesus.'

Her palm lowered. He stopped. Those words. She had heard those words before. Manoah, of course, his wife in the field, she was barren, and an angel visited her and told her she was going to give birth. Her son would be a special servant to God. She became the mother of Samson. But she was married! Her palm moved and rubbed at the frown on her forehead.

'He will be great...and called God's Son.' His voice was soft, compelling. 'His reign will be glorious and His kingdom shall never end.'

As he finished, he had risen to his feet. Somehow he had become taller, wider, fuller. Astonished, she watched him fill space.

His voice so full of weight, of authority. The words seemed to enter her very being and her body vibrated at their sound, tingling from the top of her head to the tips of her toes. She knew, without doubt, God was meeting with her, telling her something so important she must listen with every fibre of her being.

She knew, when people met with an angel, extraordinary things happened. The Spirit of God had made Zechariah, her cousin Elizabeth's husband, fall to the ground unconscious in the temple, and he woke mute. Nobody understood why. Could it be possible God wanted her to do something for Him?

'He said I will have a baby,' she mused.

'Er... Um... How can this be?' she asked. 'I have never slept with a man.'

'It will be by the Holy Spirit, Mary. Through God's power you will conceive. Therefore, He will be called the Son of God.'

What!

'What is he talking about?' Mary felt a rising panic. She didn't understand.

'Your cousin Elizabeth is already pregnant; although she is in her old age, she is now in her sixth month. God's word is always true.'

Elizabeth pregnant. How was that possible? She was too old. Everybody said so!

'If this is God,' she thought, 'then there is nothing I can do or want to do to stop it. No! All my life I have loved and followed Him, and I never want to follow anyone else.'

Slowly she removed the bag of olives from her back and dropped it. She brushed both her hands across her face and over her hair, as if removing buzzing flies, emptying her head of questions. Her eyes met those of the man and never wavered.

'I am the Lord's servant,' she answered. 'Let it be so.'

One moment he was there, the next he had gone.

She didn't move. She stood pondering his words for a long time.

Eventually she returned home, long after family and friends had eaten. She ignored all questions.

'Has anyone heard if Cousin Elizabeth is pregnant?' she asked. Laughter – the consensus was she was well past that possibility.

'Why?' they asked

'I need to see her.'[29]

Whatever our beliefs, the story of Mary and the angel in the Bible is extraordinary. A simple encounter between a young teenager and a spiritual being that encapsulates the notion of both the transcendence and the immanence of God prophesying that God will begin His human life as an egg in a young woman's uterus.

The co-existence of deeply intimate relationship alongside the beyond-understanding power of God.

Meeting the supernatural appears to induce fear. The phrase 'Do not be afraid/fear not' is used 365 times in the Bible. If a transcendent God expressed Himself to us personally, we mere mortals would do well to open our ears, shut our mouths and clothe ourselves with humility in the face of such wonder.

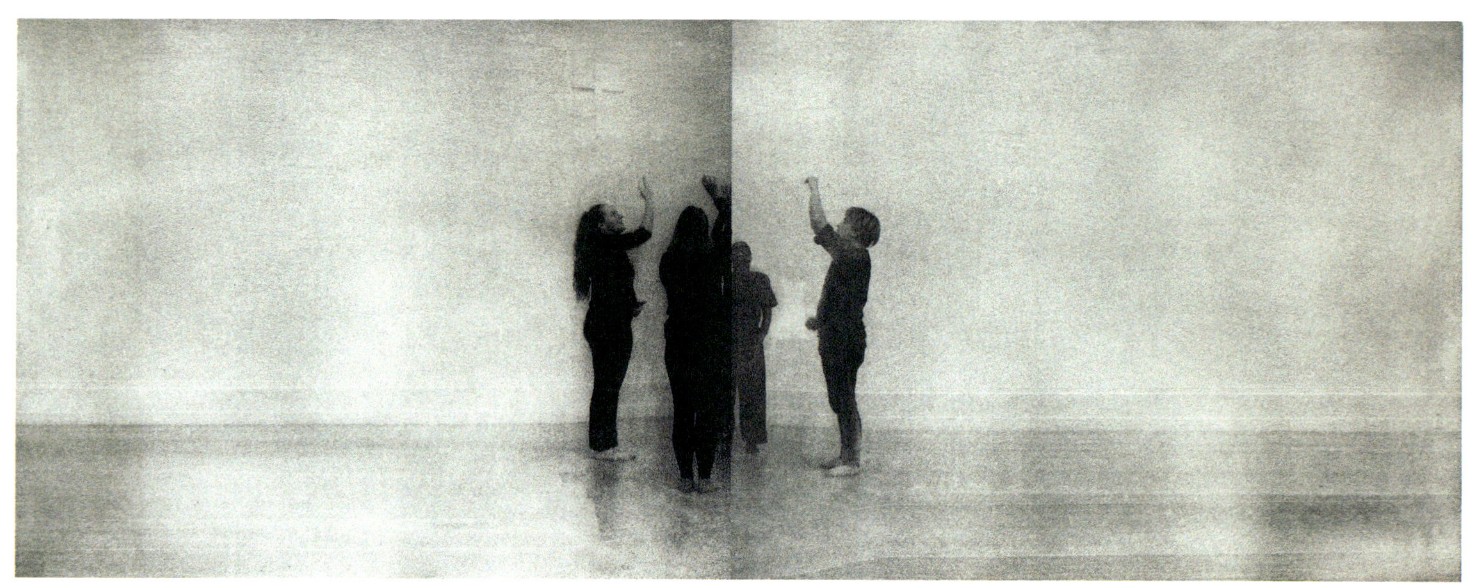

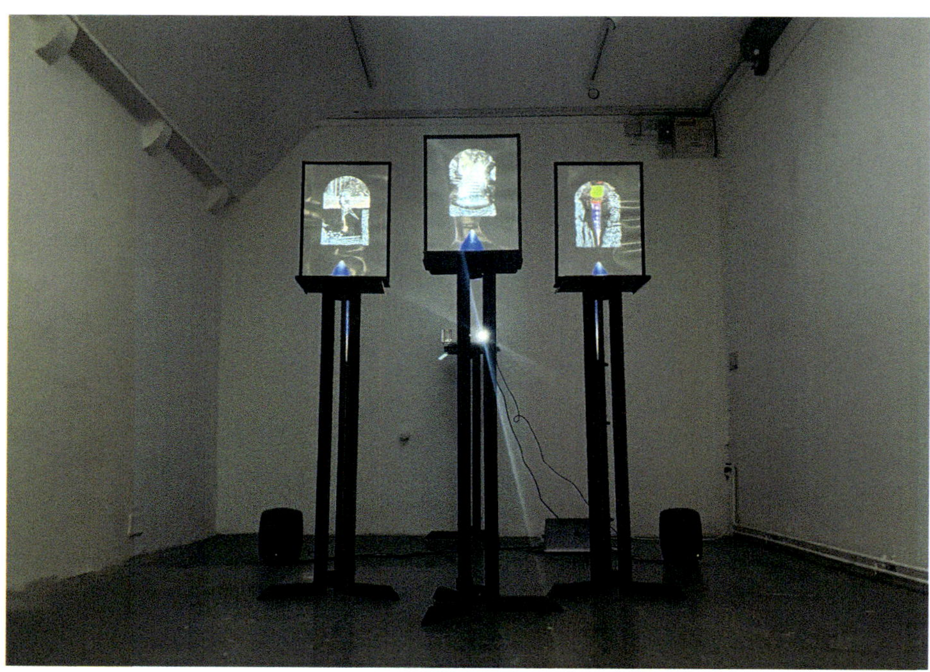

MARGARET ASHMAN

Trinity

Etching on paper

H: 60cm W: 132cm

My practice straddles many discourses incorporating the use of a language for the deaf, which locates it within disability arts. I welcomed the challenge of creating compositions using several dancers and displaying a sequence of movement. This is part of a series including a film exploring themes of inclusivity, meeting together and fellowship.

WILLIAM LOWRY

Ophanim

Digital composition of original biro drawings, prints and paintings projected onto A3 plastic, mounted in three steel frame stands, with original sound piece written and produced by the artist

H: 153cm W: 25cm
D: 25cm

Inspired by the *Ophanim* (Hebrew): magnificent, all-seeing wheels in the book of Ezekiel in the Old Testament, and drawing on cosmic and sacred imagery, the triptych offers a meditation on the fragility of human life and knowledge, and our longing to escape these limitations through artistic and technological innovation.

ROSALIND BARKER

Us-future 2022

Sculptural drawing, ash, dust, Evo-Bond, fine netting, metal rod

H: 190cm W: 180cm D: 180cm

My media is the dusty debris and residue of human DNA, data of my family and ash from family fires. Ghostly children, in the innocence of childhood, dance and play around a fragile world. Dust holds life together and is a witness to human physical and spiritual vulnerability.

JUDITH BURROWS

Fragile Earth D

Organic matter and lacquer on raw steel

H: 125cm W: 94cm

Make yourself one with dust. This is the profound identity of humanity and nature heightened by global precariousness. This prompts my dialogue between living organisms and the man-made. I search for balance and connection as I note nature's responses to human interference unbalancing the natural order and fragile ecosystems.

ANDY SIMPSON

All That I Have Left

A combination of video installation, light, sound and sculpture

Video: 1 min 40 sec

In 2015, at twenty-two months, my son Edward died. This tragedy impacted my own spirituality, making me consider my own beliefs in an afterlife. After much consideration I concluded there was no god, and all existence was light and sound travelling through space and time. The piece is constructed of Edward's light, tiny moments in time, repeated.

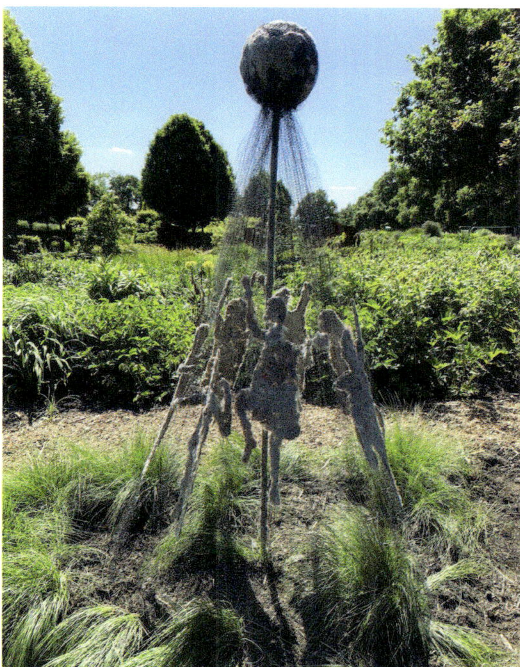

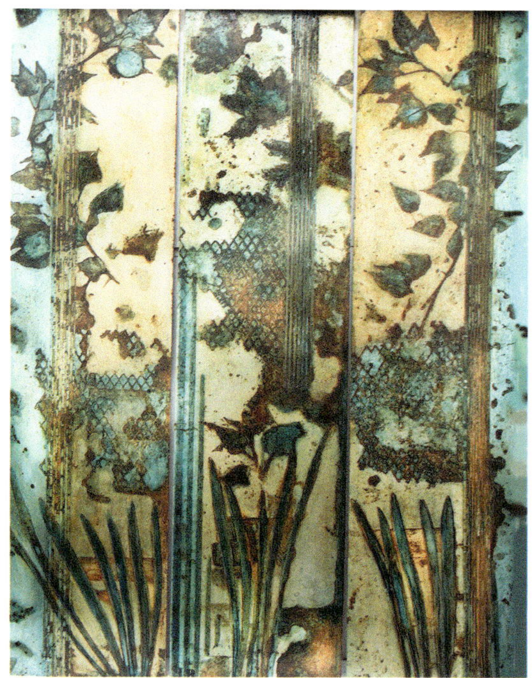

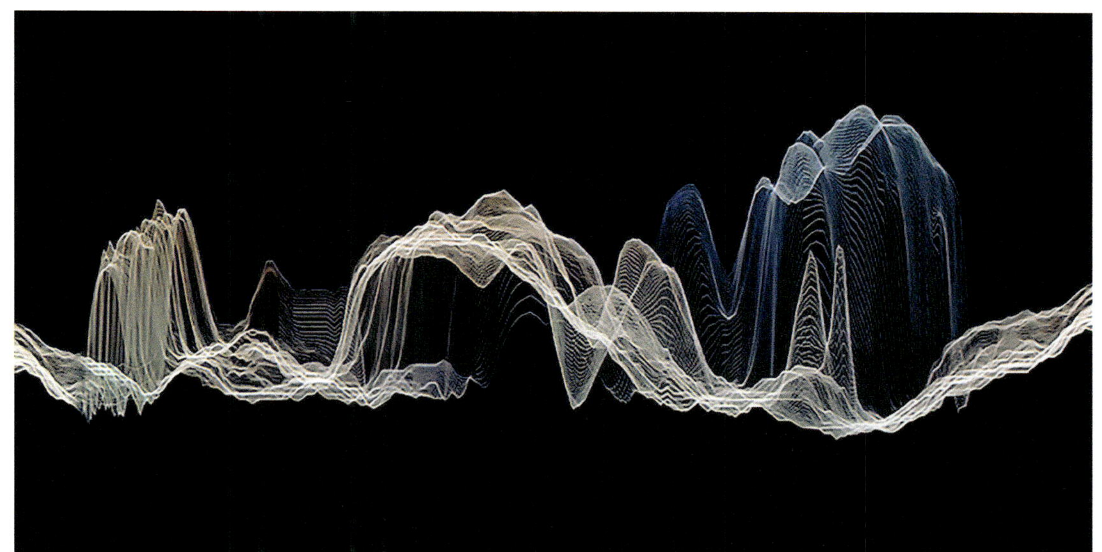

flesh and blood

'Lie still,
lie still, my
breaking heart;
My silent heart,
lie still and
break:
Life, and the
world, and
mine own self,
are changed
For a dream's
sake.'

CHRISTINA ROSSETTI[30]

'There is
something so
enchanting in
the smile of
melancholy.
It is a ray of
light in the
darkness, a
shade between
sadness
and despair,
showing the
possibility of
consolation.'

LEO TOLSTOY[31]

EXQUISITE MELANCHOLY

A woman sits silenced. She listens for something to break into her melancholy. Silence. She is surrounded by a maelstrom of things to do, but within her there is silence.

What is she waiting for?

Does she wait? For what? A husband, a friend, a connection to divert her attention? She returns to silence.

She eats, she walks, she talks, she works, she cleans, she tidies, she buys, she reads, she listens, she watches.

Still, she returns to silence.

In the dark, she turns on the light. Silence.

In the sun she lifts her face. Silence.

In the rain she closes her umbrella, opens her waterproof. Silence.

Different worms of worry eat within her. They chomp in silence.

A good life – a home, a family, but the silence remains.

It has never been silent in the past. Before there had been pathways, choices, companionship. But now silence has descended.

She has slowed to a stop. She is present but without inhabiting. Her spirit floats in space and time, untethered.

And she is cold.

People who know they have answers make speeches. Inside her, all is silent.

Nothing touches her sadness or the arena where she exists. And she is so tired.

No one knows or understands how depleted or how alone she remains in all the silence.

She closes her eyes and surveys the parameters of the land within her and asks, where is God then? Where is God for me?

Her eyes fill. Then in her mind she sees a figure walking purposefully towards her.

'You've walked far,' He says.

'How do You know?'

'I walked with you.' He smiles as He stands alongside her, joining her in her silence.

'But I didn't know,' she says.

'Truly?'

She smiles, holds out her hand, and He takes it.

'You may not be able to control all the events that happen to you, but you can decide not to be reduced by them.'

MAYA ANGELOU[32]

« **Detail** – See page 119

COLLATERAL DAMAGE

Weighted by
wilderness Russia's war,
forcing ingestion of
a sluggish poison
administered by venal warriors now
become a venomous snake.
Its mission?
The cry of a cold and hungry child;
a grandmother's pitiless rape;
the sideways topple of a father
as sniper's bullet
shreds his brain.

From where does their help come?

Life-jacketed migrants stuffed
into the sea
atop unseaworthy bloated plastic.
Stripped of means,
of dignity, of skill,
of right, of humanity.
Jettisoned,
worthless flotsam
disposed of rubbish-like
on city street
to disappear
from view.

From where does their help come?

Politicians braying and hawking
anxious to self-serve
among a people
broken by
anxiety, poverty,
ill-health.
Frenzied,
demobbed systems
their outer ears lost,
able only to herd the
panicked mob –
running in circles
searching for safety.

From where does our help come?

The uncertainty of home,
creeping insolvency,
families determined to endure the
freeze of
winter's indulgence.
Sirens blare but
there is a new normal.
Did you not know?
Did you not see?
If we become less than human,
become things –
our disposable society
will dispose of itself.

From where does our help come?

'The oneness of human beings is the basic ethical thread that holds us together.'

MUHAMMAD YUNUS[33]

THE EAR

Without warning, an ear concluded it was the most important part of a body. It was very certain it contributed more than any other section. The rest of the body parts took no notice, continuing to work together at their different functions.

Stomach, although often believed itself misunderstood, never stopped, but felt increasingly isolated. It thought the ear superior and clever because of all the things it heard, understood and communicated. The ear, because it listened to everything inside and outside the body, also deemed itself intelligent and wise.

One day the ear, in fervent energy-saving mode, decided the stomach was of little use to the body and 'the right thing to do' was for it to cease working. The stomach was thrilled at being noticed but began to shut down.

Before long, other parts of the body broke down. The ear became very concerned because it found it could hear less and less. Every part of the body put down the cause to the non-functioning stomach and agreed the entire body was dying.

Ear panicked as it realised it meant it too would die. It shouted at the stomach in no uncertain terms to work again.

But the stomach had given up.

Contrite and recognising its own helplessness, the ear took a different tack.

'But stomach,' said the ear, 'you are unseen yet so significant. You help all of us to be our best. Forgive me, dear stomach. You are one of the most important parts of the body, vital to the life of us all. Drink a little. Please...'

And the stomach tried.

'If I stopped working,' said the ear, 'the body wouldn't die. My role is much less important than yours. Please eat a little.'

And the stomach did.

Slowly life inched back into the body and every part expressed their appreciation to the previously unheralded stomach.

As for the ear, having learned humility and gratitude, he quietened and simply took his place and made his contribution.

'My humanity is bound up in yours, for we can only be human together.'

DESMOND TUTU[34]

'You should not underestimate the power you have to affirm the humanity and dignity of the people around you. When you do that, they will teach you something about what you need to learn about human dignity, but also what you can do to be a change agent.'

BRYAN STEVENSON[35]

» **Detail** – See page 122

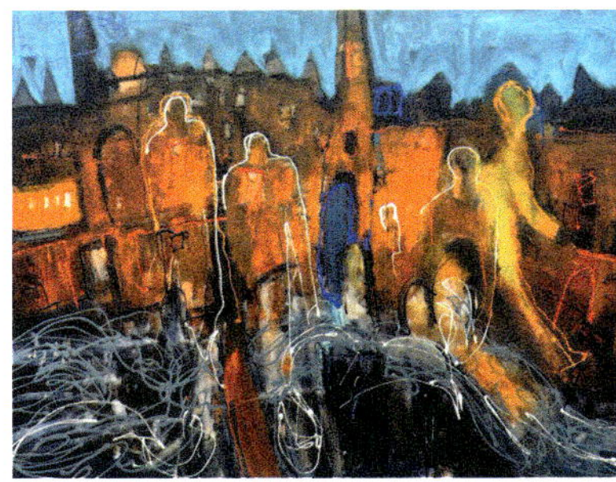
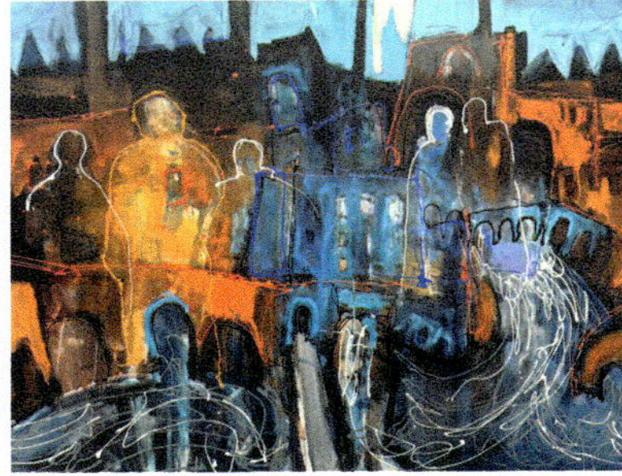
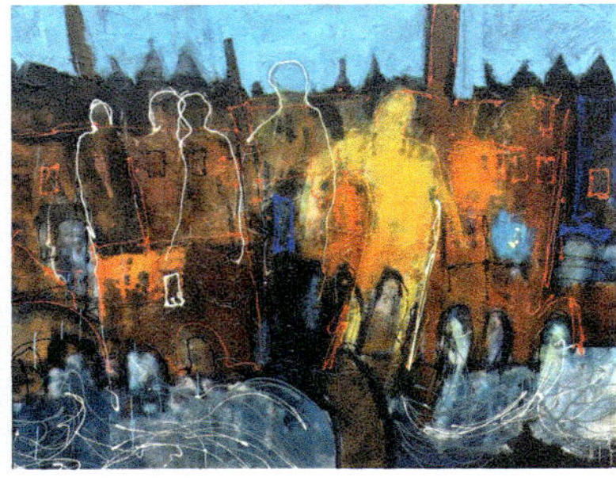
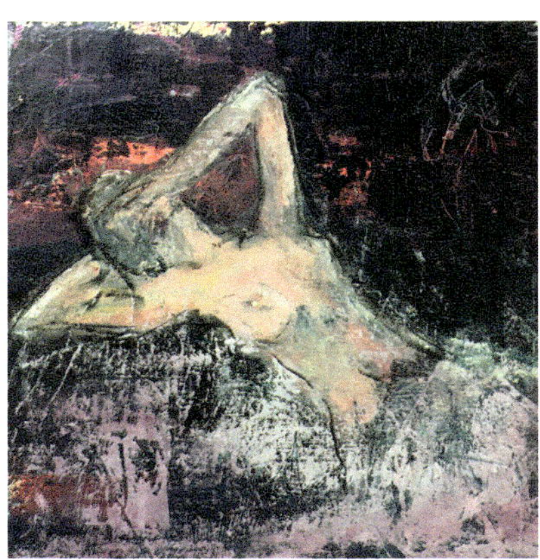
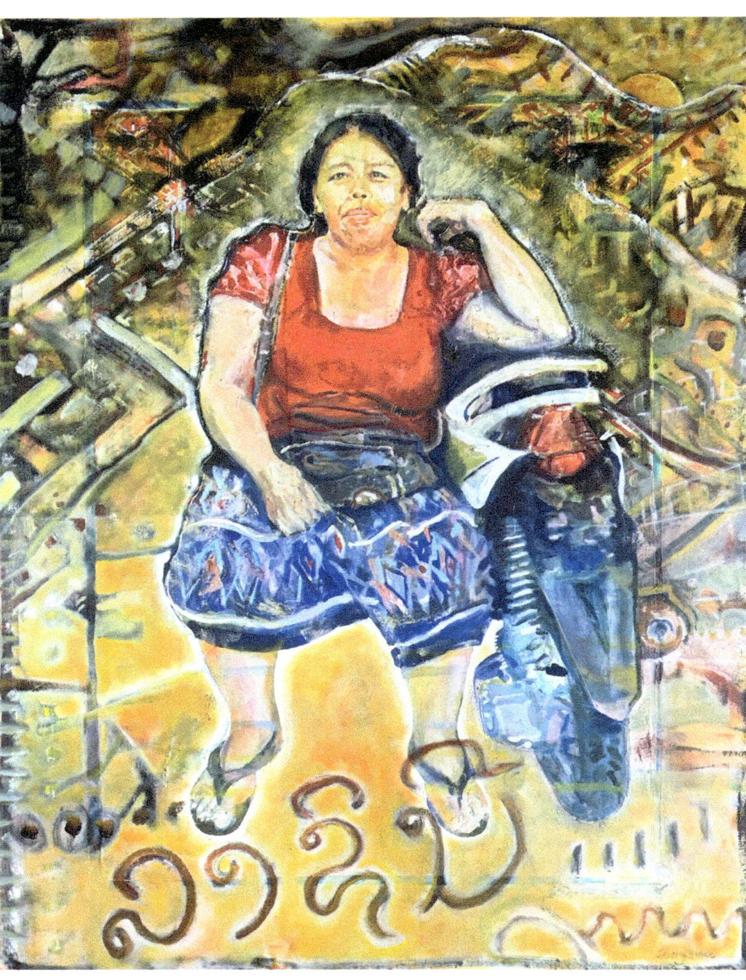

MARTIN KINNEAR

Lethe

Oil on canvas triptych

H: 125cm W: 450cm

In Greek legend the dead drank from the River Lethe, to forget their past lives and be reborn. The painting illustrates the people we loved and remember, their lives echoing into our life choices. Haunted by a family suicide, my grandparents' sadness cascaded down through the generations. The past ripples into our future, yet opportunity beckons to make new lives.

TRINA HART

A Woman in Life

Acrylic on canvas

H: 30cm W: 30cm

Women are the puzzle piece that holds all together. Awesome givers of life. Post-ecstasy, the woman is deep in thought, navigating the journey of her life. Humankind is fragile, yet women are strong, and it is that strength that keeps us all connected.

JEREMY BUNCE

Portrait of Gin

Oil on canvas

H: 122cm W: 91cm

A portrait of Gin, a friend and a mother from a poor community in the Far East. For her, no fancy, rich clothing; no car; no expensive jewellery; no high-priced house. Yet Gin is a work of sheer beauty. She's royalty.

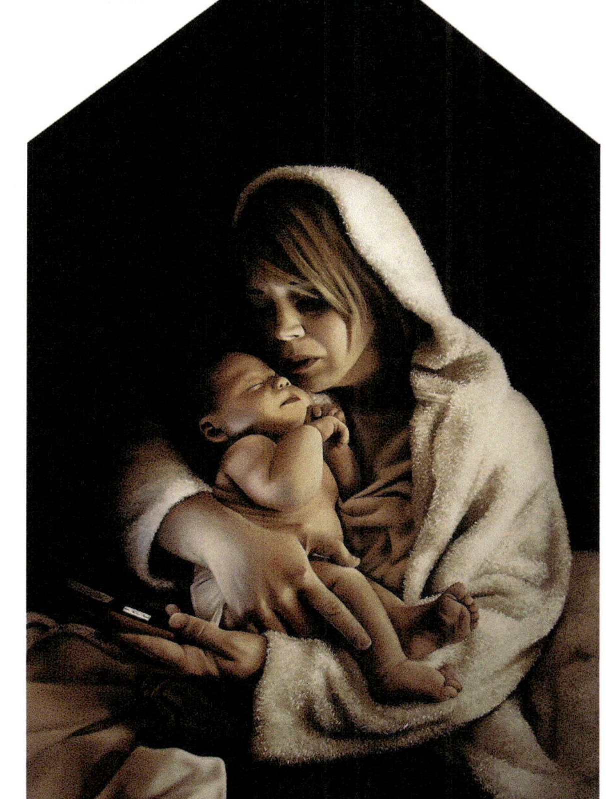

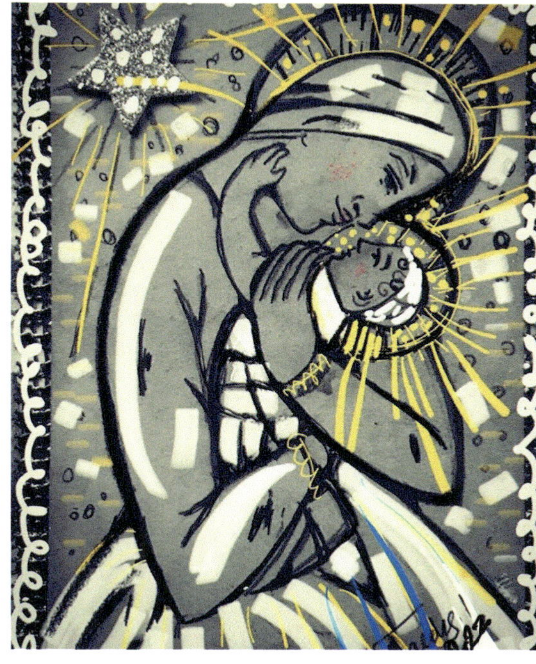

OLIVER JONES

#motherandchild

Pastel on stretched paper

H: 160cm W: 100cm

Composed visibly as an icon or Florentine altar piece and most identifiably with the 'Madonna and Child' by Giovanni Battista Salvi, #motherandchild draws upon the narrative surrounding the Mother and Child, emotively engaging us with notions of motherliness, love and devotion.

MONICA JACOBS

Hold On

Lino block, digital overlay on canvas

H: 86cm W: 55cm

A meditation on the word 'iconic'. Throughout the history of Christendom, the embrace of the Madonna and Child continues as a prayerful means of meditation for generation after generation. Icons translate the power of love into all cultures, embracing each family expression with a simple gaze.

DOHYUN BAEK

Birth of Venus

Acrylic on canvas

H: 162cm W: 113cm

Inspired by mythology and a Christian exploration of being human, this dramatic birth of 'Doodooism' is the antithesis of Venus' birth's traditional representation. 'Doodooism' is a concept developed in response to my generation's angst. Crowned with Disney-princess hair, Venus holds Time and, in her distress, defecates. Poo, the great equaliser, evokes reactions: disgust, embarrassment, laughter – encapsulating our shared vulnerability.

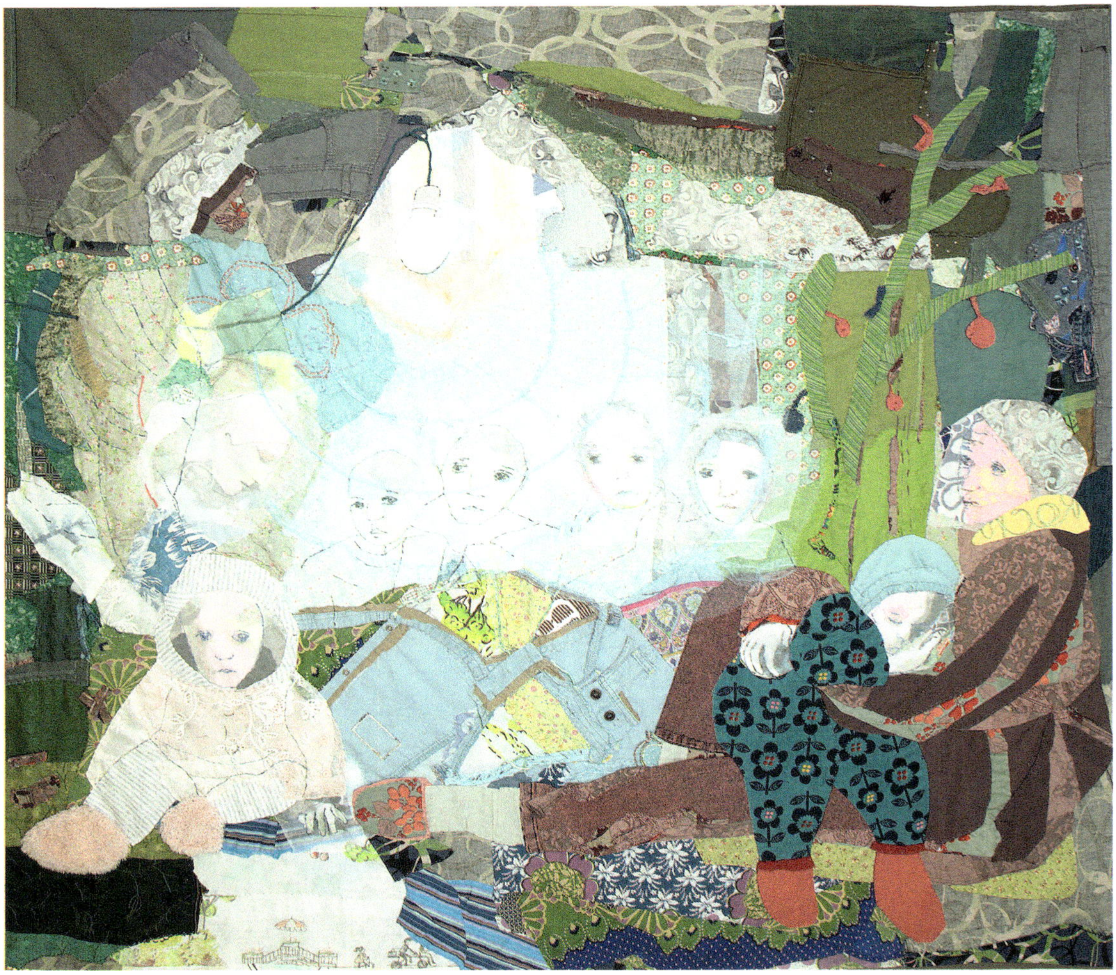

ANNE SMITH

Space

Fabric quilt (recycled clothing: cotton, linen, mixed blends), hand-pieced, appliquéd, hand-embroidered, hand-quilted

H: 152cm W: 138cm

Standing with solidarity, in a parallel space of a tiny studio, I watched the desperate fear and worry on the faces of mothers and children fleeing the Ukraine war. For the four months I lived with their faces, quiet and hopeful, waiting to be created from recycled fabric, I co-existed with the fear and hope of others.

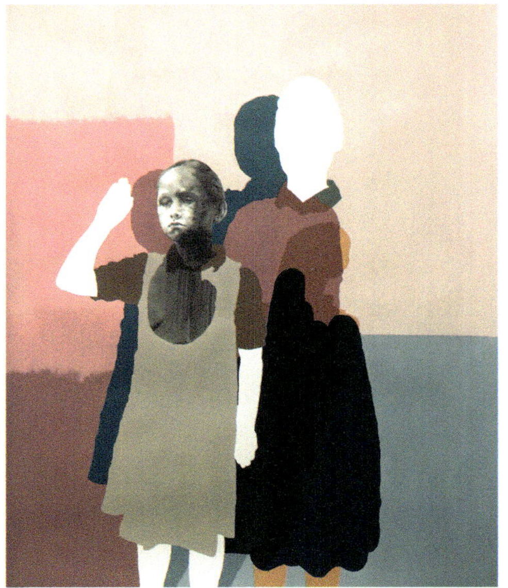

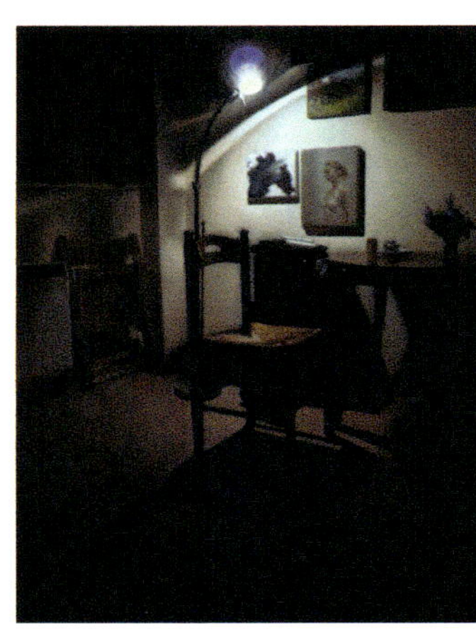

PATRICK MORALES-LEE

Covenant

Pencil, acrylic paint, charcoal powder and chemical spray on 300gsm paper

H: 156cm W: 123cm

Exploring themes of belonging, identity and belief emanating from being fostered. The artist's daughter portrayed participating in a liminal ceremony. The authentic and sacred moment of leaving one family, joining a new one and forging new agreements.

ALAIN E BRESSAN

Death

Oil on canvas

H: 108cm W: 82cm

A representation of the absence and the emptiness that replaces everyone who dies. No voice, no smell, no warm breath near the ear – no more. Those who stay must watch the others go. Are we life prisoners? Is ignorance our inheritance?

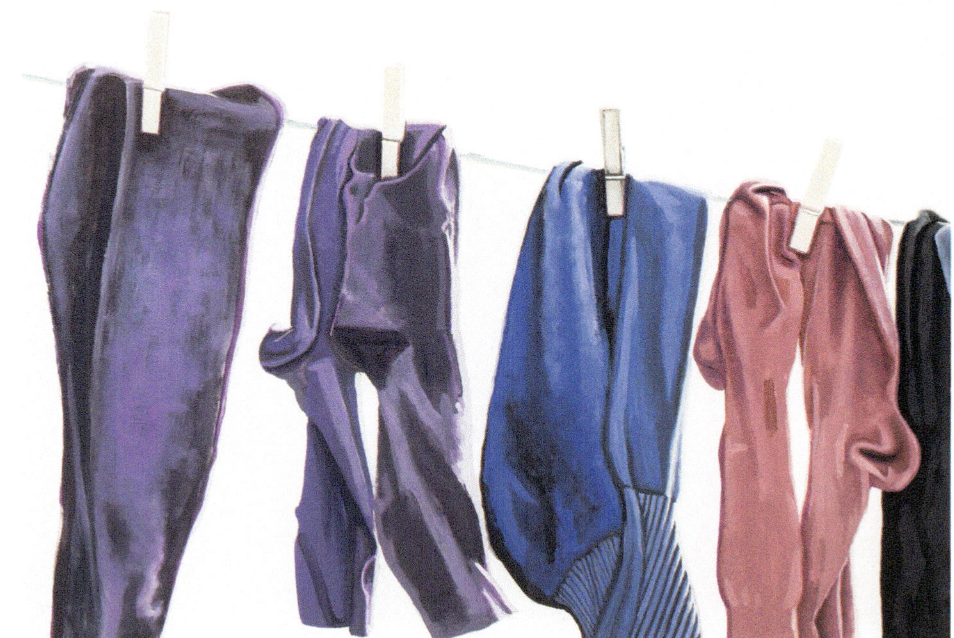

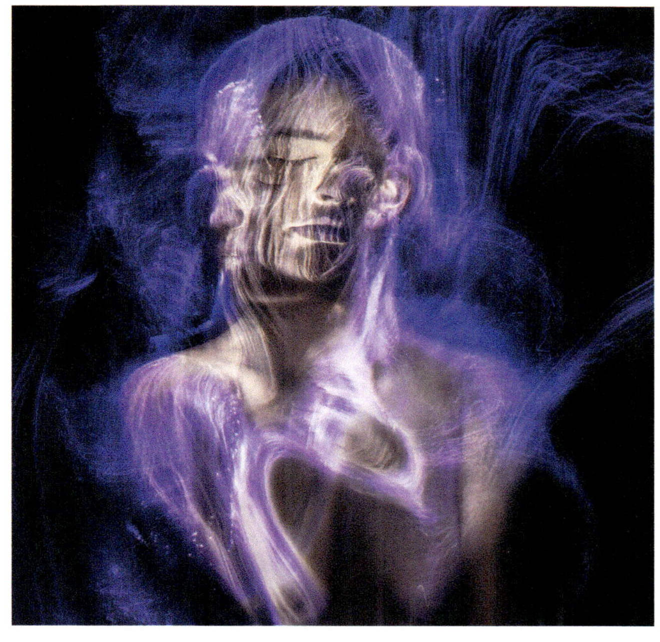

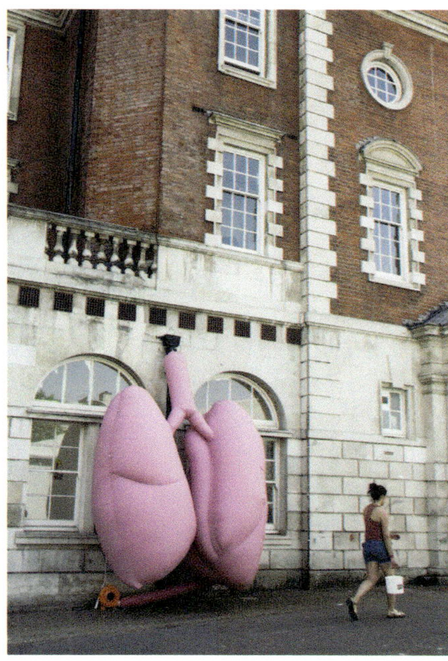

DEBORAH SEDGWICK

Spiritual Aspirations

Oil on primed paper (framed)

H: 54cm W: 64cm

A fascination with laundry grew when I was too ill to paint. Colours, patterns, the simplicity of socks, evoked the concept of the relationship between cleanliness and spirituality. Muse on the notion: dirty marks on a surface signify impermanence in all its unique splendour and don't require cleaning to 'perfection'.

KAROLINA SKOREK

Transcendencee

Digital photography

H: 60cm W: 60cm

Created to evoke the meditative state and outer body experience people describe during meditation.

YEN-HSU CHOU

Suffering

Huge lungs use canvas balloons to inflate and deflate to simulate the feeling of breathing

H: 300cm W: 180cm D: 180cm

Lungs, the organs of the human respiratory system. Organs are fragile and easily damaged by external pollution. The work expresses the seriousness of the body's circulation and, in Covid times, the difficulty of restoration. The enlarged scale perhaps emphasises their fragility along with their great importance.

pixels

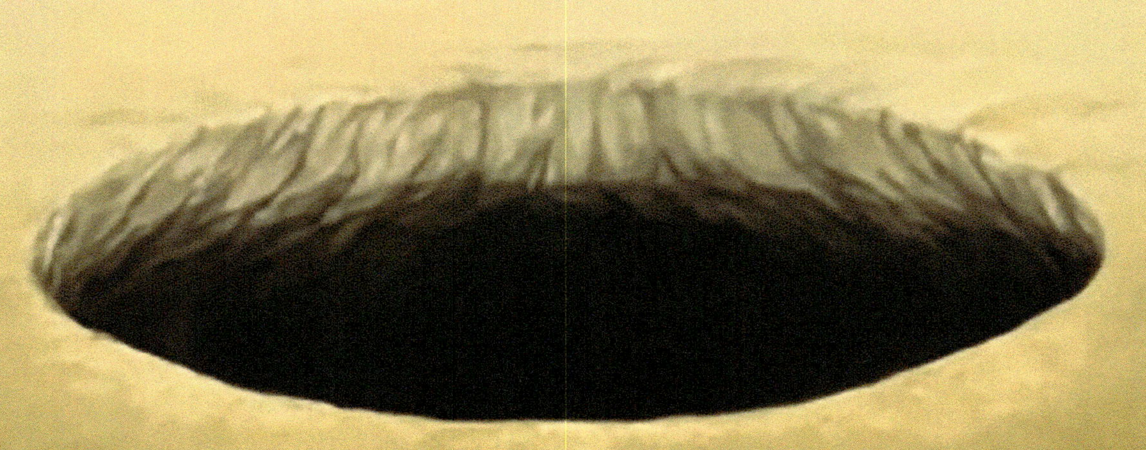

'Artists are low key astronauts.

Instead of going to the moon, they sit back in their studio and make the moon.'

MICHAEL BASSEY JOHNSON[36]

&portals

THE OVERVIEW EFFECT

ON 16TH NOVEMBER 2022, Artemis 1's four liquid-fuel cryogenic rocket RS-25 engines ignited at Kennedy Space Center, marking the return of lunar exploration for NASA and partners. It was the first integrated flight test of the Orion Spacecraft and Space Launch System rocket.

Two extended, solid rocket boosters generating 16 million pounds of thrust sent the space capsule Orion skyward, travelling at more than 2,000mph. The beefiest rocket ever to leave the ground, Artemis weighed 5.75 million pounds when fully fuelled for launch, yet would climb nearly 500ft straight up in seven seconds.

After two minutes there were two jettison events. The two boosters, their propellent gone, ejected. Once in space, the three protective fairings also ejected, followed by the Launch Abort System. When emptied of propellant the main rocket, the Main Engine Cut Off, dropped away. This turned the propulsion into the Interim Cryogenic Propulsion Stage (ICPS).

Eight minutes after lift-off the rocket moved at around 18,000mph. The rocket's upper stage increased velocity to 22,600mph.

Orion then orbited around the earth while the entire system function was checked prior to propelling it to encircle the moon. Once given the all-clear, the Translunar Injection fired from the ICPS upper stage every twenty minutes. This gave Orion enough energy to get out of the lower

« Detail — See page 85

earth orbit and make its way to the moon. Shortly after this, the ICPS separated, as its job of pushing Orion was done.

The ICPS carried secondary payloads and would deploy satellites before sending itself on a moon trajectory prior to escaping into orbit around the sun.

Orion continued onwards towards its goal, making corrective burns as it fine-tuned its path. It would undertake a lunar flyby, coming within sixty nautical miles of the moon's surface, and then be sent on Distant Retrograde Orbit (DRO). The aim of this was to allow scientists to learn as much as possible about Orion itself.

It spent three weeks in space, including six days in DRO around the moon. It orbited within approximately 80 miles (130km) of the lunar surface and achieved a maximum distance from the earth of 268,563 miles (432,210km). After a final flyby of the moon on 5th December, it was time to return home. The path home to re-enter the atmosphere then required pitch-perfect fine-tuning.

After this there was further spacecraft separation. The service module, now superfluous, broke away to burn up in the atmosphere. On the breakaway, the heat shield, an extensive structure covering the base of Orion, revealed itself. The testing of this was the number one goal for the Artemis 1 flight.

The craft was built to re-enter the earth's atmosphere at an approximate speed of 25,000mph. This was faster than the re-entry from the International Space Station and meant the heat of the base would rise to about 5,000°F. This is half the temperature of standing on the surface of the sun. Testing this accurately was vital as the next flight would carry astronauts, and the ability to bring them home safely was of paramount importance.

Artemis' future missions will seek to re-establish a human presence on the moon from which a future exploration of Mars can be made possible.

After its 1.4 million-mile journey to beyond the moon and back, the uncrewed Orion spacecraft for the Artemis 1 mission completed a parachute-assisted splash-down near Guadalupe Island at 9.40 PST on 11th December 2022 after a 25.5 day mission, and was picked up by US navy ship *USS Portland.*

Every moment of this ground-breaking expedition was recorded on the NASA website. Look and be awestruck at the high-definition images of earth seen from orbiting the moon.[37]

The intelligence, creativity, sheer determination for exploration and accumulation of knowledge that makes possible such an event as Artemis 1 is almost beyond articulation. The capacity for thousands of individual human brains to work together to make this happen is astonishing.

One pristine photograph shows the lunar surface in the foreground with the earth, a blue glass marble, rising in the distance, each suspended in unending, ever expanding, space.

The Overview Effect is experienced by every astronaut. Read their quotes as they try to find words for their transforming journey which altered their perspective and caused them to reflect on humankind's place on a shared, tiny, vulnerable, fragile, planet which they and we call Home.

» **Detail** — See page 112

'A tiny, fragile ball of life "hanging in the void", shielded and nourished by a paper-thin atmosphere.'

UNKNOWN[38]

'When you study images of earth... you're struck with such a gladness at that beauty and the originality of it, that you don't have time to think about how is it going to turn out. All you know is you'll serve it... to the last breath.'

JOANNA MACY,
PHILOSOPHER AND ECOLOGIST[39]

'There was a startling recognition that the nature of the universe was not as I had been taught... I not only saw the connectedness, I felt it.... I was overwhelmed with the sensation of physically and mentally extending out into the cosmos. I realized that this was a biological response of my brain attempting to reorganize and give meaning to information about the wonderful and awesome processes that I was privileged to view.'

EDGAR MITCHELL,
SIXTH MAN ON THE MOON[40]

'Everything is connected on this planet and everything I do affects it in some way.'

NICOLE STOTT,
ASTRONAUT[41]

'The thing that really surprised me was that it [Earth] projected an air of fragility. And why, I don't know. I don't know to this day. I had a feeling it's tiny, it's shiny, it's beautiful, it's home, and it's fragile.'

MICHAEL COLLINS,
APOLLO 11[42]

'It suddenly struck me that that tiny pea, pretty and blue, was the Earth. I put up my thumb and shut one eye, and my thumb blotted out the planet Earth. I didn't feel like a giant. I felt very, very small.'

NEIL ARMSTRONG,
APOLLO 11[43]

'I find it curious that I never heard any astronaut say that he wanted to go to the Moon so he would be able to look back and see the Earth. We all wanted to see what the Moon looked like close up. Yet, for most of us, the most memorable sight was not of the Moon but of our beautiful blue and white home, moving majestically around the sun, all alone and infinite black space.'

ALAN BEAN,
SKYLAB COMMANDER, ASTRONAUT[44]

'To look out at this kind of creation out here and not believe in God is to me impossible.'

JOHN GLENN,
ASTRONAUT[45]

'I looked and looked but I didn't see God.'

YURI GAGARIN,
FIRST MAN IN SPACE[46]

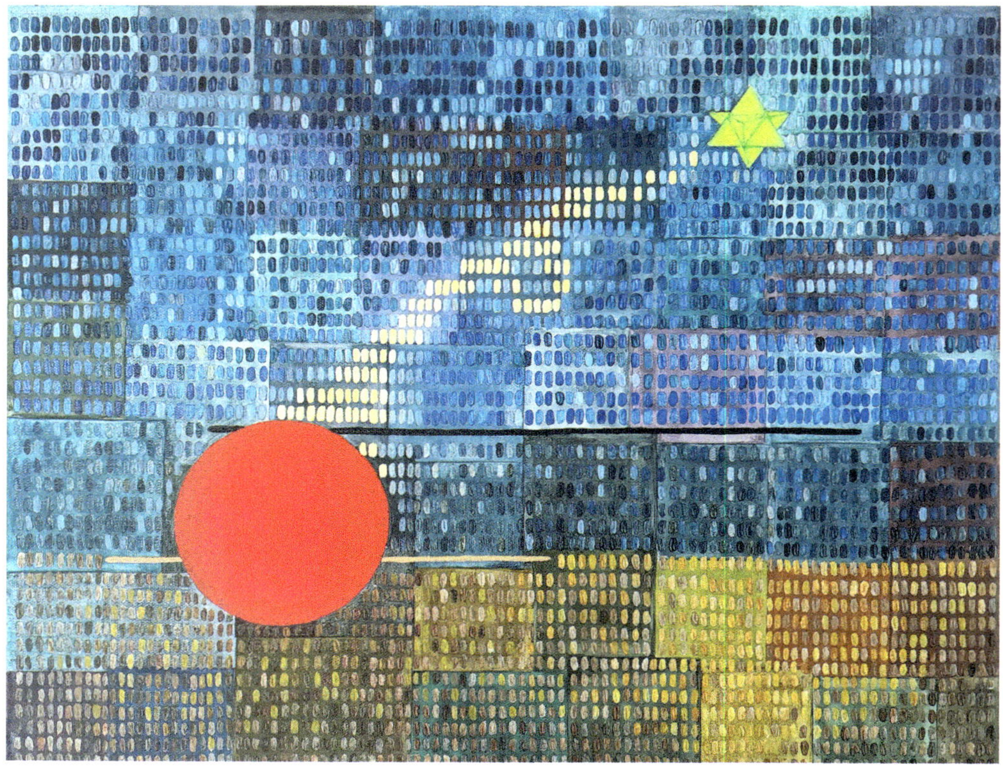

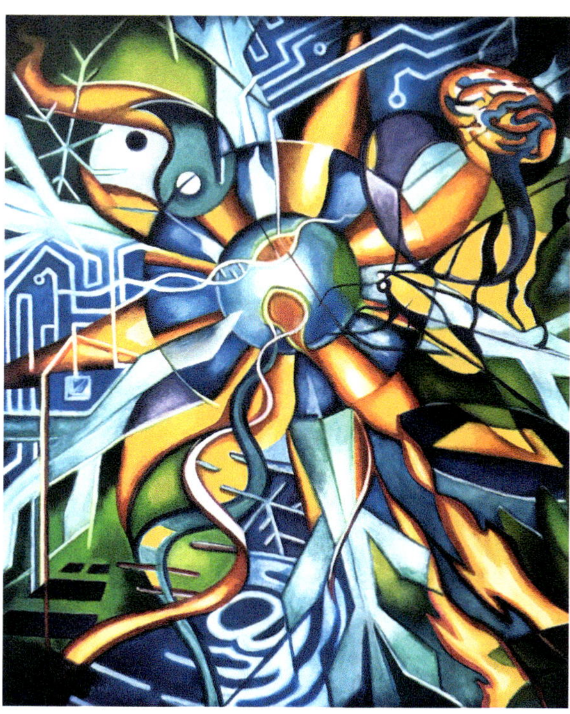

PAUL JAMES

Odyssey

Acrylic on canvas

H: 40cm W: 50cm

The Merkaba (mer-ka-ba = light-spirit-body) consists of upward and downward tetrahedrons, spinning in opposite directions to create a three-dimensional energy field (toroid) in which everything exists. Merkaba meditation consists of eighteen spherical breaths to open the heart to the realm of oneness. 'Odyssey' is an abstract and fantastical representation of the Merkaba, a surreal vision of unity and afterlife.

SUZANNE GIBBS

Nature and Technology

Oil on canvas

H: 76cm W: 61cm

Inspired by Kandinsky's surrealist paintings, the work invites travel around the picture plane, awakening spiritual awareness, transcending our response to the outer world and transforming it to view the inner world. An abstract feeling gained from the manifestation of natural harmony, symmetry and balance in the universe.

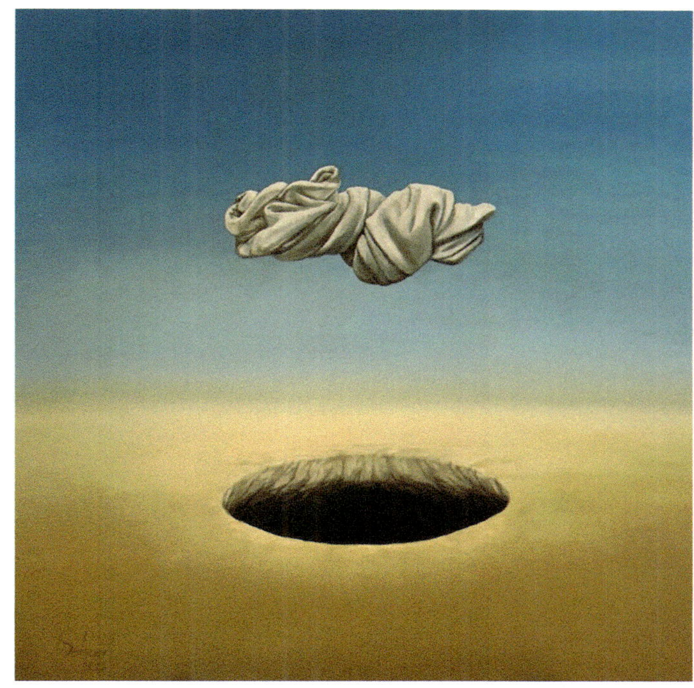

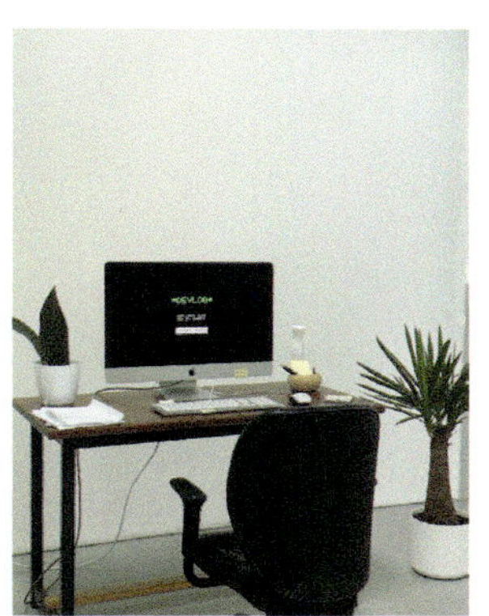

SAHAR KHOSROJERDI

In Absence of Adam and Eve

Oil on canvas

H: 130cm W: 150cm

An immigrant to the UK, leaving everything, I express a world beyond conventional boundaries, creating a safe zone of dreams. To challenge rules and the conventional codes of racial and geographical limitations. We are something beyond the coordinates of a body and factual reality.

DUMO GUO

Devlog

Video installation

A video game about making a video game using the game engine Unity to document the journey, providing real-time engagement for the viewer/player. An evolving collection of inspiration and a place for exchanging ideas. Various features can be activated allowing co-creation and development possibilities. The finished video game will be produced separately.

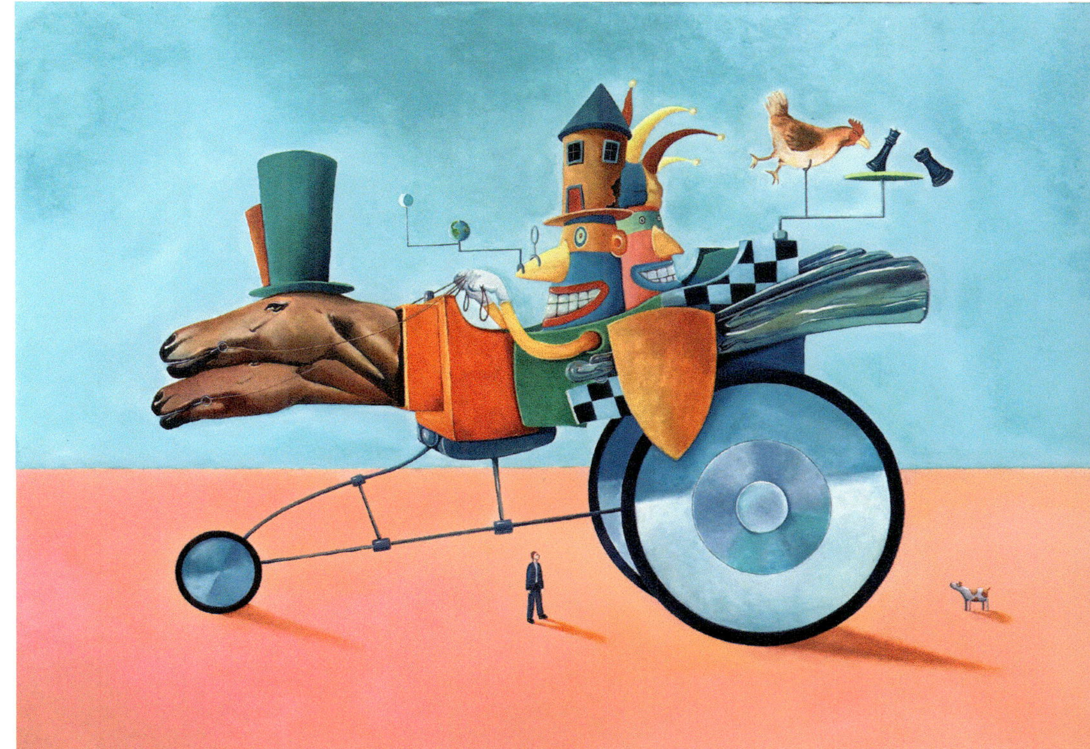

DAVID GARRATT

Living Creatures and Mechanical Parts

Acrylic on card

H: 41cm W: 59cm

The man and the dog look at a strange combination of living creatures and mechanics. The mixture of extraordinary elements is quite common in the Bible. The strangeness and awesomeness of some of the biblical images defy expectation and must cause us to question our limited, uncreative view of God.

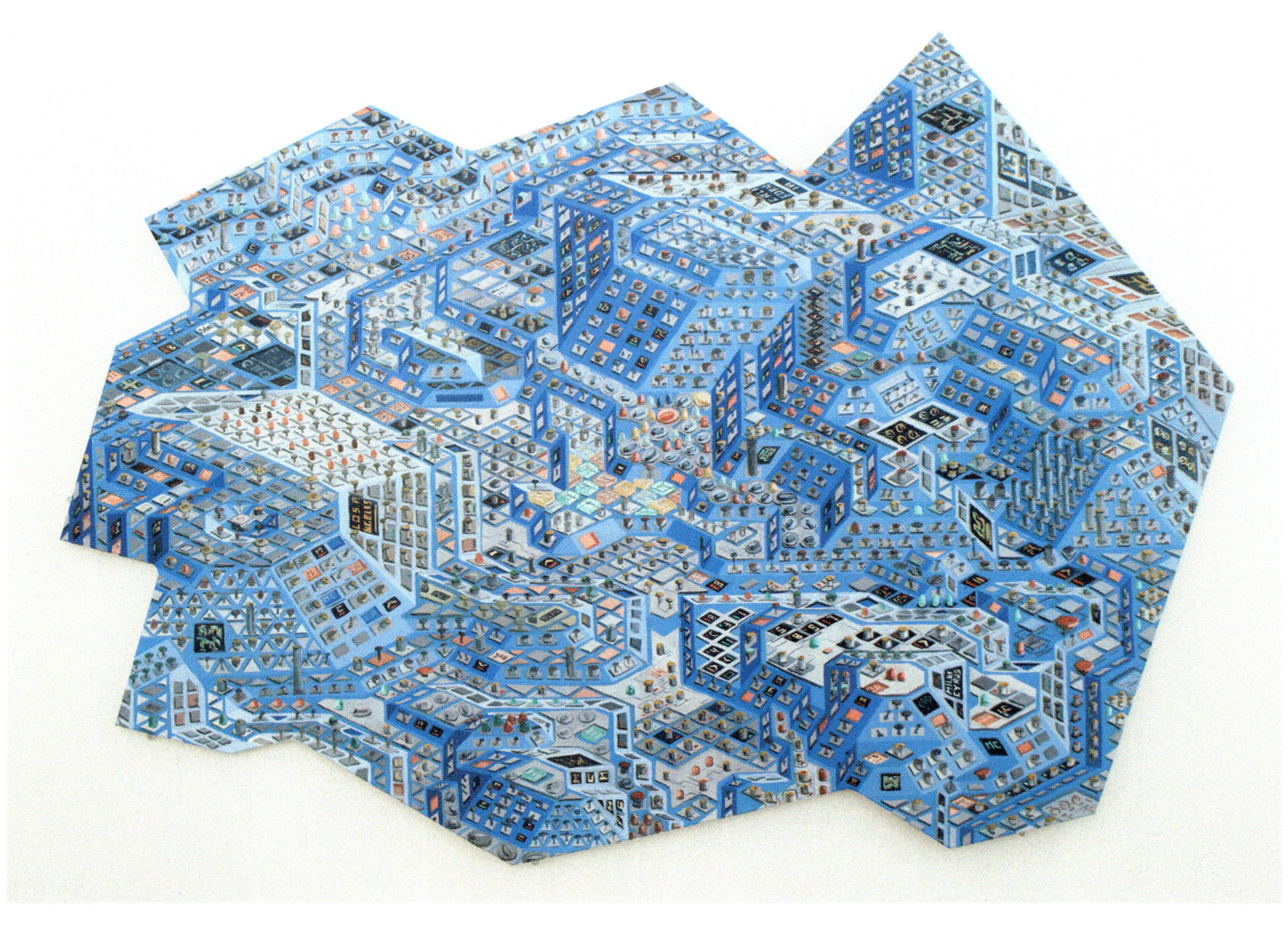

MICHAEL COPPELOV

Silicon Valley

Oil on eighteen-sided stretched canvas

H: 190cm W: 265cm

An isometric grid structure elevates us to a God's-eye perspective. This system, used by the 1990s computer game designers, removes perspectives and horizons and renders the landscape infinite in all directions. Like this absurd landscape, the climate emergency proves everything is connected – the world a system of interacting systems expressing the beauty, brilliance and magnitude of the Maker.

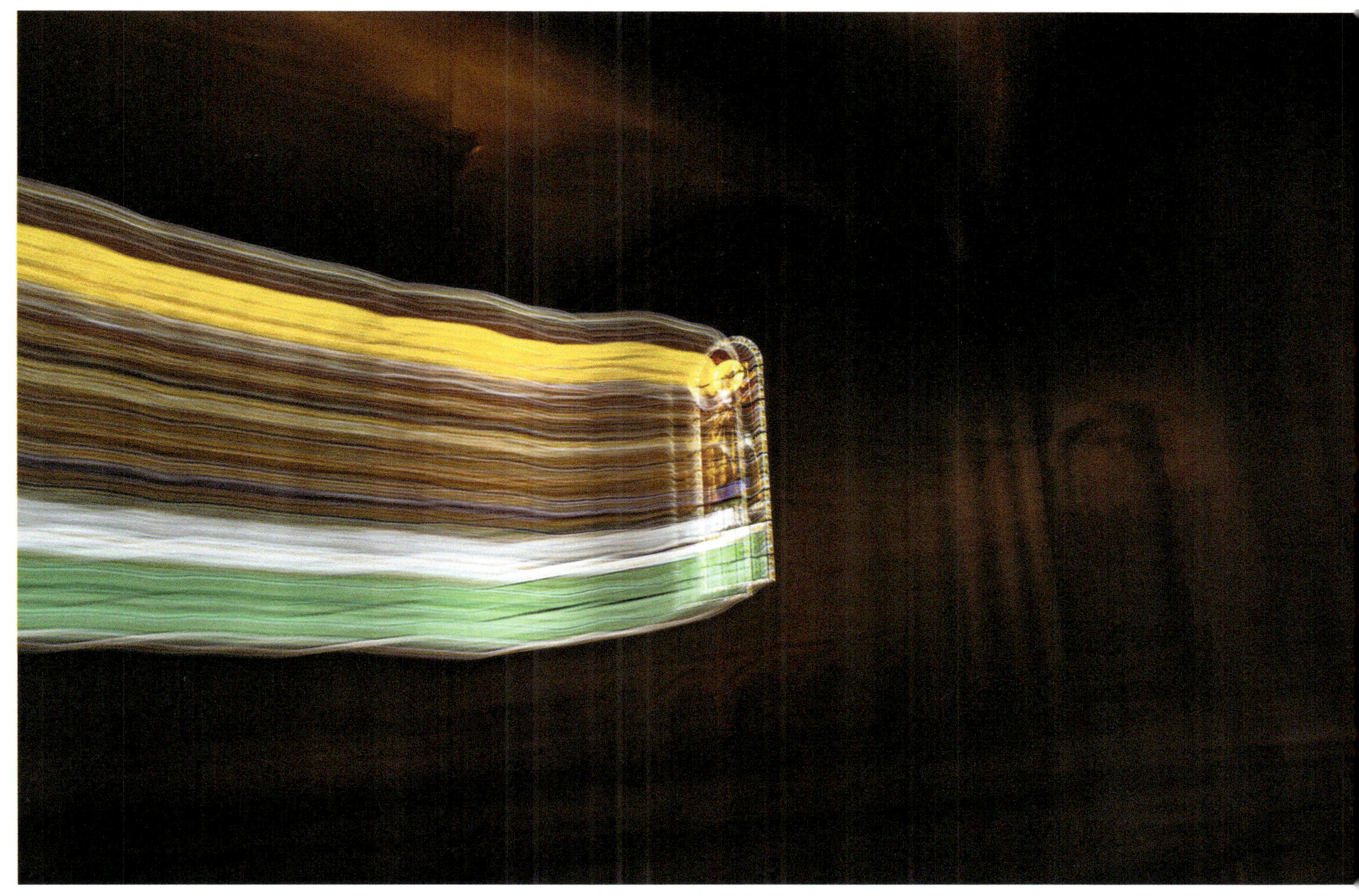

MARIA SCARD

From One Degree of Glory to Another

Photographic image mounted behind HD acrylic in a black wood tray frame. One of fifteen

H: 76cm W: 114cm

A spiritual journey exploring thin places. A Celtic term for locations where the veil between the physical and the spiritual is almost transparent. These liminal (threshold) places include gifts of a glimmer of light, a whisper, a strength, a presence and peace. The St Brice window, in the chapel of St Andrew, Norwich Cathedral.

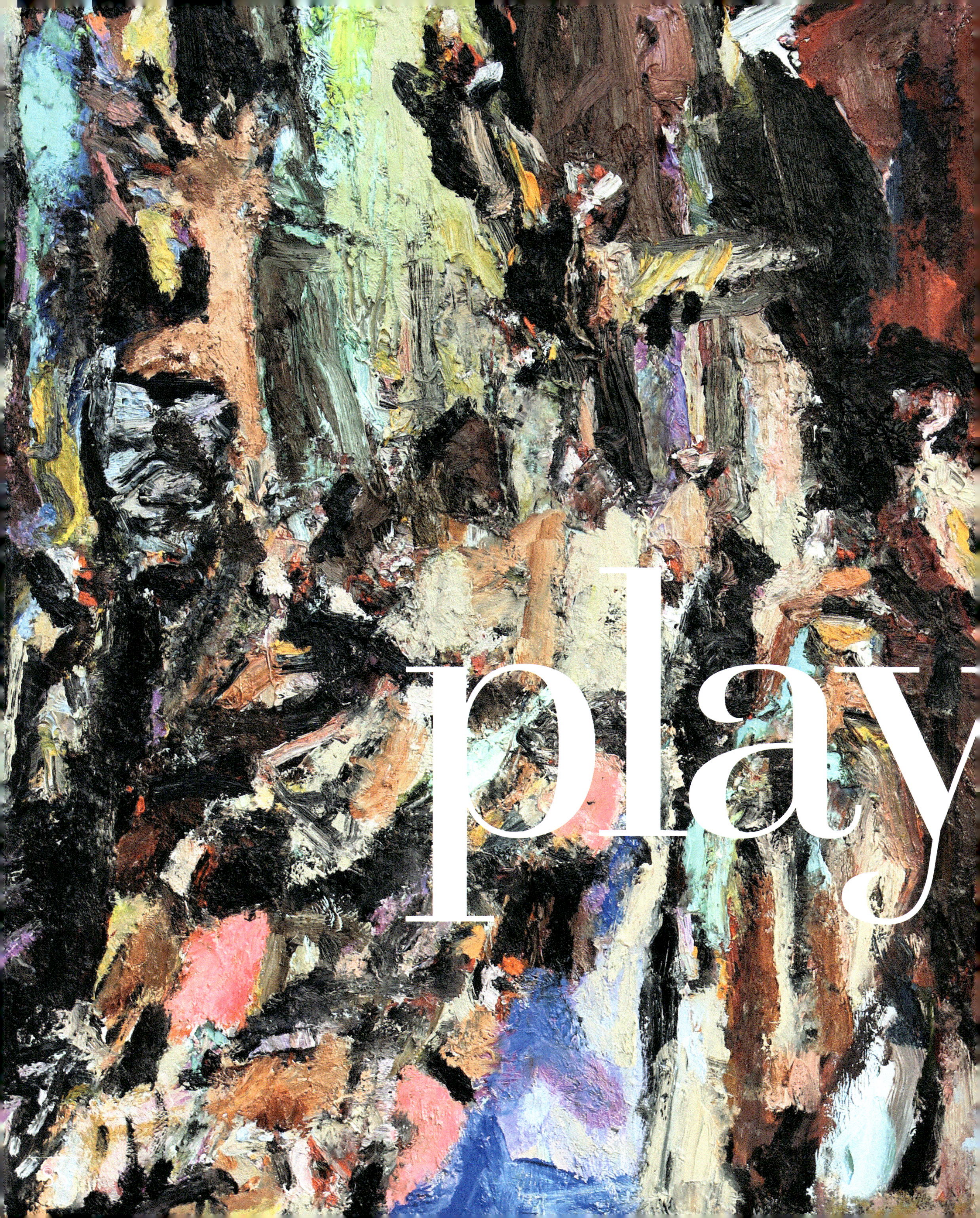
play

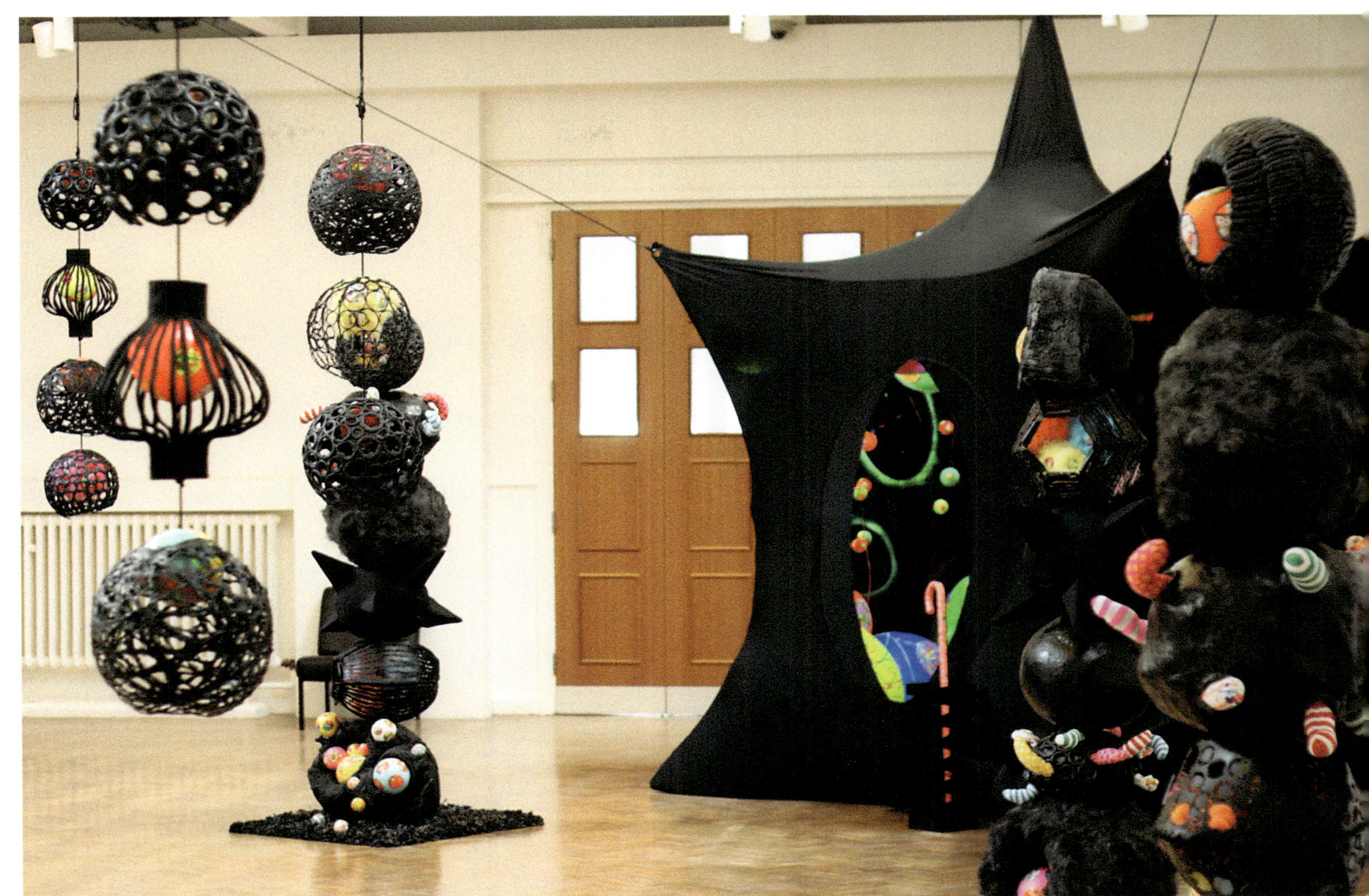

KATE GREEN

Emerge

An installation space involving a collection of sculptural elements, created from a variety of mixed media, many of which are recycled

H: 320cm W: 500cm D: 700cm

Unseen potential and unique value lie beneath the surface of every one of us, each an individual, handcrafted, weird and wonderful creation – but circumstances can threaten to suffocate us. Inspired by seedpods, the piece speaks of surfacing, arising, overcoming, birthing, of becoming. What is dying, what is coming alive?

« **Detail** – See page 24

THE SWIFT

Swifts fly on the wing for most of their lives, covering around 7,000 miles per year, eating, sleeping and mating in flight for perhaps ten months at a time or longer, stopping only to create a nest and populate it with chicks to feed.

They are perfectly formed for flight, with long, scythe-shaped wings, their forked tails closing in flight, allowing them speeds of up to 69mph. Few predators can catch them.

Their delightful, chattering play as they swoop and dart together over smooth water to drink, to bathe, to catch the odd insect communicates an infectious happiness.

Social birds, they might gather in a 'scream' (they are vocal) of 2,000 in a feeding party.

Joyful, vivacious birds, wonderful to watch.

'The creation of something new is not accomplished by the intellect but by the play instinct.'

CARL JUNG[47]

Adults need to play. The stresses and strains of life overtake us too easily. We forget how to laugh. We stop giggling and determine to 'be sensible'.

Out of play comes social connection, creativity, energy, youthfulness, happiness and an overall sense of well-being.

What do we find fun? When did we last ask ourselves that question?

Generate a list and determine to make its contents happen regularly.

Identify a fun person who likes to play and develop a friendship.

Get to know a friend's kids and play with them.

The absolute best game for me is swimming in the sea with my husband, particularly if it involves a Greek beach. We own an ancient ball that fits in the palm of the hand. The game is to throw it to each other from a distance. It makes us yell, laugh, half-drown as we throw ourselves without thought to make the catch. A missed catch engenders frequent giggling at the ensuing explanations. So simple. We have been playing it for more than forty years and continue to laugh and shout at each other. And – my catching and throwing are dazzlingly good. So much practice!

Think about playing more. It is so good for the soul.

'Those who play rarely become brittle in the face of stress or lose the healing capacity for humor.'

DR STUART BROWN, MD[48]

» **Detail** – See page 108

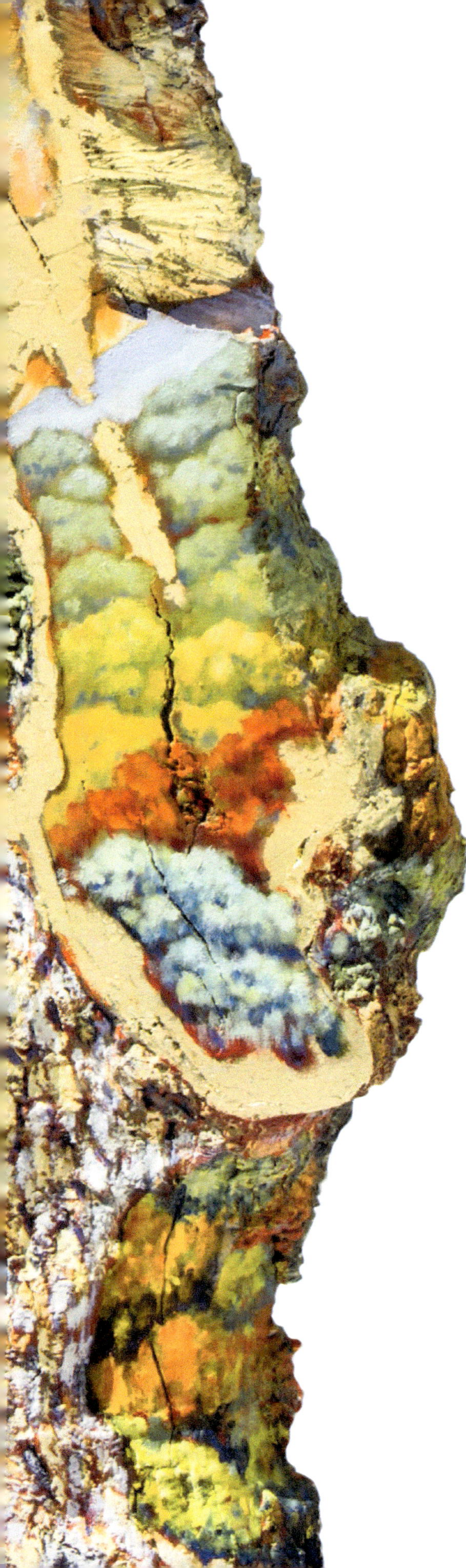

BUSSING

I push through everyone waiting, surging, paying, sitting, standing, climbing to the upper floor, all wanting to get somewhere for myriad reasons. Packs of schoolkids shouting, eating, joking, listening – uninhibited noise! There's an entire world on a bus and I always want to walk upstairs and sit at the front.

Some people hate public transport and will only go by car. I don't have a car now and it's been an education. Where I live in west London, the transport system is amazing.

I have learned to love this world where we're all thrown together for a moment in time, but my grandchildren love it more. To them there's nothing better than to sit on the top of a double-decker in the front seat and count buses, emergency vehicles, refuse trucks and cranes. They don't think about getting anywhere when they're on a bus. They go for the sheer enjoyment of the ride. To them it's play. That challenges me, and it's why even without them I climb the steps to count, watch and smile.

Uninhibited play promotes unbridled joy. Joy to me is all about the moment; when I forget everything except what I am doing in the now. Rather than allowing myself to become a dumping ground for things that must be done, play allows me laughter, joking, high-five moments with complete strangers. It's like oxygen when you're drowning, heat when you're freezing, life when you're dying.

There's something about childlikeness I never want to lose. It is also something, I have learned with surprise, other people love to join in with.

Maybe it's true – laugh and the world will laugh with you![49]

'We don't stop playing because we grow old; we grow old because we stop playing.'

GEORGE BERNARD SHAW[50]

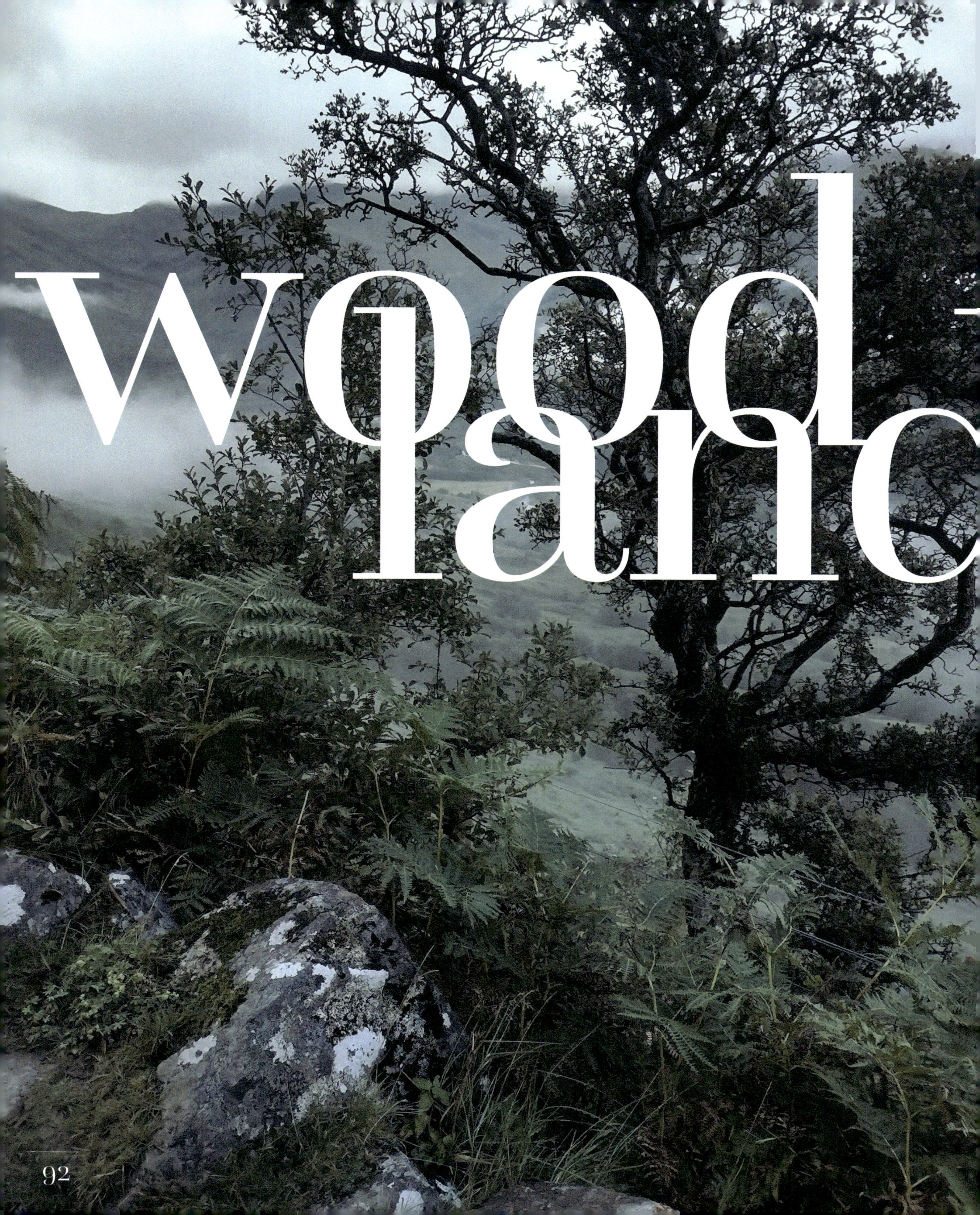
wood-
land

vhispers

'To see a World
in a Grain of Sand
And a Heaven
in a Wild Flower
Hold Infinity in the
palm of your hand
And Eternity
in an hour.'

WILLIAM BLAKE[51]

'I took a
walk in
the woods
and came
out taller
than the
trees.'

HENRY DAVID
THOREAU[52]

« Detail — See page 96

SUSPENSION

DESPITE THE MORASS in his being, the first thing he noticed was an auburn leaf suspended in mid-air. Closer inspection revealed its attachment to a single spider's thread, its levitation magical in its own way as it swayed to a backdrop of mysterious woodland full of the sound of birdsong.

He hunted for a web and located it, resplendent with dew, in the centre of which, motionless, sat a sizeable, common diadem spider. The first shafts of autumn sunlight broke behind him, turning the dewdrops into precious diamonds fit for a crown.

Lifting his body and his eyes, he surveyed the trees ahead of him; shadows playing as he upturned his head to the tree canopy and walked forward to immerse himself in another living world.

His feet slurped on mud, slapped on a carpet of forest detritus including freshly fallen leaves. He breathed in deeply, enjoying the smell of vegetation, mud, tree, fullness. His insides met his outsides as they expanded gleefully into the vibrant space.

He knew this place. Its spirituality fed and watered him.

He walked and walked, filling his being with the sounds of the woodland, hearing his own breath, his own body, his own disquiet.

Satisfyingly, he found the stump at the centre of the forest, damp with dew, remained. He wiped it with his hand, sat upon his humble throne, and stilled himself.

A female blackbird rewarded his patience, landing a few feet from him. Her mate soon joined her, overseeing her foraging. The drumming of an insistent woodpecker broke through the sounds. He lifted his eyes, slowly turning his head, pleased to locate black and white plumage with a bright red flash. A bluetit flew across his vision, unsure whether to land. He hoped the spider was alert to its predator. Then a bullfinch, its pinkish-red breast adding to the early autumnal colours.

At his feet, ants were exploring his shoe, and to his delight, a little rose chafer beetle, displaying its beautiful iridescent sheen. He placed his finger in its path, which it politely accepted, scrambling upon his skin. He lifted it to his face, enjoying its glory, before carefully placing his digit on a leaf for it to clamber upon.

The woodpecker's insistence interrupted his thoughts. It must have found a delectable ant and insect colony, he reasoned.

The sun broke through above him and turned mystery into magic. The sunlight not only made everything around him vibrate with colour, but it also infused light into his soul. As his spirit fed on the richness, so the wind whispered through the trees, their banter filling his senses. It was here, among nature, a familiar and longed-for sense of wonder overcame him. He, a mere speck in the midst of magical life, present to attempt to rediscover proportion. Woodland beauty always enriched him, and he felt grateful to be included in the whispery conversation.

He watched the falling leaves that symbolised the end of their season. Their barky host, rich with energy and vitality would, in their de-mobbed state, release fresh, overflowing growth in spring. He needed a new season, a new beginning. The thought that springtime must come lifted his spirit. Winter had been so long, so hard. Whatever he had grown now lay trampled or cut down. He took heart that from his deep roots, fresh life must emerge.

The sounds of the forest melded into chords, into song, into words of a song enfolding him. 'Hold on,' it sang, 'hold on.'

'Hold on to what?' he thought.

He sat, he stood, he walked, he listened, he stayed, allowing the woodland calm to fill him.

As twilight gathered darkness, he emptied the contents of a small bag out of his pocket. Birdseed. A tiny oblation to beauty.

Then he left the wood, deciding to cut across the farmland.

He heard him first. The shriek in the inert air. Moving only his eyes, he scanned the expanse of farmland before him.

There! He recognised the white chest. The long, broad, rounded, undulating wings revealing the whiteness of his sweet belly. His heart-shaped white face and dark eyes followed the sounds only he could hear.

The man waited. Silent. Watching the acoustic predator, awestruck.

Flying low, the barn owl swooped over the field, back and forth. Then he rose in the sky and hovered almost above him. Dropping like a stone headfirst onto the field, he pounced, perhaps ten feet away. Astonished at his nearness, the man watched him dive into a patch of field-margin rough grass. At the last moment, the owl pulled his head upwards, outstretched his talons and grabbed his prey. Without pausing, he rose again, his prey imprisoned, and flew to the edge of the field to disappear into a tree to eat his quarry whole.

> 'Hope is patience with the lamp lit.'
>
> TERTULLIAN[53]

To have a ringside view of a barn owl hunting was rare. The sheer beauty of the hunter overwhelmed him. The immensity of his unexpected gift washed him in awe, hope and grace.

« **Detail** – See page 116

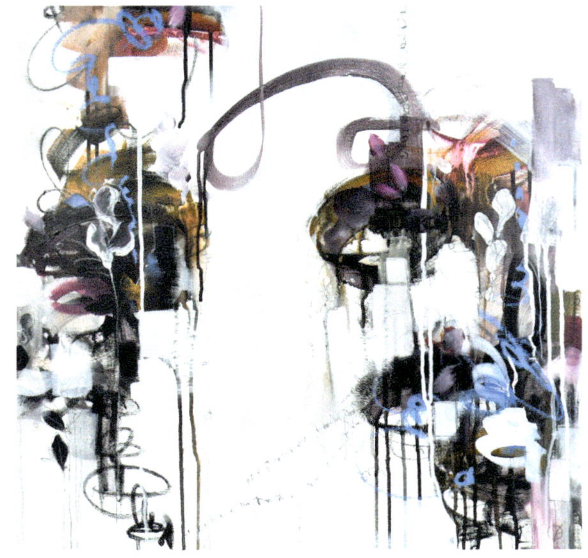

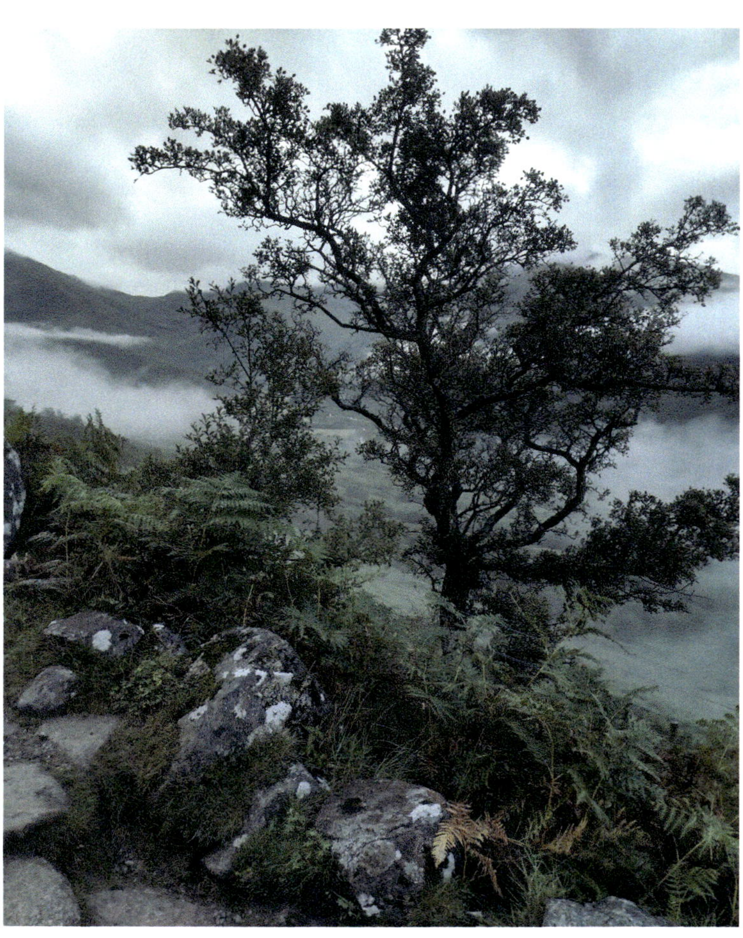

AM THOMAS

Memento Mori III

Mixed media on stretched canvas

H: 60cm W: 60cm

An expression of my honesty alongside mixed feelings of dread of failure. What transpired in the making was the surprise and joy in the creation. We only get one chance at this life, so live it to the fullest, fear and all.

ANN LOSCOMBE

Ben Nevis in the Clouds

Photograph

H: 76cm W: 56cm

The ethereal hues of morning light, sunsets and storms; the colour and *chiaroscuro* of nature which can take one's breath away with its magic. To capture a moment of such magisterial splendour in a photograph makes my soul sing and look at life and the world with awe and wonder.

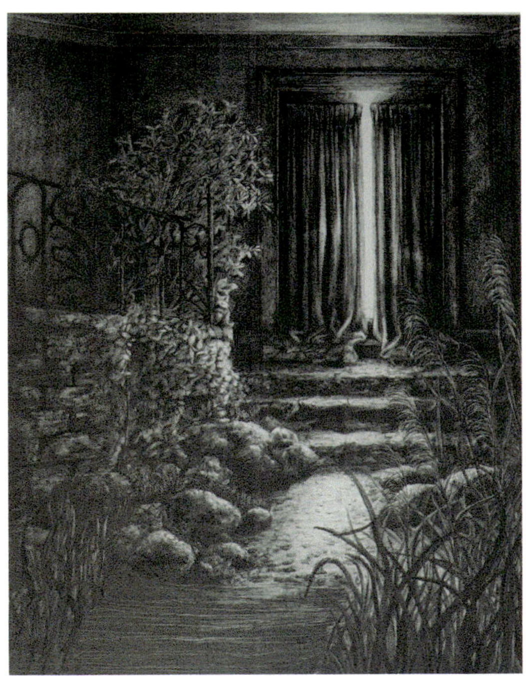

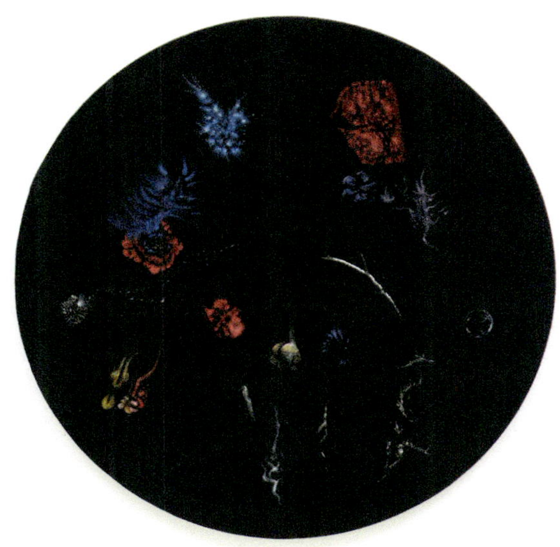

EMMA CLIFTON-BROWN

Unfolding Journey

Graphite on paper

H: 45cm W: 35cm

Through the grit and grime of life, I travel into the wild borderlands of the soul. Chinks of light cast their shadow on yesterday, keeping the mystery of unknown possibilities alive. Since a young child I have ached for a deeper connection with God, to grapple with the journey of faith and the wilderness of the soul's landscape.

IAN DOUGLASS

Sub Rosa

Oil and indium-gallium on velvet

H: 54cm W: 54cm

Sub rosa means 'under the rose' in Latin: something done in secret. The core of the mystical dimension is a secret which cannot be known or told. Using indium-gallium, a metal which melts at the temperature of the human body, a mystical alchemy takes place in the creation process. It represents the bounty of nature and existence.

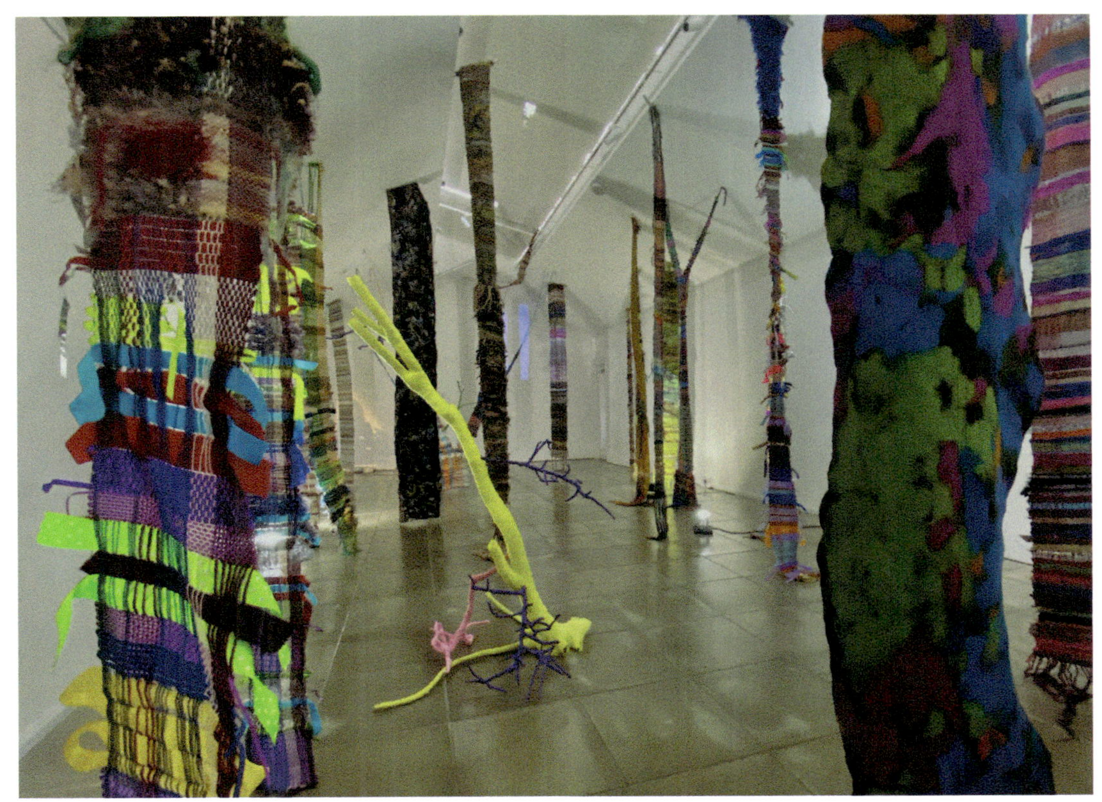

TOM HALL

Into the Dark Woods 2

Woven, cast and felted trees, theatrically lit with a shadow projection and quiet soundtrack

H: 250cm W: 300cm D: 600cm

Woods hold a significant place in our history and folklore as sites of caution, the unknown and danger. The work represents an experimental collaboration between material-based artists creating a metaphor for the dark pandemic times we inhabited. Made of woven 'trees' extending the forest outwards, beyond its physical bounds towards imagined narratives.

journey marking

THE CHAIR

IT WAS A THREAD, a
simple thread
that caught her attention.
She stooped down, took it
between her fingers
and pulled.
It grew and grew and
grew.
She lifted and looked –
She upended and stared –
Threads had fallen from the
middle unnoticed.
A centre undone
threatens structure.

Why care?
She had sat,
read,
thought,
written,
upon the secret unravelling,
hiding deterioration
in inauthentic calm.

She bemoaned her basic
repair skills,
railed against her mother's
inattention,
her father's disassociation,
her sibling separation.
How to remedy its
disembowelling?
YouTube talked of history,
age, creation,
introduced unknown tools
to cut, uncover, discover,
a jolly voice of
encouragement
underpinning,
to unlearned eyes,
imminent destruction.

But unimagined courage
spurred her.
Carefully she fingered
every nook and crevice
marvelling at structure and
composition,
creativity and spirit
and began.

Her electronic tutor spoke
against fear with faith –
modelled anxiety into
believing –
transformed dread into
learning and loving –
the tools of regeneration.
She nailed, she replaced,
she sewed and mended.
Her growing expertise
wove
a tapestry of health deep
within
and time begat the inside
and the outside
as she dressed it
in long-lasting fabric,
impregnated with non-
staining
properties,
made to dismiss spills
with a wipe, or energetic
blotting.

She grew to love her chair,
to relish its embrace.
And others
Seeing it
longed to try it, and often
rested in its arms.
It grew old and worn, but
never lost its strength,
or comfort.

'Aim for the sky, but move slowly, enjoying every step along the way.

It is all those little steps that make the journey complete.'

CHANDA KOCHHAR[54]

« **Detail** — See page 71

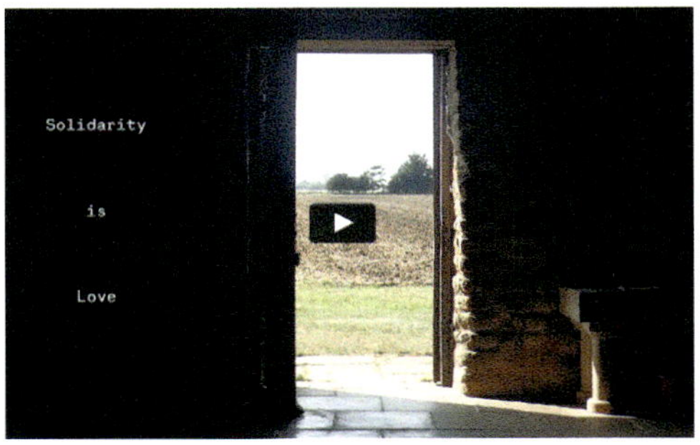

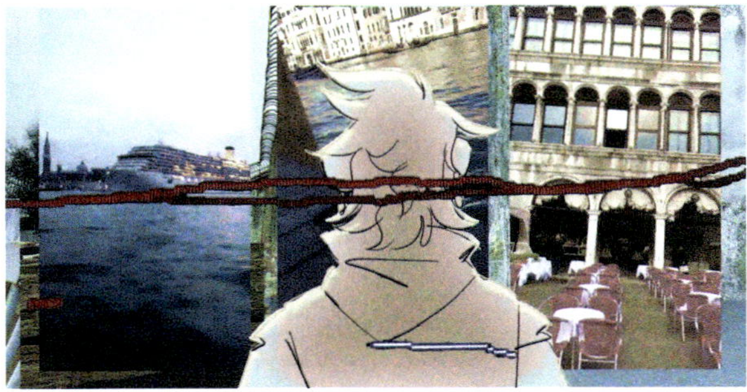

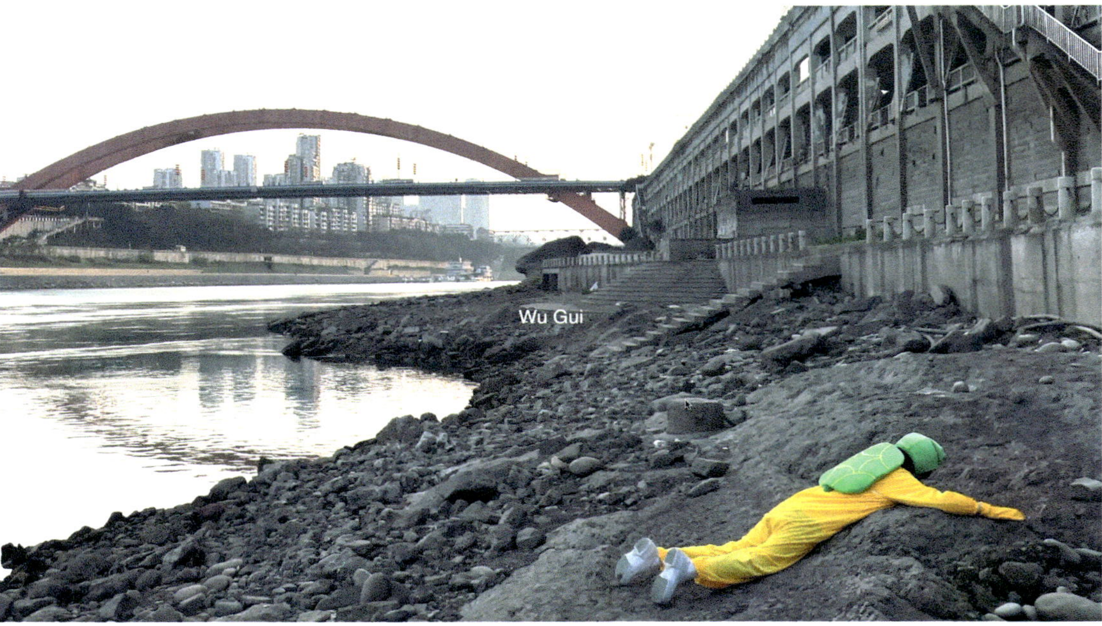

SIMON BALL

Solidarity is Love

Video: 2 min 48 sec

Questing for meaning and understanding, I met Stavros. This spun me into a wild adventure within a world of collective artwork. I enjoyed the power of creation, linking disparate images and places, celebrating the grand mystery of life. These fragments are pieced together with love, a paean of coming together in the service of something greater.

DEAN DE BARROS

Parallels

Photography, video, digital art, generated sound

Video: 2 min 57 sec

A journey to Erith on the shore of the Thames parallels a journey to Venice with my grandmother. The parallel journeys remind me of how I have changed. Remembering my grandparents, their habits and mine, my grandfather's gifted green scarf, trying to revive their memory in Erith. It is a haunting activity to revive memories from a distance.

XINYAO YU

Wu Gui

Video: 2 min 52 sec

When Wu Gui* woke up, they realised that identities and languages are fake parodies to discipline individuals. They re-identified themselves, wandering as ghosts, exiled from the symbolic to the real. They found divinity inside everything, even the world they had disassociated from. They choose to be involved again.

*reclaiming the word 'turtle' in Chinese

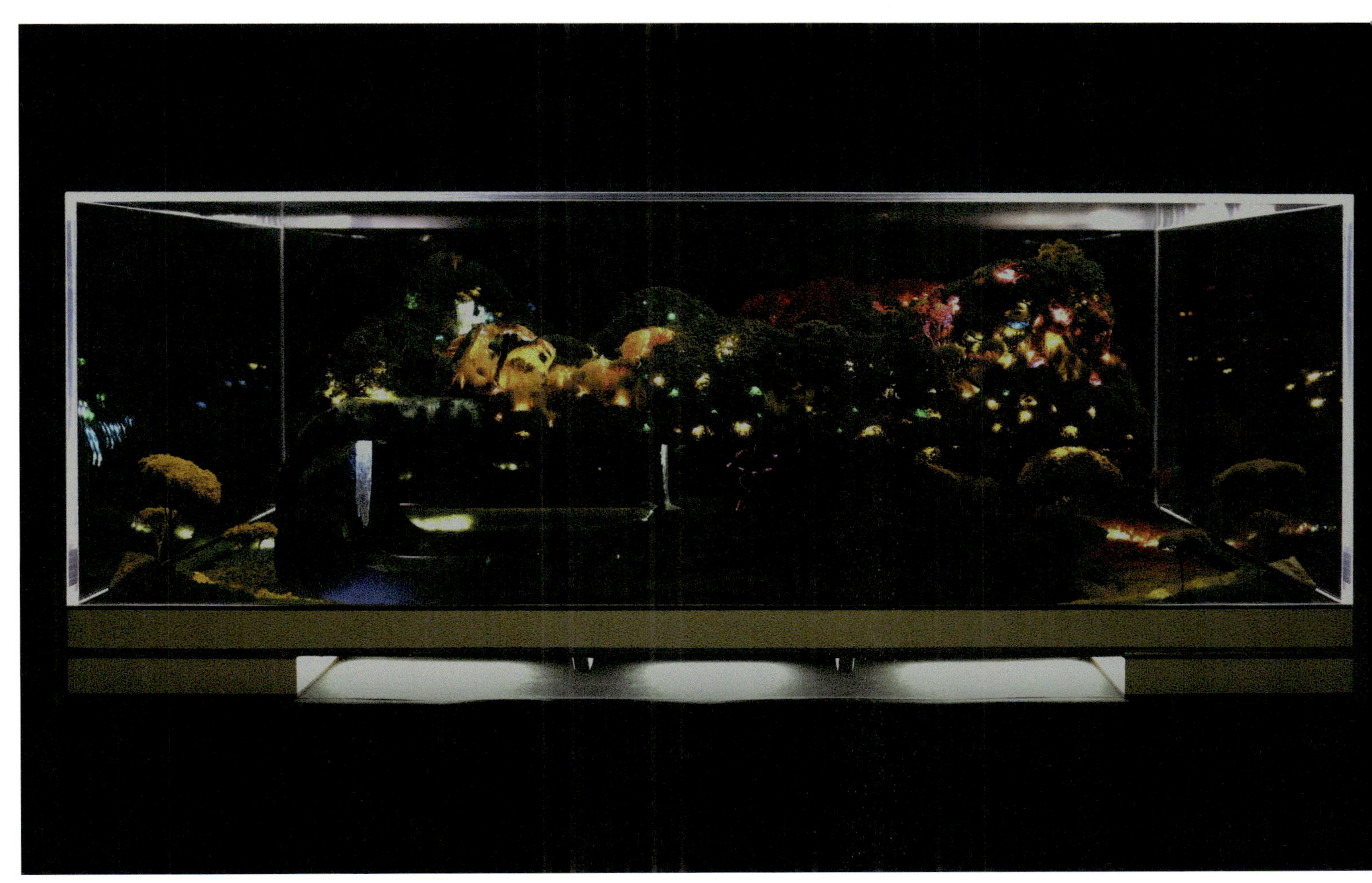

WIKTOR KUTA

Paradise

Sculpture/mixed media, materials including resin, electronics, wood, man-made fibres, acrylic paint, dried plants

H: 46cm W: 113cm
D: 71cm

This explores the state of paradise; a state of beauty, happiness, harmony, bliss, wonder and fulfilment. It delves into the materialistic and energetic realm of our existence.

force of nature

'You must choose to take hold of what you can control and let go of what you cannot. You cannot control your circumstances, but you can control your character. You cannot control the actions of others, but you can control the choices you make. You cannot control the outcome, but you can control the process.'

ERWIN RAPHAEL MCMANUS[55]

NAZARÉ

STANDING ALONE on a beach, overlooking the ocean, whether calm or choppy, with rising swell or wild open space, permeates the mind, the spirit and the soul with wonder. Lungs expand with the whipping wind, nostrils widen enriched with the smell of salt, face is cleansed as it lifts to feel the sun's rays. The vast expanse of sky decorated by clouds; white or dipped in grey; wispy with winds; mackerel-scaled; suspended or scudding; paint the heavens with shapes we reimagine anthropomorphically.

We breathe deeper, wider, fuller. Our body tenses against the cold and wind, or perhaps relaxes, receptive to the warmth and space. Whatever our experience, something beckons in the whispering gusts, a sense of the pinprick of our existence within ever-enlarging space. For most of us, this multifaceted sighting of awe-inspiring natural phenomenon feeds and satisfies our soul.

Some want more. Their well-being, their energy, longs for experience. Being in the sea is not enough. Being on the sea is not enough. Somehow, they must be at one with its fearful power – to 'ride' it. The professional surfers.

There are few places in the world where conditions are perfect for extraordinary waves. A storm is required, with winds blowing in the ideal direction. The sea surge must optimise. Preferably, there needs to be a type of unique underwater formation as the swell travels towards its landfall.

There is a place with an undersea canyon half the length of the Grand Canyon. It runs for 143 miles offshore right up to the beach with a maximum depth of three miles. This has a major effect on incoming swells. As water approaches the land, the wave splits; accelerates; turns inward towards the canyon side, hits the wall, which then forces it upwards. The resulting humongous waves can be more than 100 feet high. The combination of the weather, the natural structural formation of land and sea creates the ideal environment for the perfect wave.

The big wave surfers found Nazaré in Portugal in 2011.

For generations, Nazaré was a fishing village with a reputation as a dangerous place to fish as the work robbed many families of brothers, sons and husbands. Historically the villagers fished by line-casting, but the seas emptied courtesy of trawlers with monster catches. Nazaré's twentieth-century 'catch' became the tourists and the professional 'big wave surfers'.

The waves are overseen by a lighthouse built on an extension into the sea, one side overlooking the balmy visitor beach, the other the Praia do Norte where nobody from Nazaré ever ventures because of its inherent danger.

Today, autumn through to spring you can stand on the lighthouse terrace, spellbound, experiencing the fearsome power of the largest waves in the world. Watch terror-filled as professional surfers risk everything to ride 'the big one'.

Nature's ferocious and uncontrollable display reminds us of our fragile humanity.

« **Detail** – See page 113

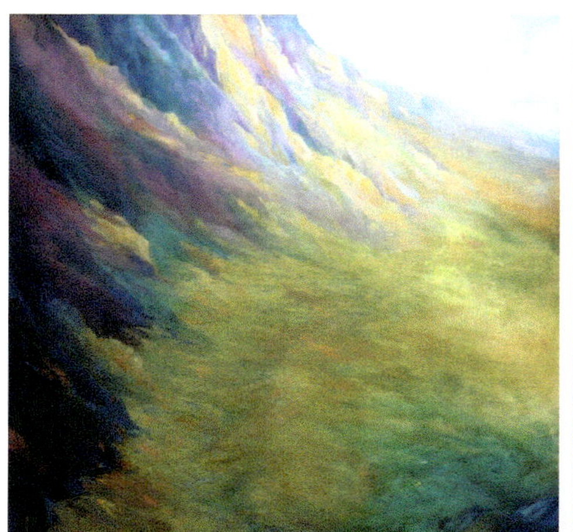
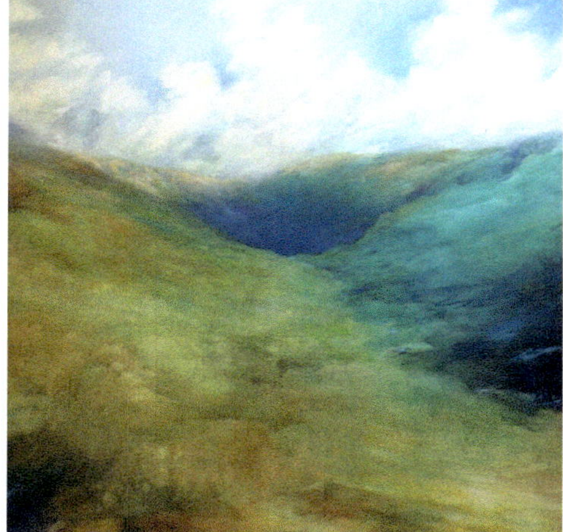
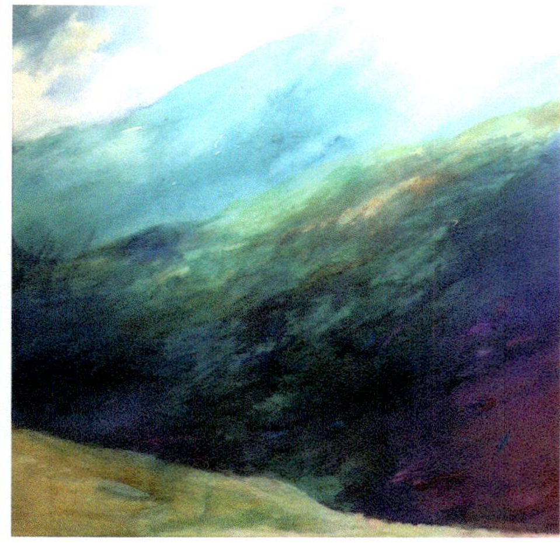
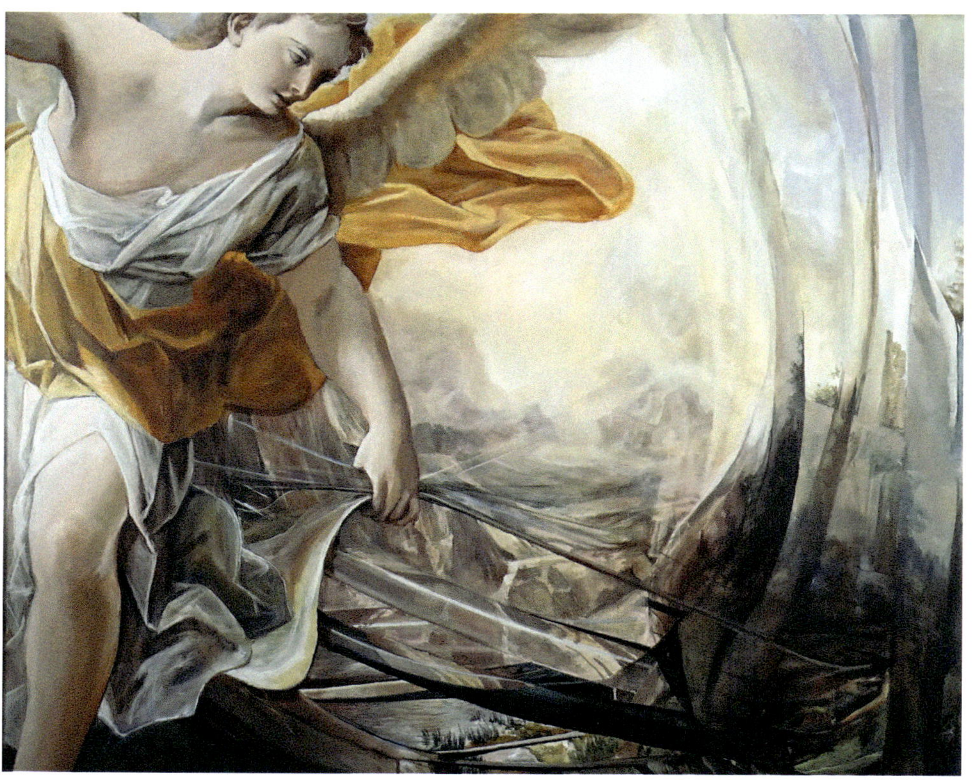

JANINE ELIZABETH
Earth

Triptych – mixed media on canvas acrylic, oil, pencil and pastel

H: 100cm W: 300cm

Sunlight reveals the form and colour of a mountain landscape in the Lake District. A distant valley carved by ancient ice curves beneath summer sky. The mountains call to our sense of wildness – the place of solitude within where God speaks. Vast landscapes echo with power. They inspire intimate awe, silence and wonder.

LARAIN BRIGGS
Tahafucha

Historical artwork is appropriated, digitally fragmented, distorted and then transposed into a physical painting on canvas

H: 104cm W: 124cm

Tahafucha: Hebrew – 'upheaval'. The global impact of technology on humanity and the environment engenders anxiety and a sense of danger alongside awesome might. This orientates me towards the philosophy of the sublime. Marcantonio Franceschini's 'The Guardian Angel' is appropriated and used to relate an apocalyptic message of disruption to reality, time and space.

KENDRICK SNODIN

Barkby 244

Mixed media, watercolour, acrylic, gouache, pastels

H: 32cm W: 48cm

Inspired by the sunset over Holt Lane, Barkby, Leicestershire, an area I have visited many times throughout my life; it provides a constant inspiration and opens up a world of internal possibilities.

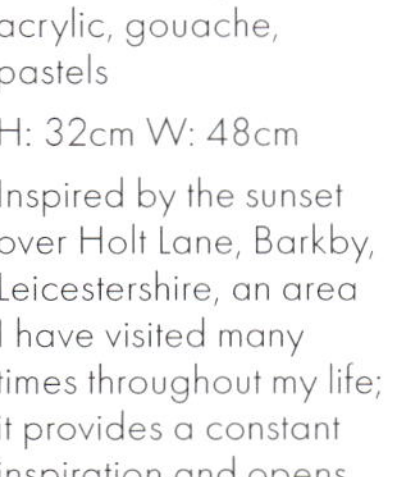

TOM HALL

The Circle

Film

Video: 6 min 6 sec

'The Circle' is made in collaboration with scientists working on experiments in the Large Hadron Collider at CERN in Switzerland/France. It attempts to reconcile the difference in how time works between the quantum and Newtonian worlds. The Space Shaman transcends and walks both in our Newtonian world of measurable distance, past and future, here and now and the timeless quantum realm.

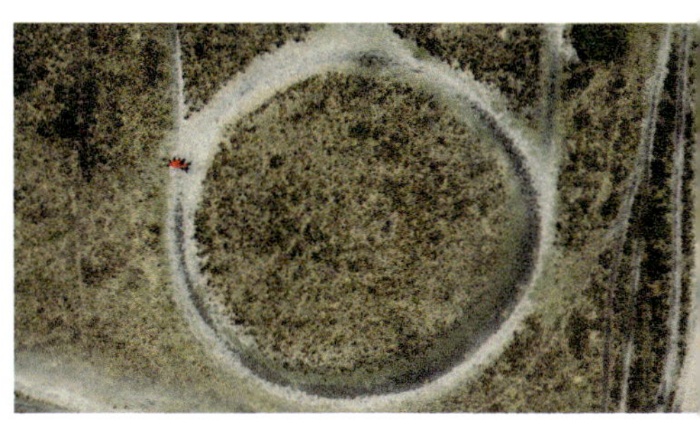

NICOLA BEATTIE

Aeris

Alabaster on granite

H: 71cm W: 42cm D: 28cm

I thought the cloudy-marked piece of alabaster perfectly illustrated the skies. I was then inspired by a glimpse of heaven through a narrow-lit opening, reminiscent of 'the narrow way' as the path to eternal life. Hollowed out at the back to allow the light to shine through, the opening in the sculpture appears as a sunlit entrance within the clouds.

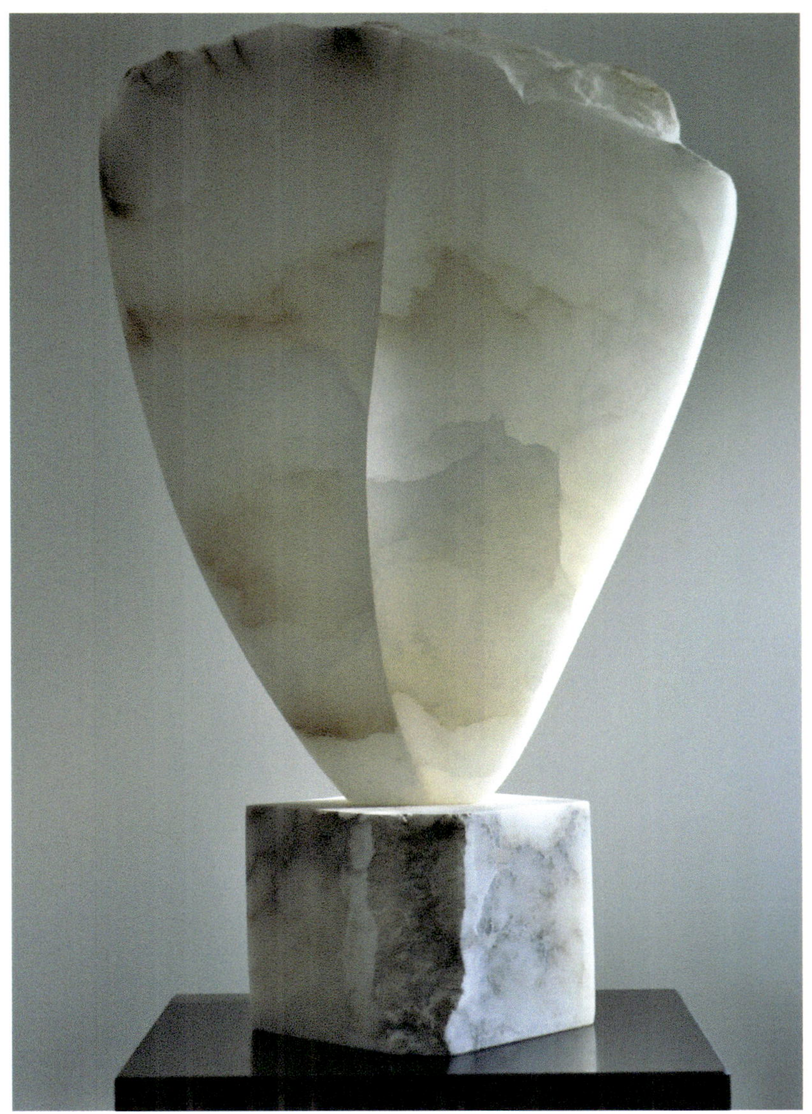

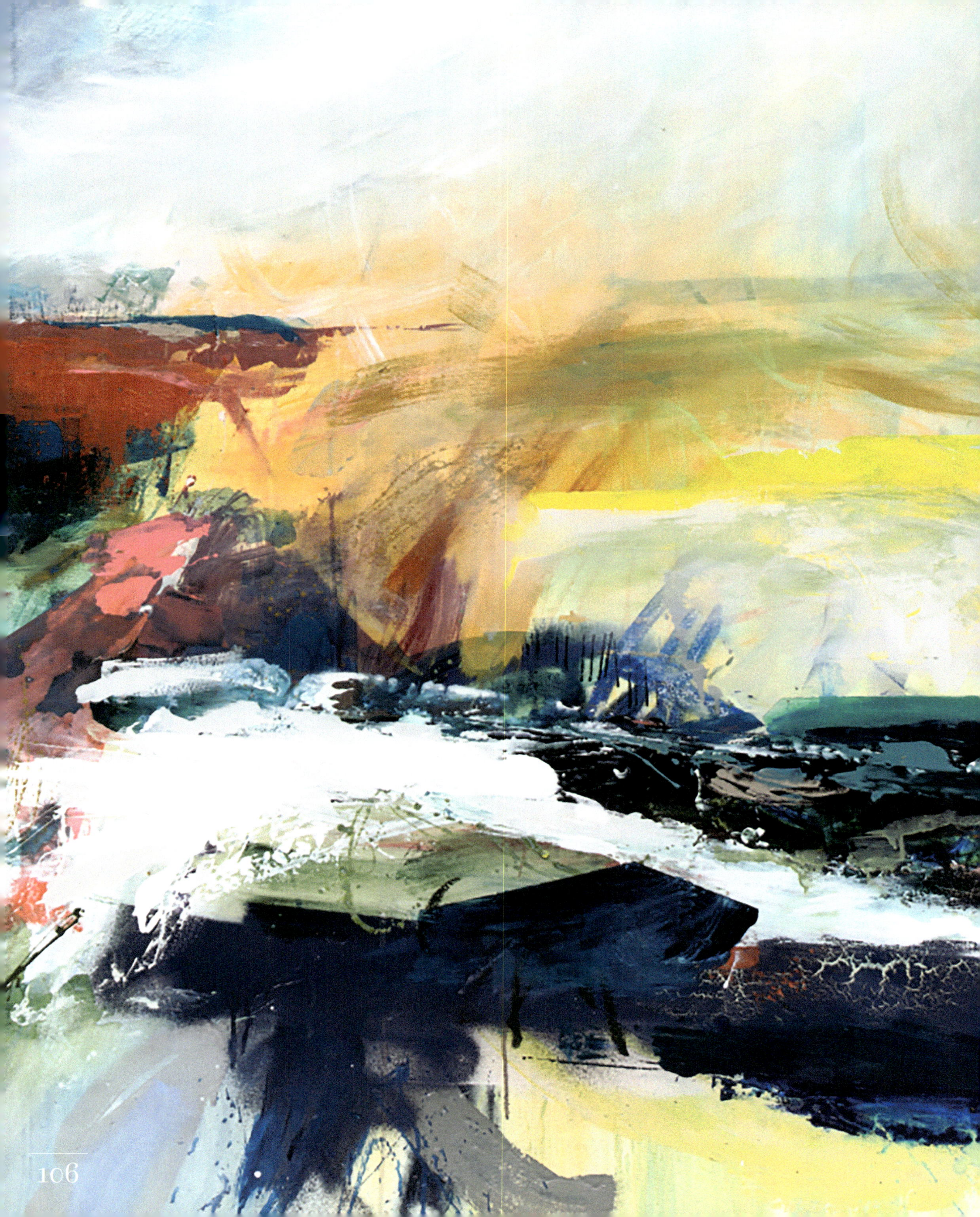

THE FRAGRANCE OF CHANGE

CAN YOU REMEMBER a time when life stopped – a diagnosis, a death, a break-up with a friend, family member or lover? It's usually loss that opens windows into self. However, the joy of others can also loosen the small protections we've put in place for safety. Comparison brings a perception of less, not more. Moving forward, if we are rudderless or have no perception of our own North Star, is challenging.

The coping strategies we often employ don't help – self-pity demoralises; grabbing for any appeasement becomes bilious, and blaming others isolates and allows bitterness.

What about humility? Allowing its delicate scent to permeate our self-protection brings deep reflection, permits crucial questions to surface and unlocks courage to ask for help.

Whatever our story, we can choose to remain a victim or fearlessly take ownership of ourselves. Do we believe our life is our responsibility or do we relinquish it to those who've damaged us?

A deep draught of humility can set us on the cusp of transformation. We don't know all the answers, nor should we expect that of ourselves. Life's flowering and fragrance offer us development in wisdom and understanding.

Change appears sluggish, its snail-like increments causing us to wonder if anything is shifting.

Simply begin.

After implementing one small change, live in it. Then add a second, then a third. Expect, over time, to have grown skills as you thrive in the abundant fruit of humility and the change it augured.

As legitimate questions surface, we will require courage and fortitude to listen to them.

Searching for ways forward requires resilience. Nothing worthwhile in our lives manifests without pain. Persist – the rewards are wonderful.

‘You can't be brave if you're not scared.’

ANN CLIFFORD[56]

« **Detail** – See page 25

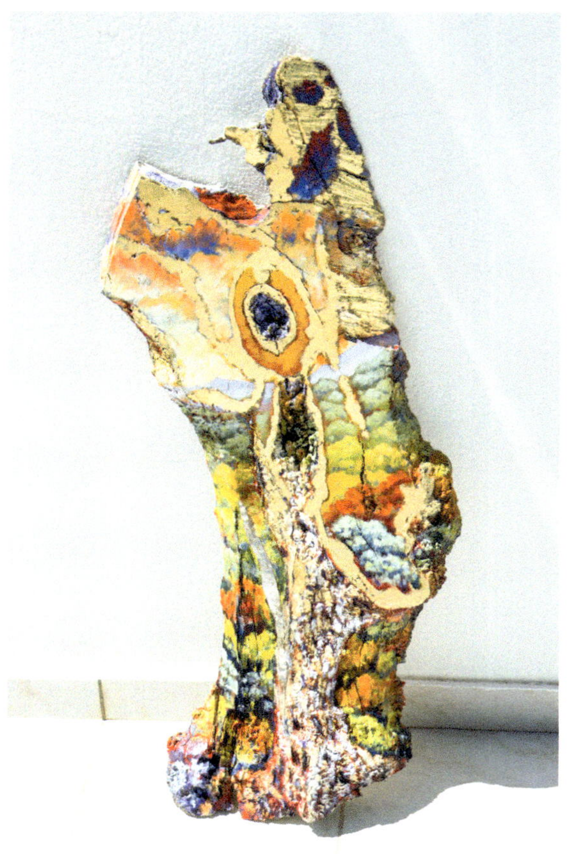

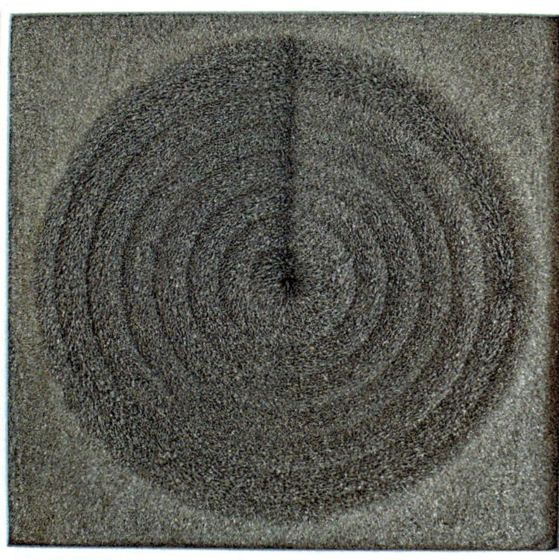

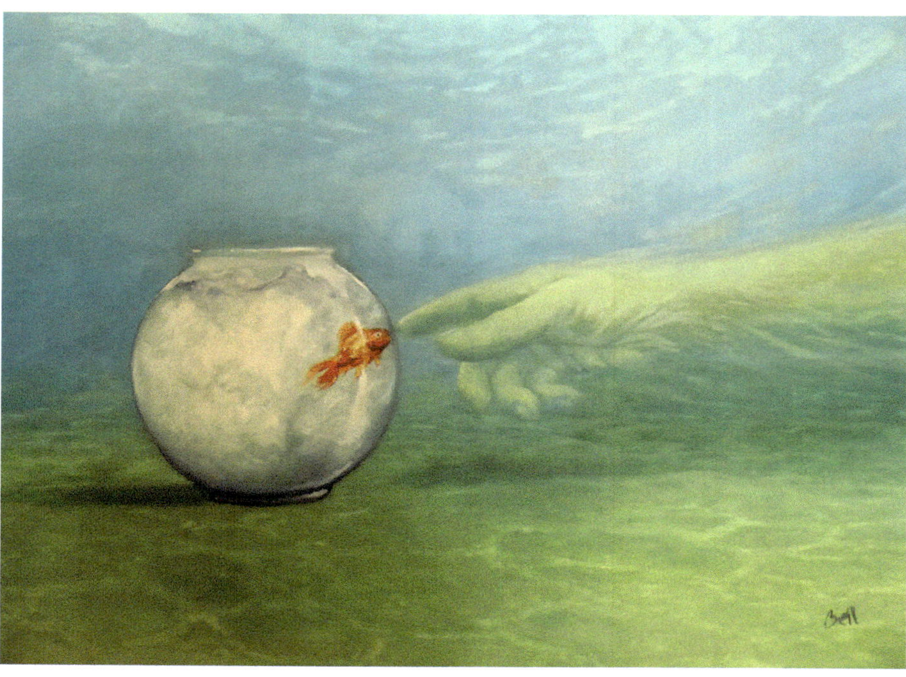

JOHN HEDLEY

Ascending Olive Tree

Oil with gold and silver leaf on olive wood

H: 91cm W: 30cm D: 4cm

A visual representation of art's relationship to nature, symbolism and our place in the natural and constructed world. Both in contrast to and comparable to the veneration of Byzantine icons, we are reminded to humble ourselves in awe and wonder of that which stands before us – the natural world that created us and inspired art.

JO FAIRFAX

Japanese Zen Garden

Interactive drawing machine, made from MDF, Perspex, Arduino, stepper motor

H: 20cm W: 22cm D: 22 cm

An interactive drawing machine triggered as someone approaches, inspired by an interview with a Japanese Zen gardener talking about the spirit of matter. I loved the way nature and humankind were seamlessly one spirit, and wanted to create a sense of awe and wonder from this beautiful union.

JENNIFER BELL

The Visionary

Oil on board

H: 49cm W: 69cm

The visionary is one who can glimpse further than the confines of this finite world. What is beyond could be made of the same elements, but immeasurably more so.

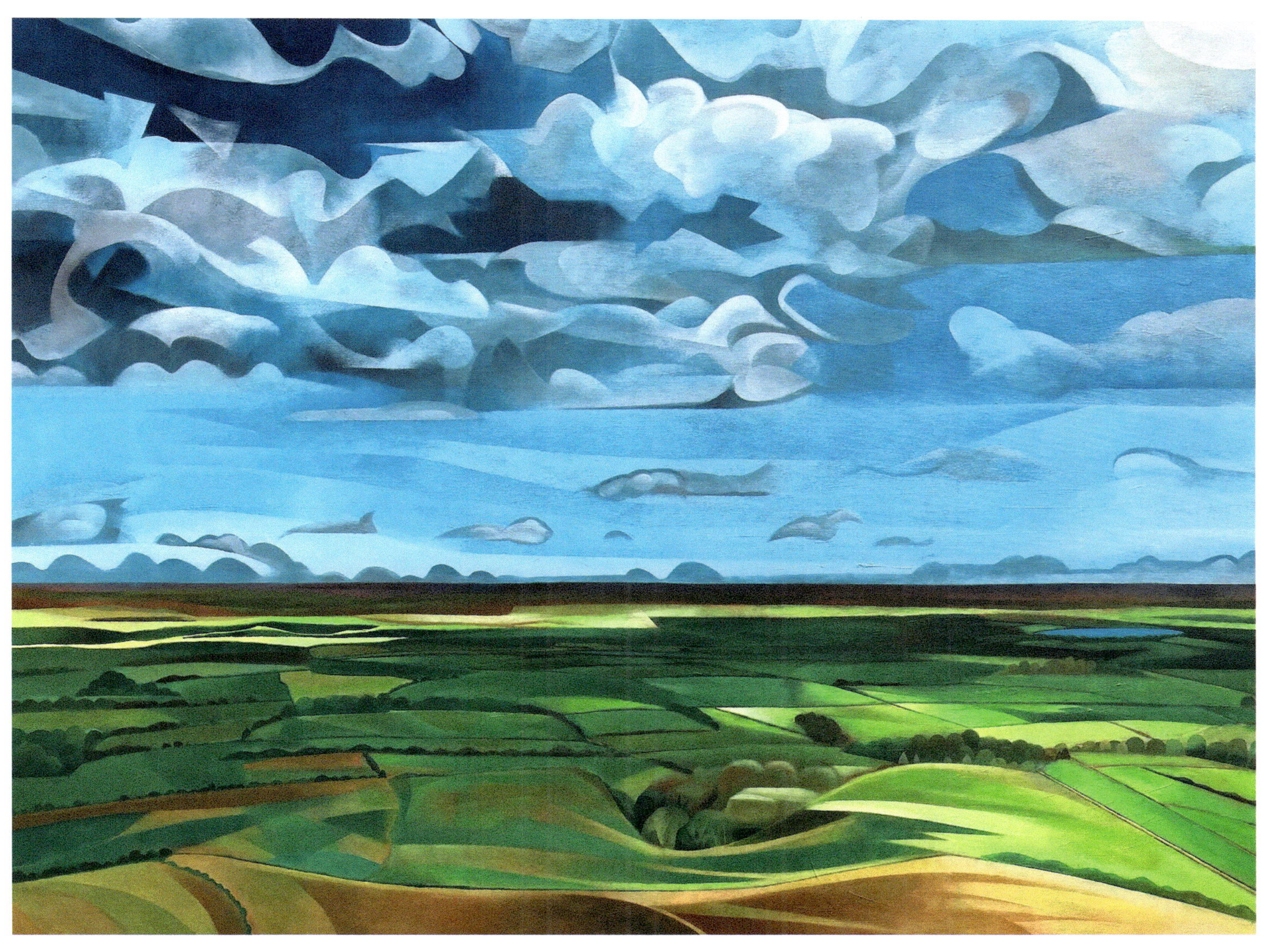

DAVID GARRATT

Firmament and Fields

Acrylic on canvas

H: 100cm W: 120cm

The view is towards Arlington Reservoir in East Sussex. The more the artist looks, the more he sees, appreciating the extraordinary complexity in the simplest and most familiar of sights.

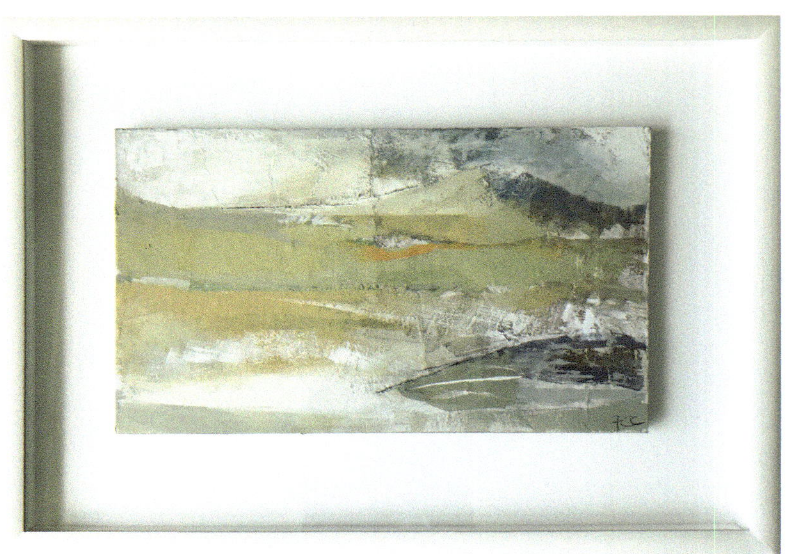

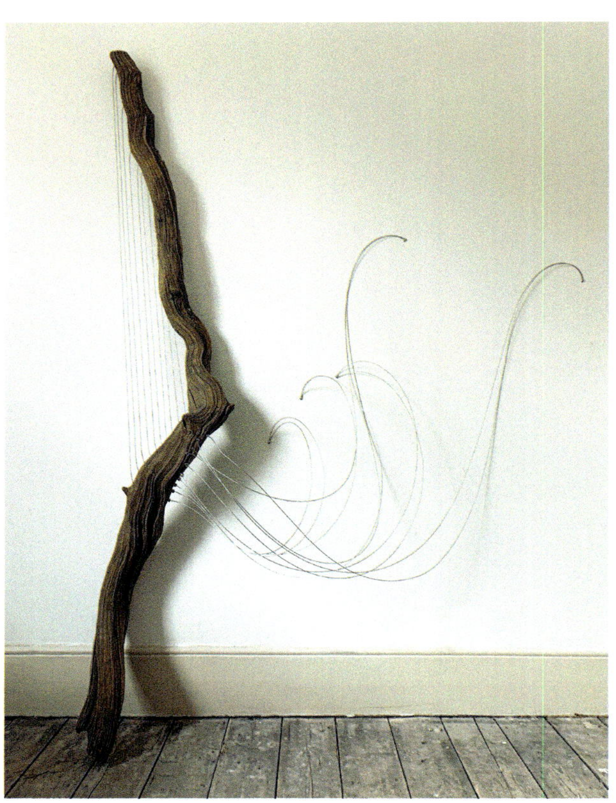

FIONA CHARIS CARSWELL

Golden Hill, Hidden Pool

Mixed media – white box frame and mount

H: 58cm W: 81cm

Vastness and the feeling of smallness, overcome by step-by-step progress. Awareness of the leading of the Spirit advances my transportation and appreciation of the incredible natural world.

ANNIE TREVORAH

Rhythm

Japanese cedarwood and steel strings

H: 213cm W: 760cm D: 9cm

This work looks at themes of temporality, slowness and rhythm.

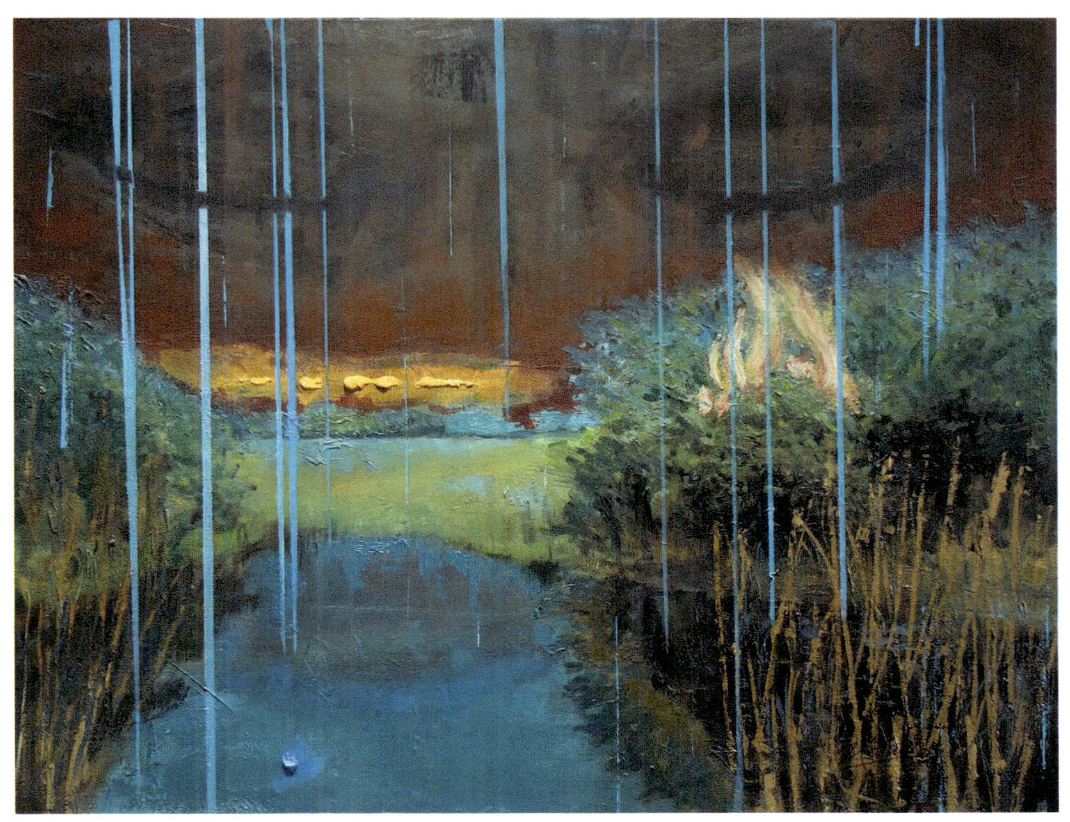

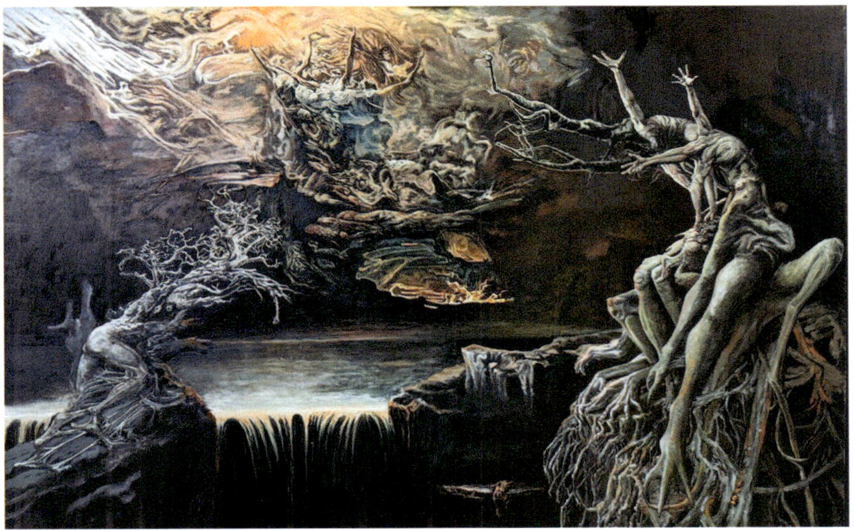

CSABA TIBOR PALOTAS

Awakening – I Am That I Am

Oil on canvas

H: 65cm W: 85cm

When God appeared to Moses in the burning bush, He uttered, 'I am that I am.' 'I' revels in life itself, in what binds every living creature together, total existence, the vigour of the heart, the pulse of nature and the purest awareness of mind.

ANDREW COWIE

Uprooted Reach

Oil on wood

H: 80cm W: 120cm

Inspired by my wanderings through the Ashdown Forest, East Sussex, in the dark winter months, feeling akin to the fallen, uprooted trees, with their limbs outstretched, reaching for the fleeting glimpses of light. Reverential respect mixed with fear reaching for the light in the darkness.

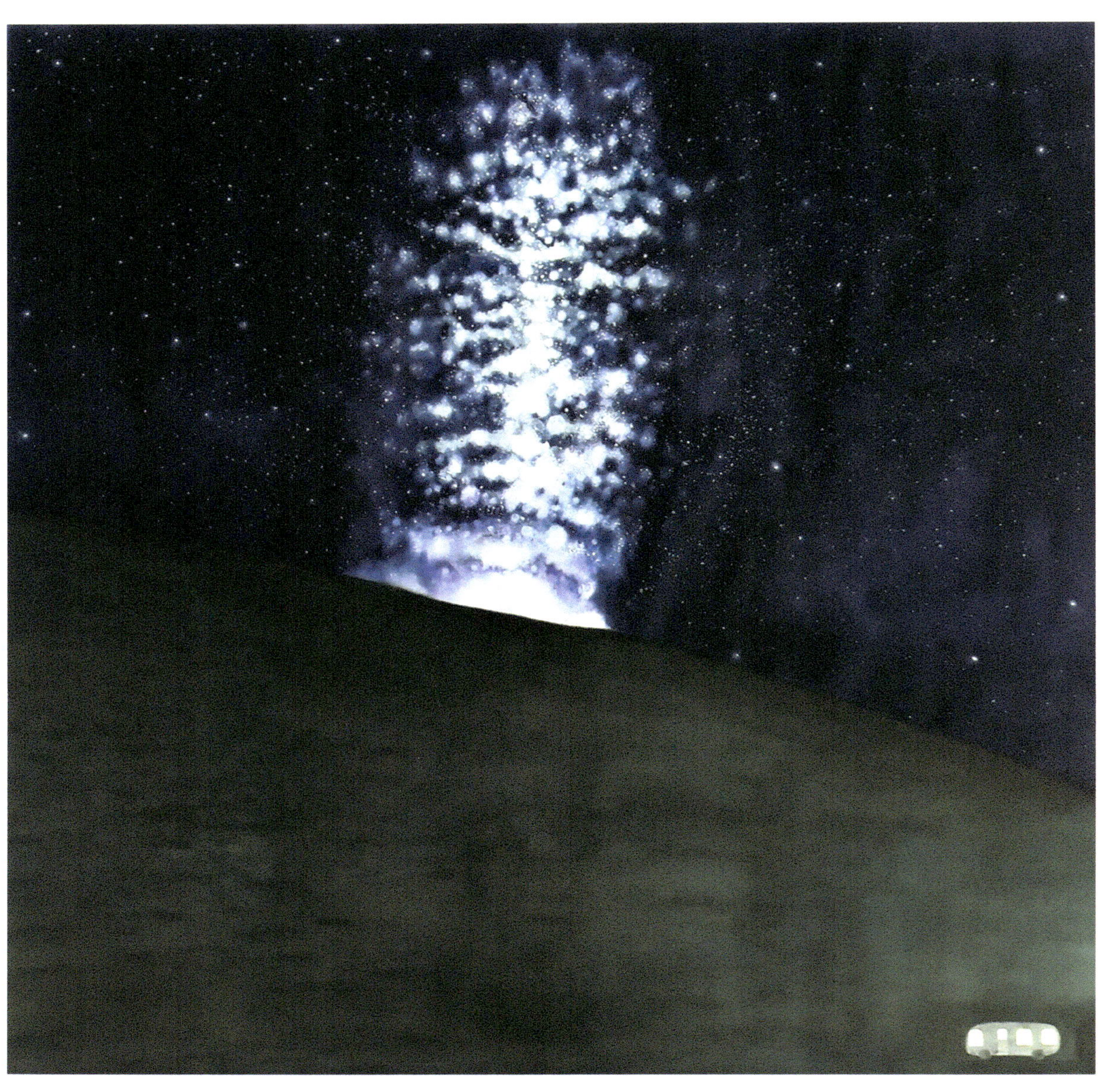

SARA AZIZ

Milky Way Over West Penwith (Winter at the Caravan)

Watercolour and mixed media on paper

H: 112cm W: 109cm

Winter at the caravan, I stepped outside in the night, grumbling; inside is warm but a trip to the outhouse is needed! Cold and dark and... emerging... all words stop dead. I am greeted by more stars than I have ever seen. Surrounded by the Milky Way. It is pure magic.

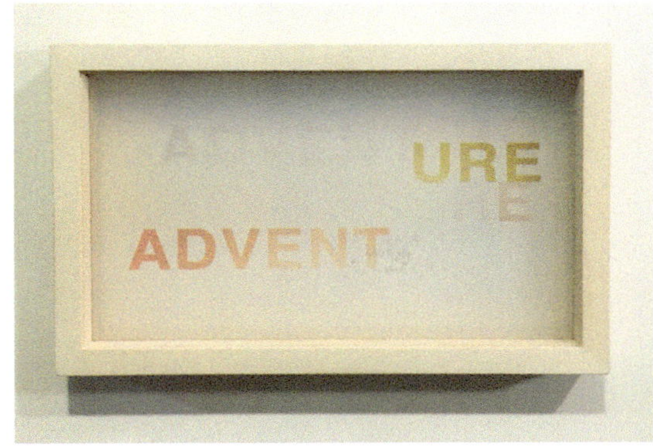

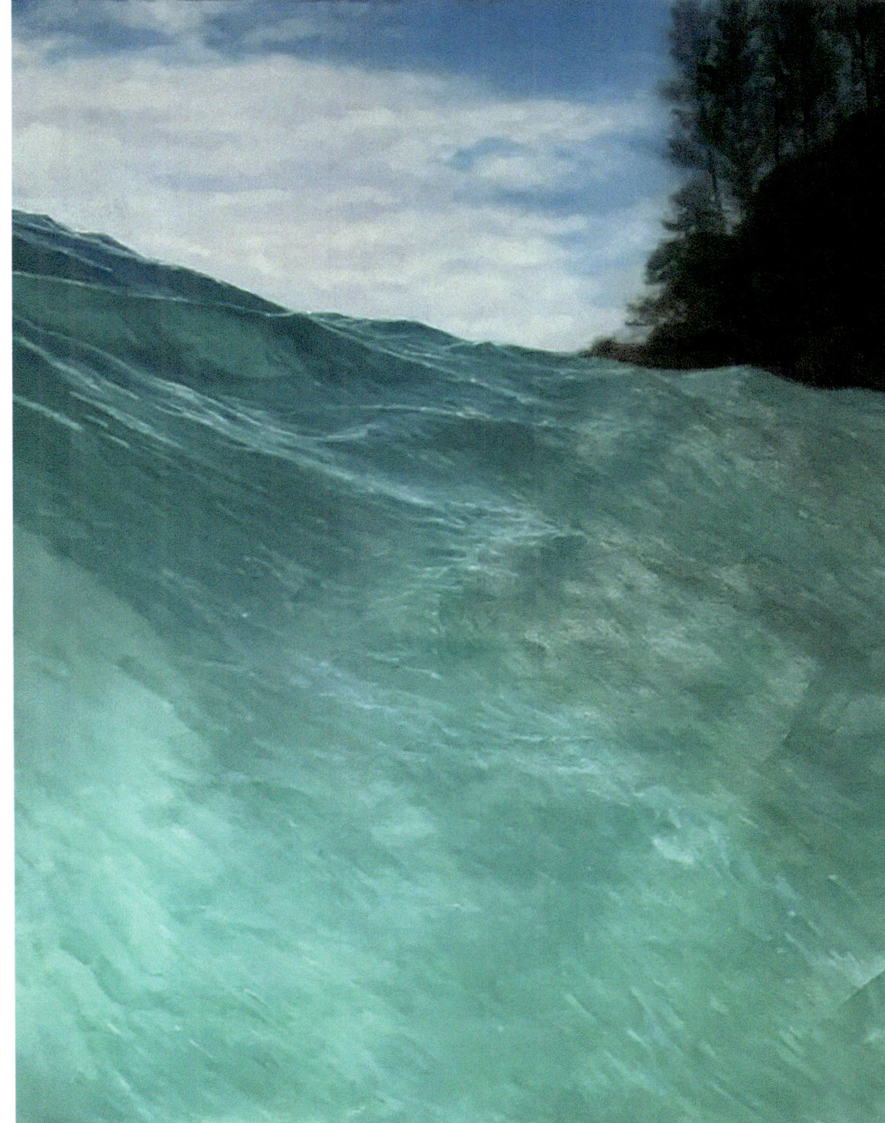

DAVID MCCULLOCH

Advent(ure)

Framed lenticular print

H: 9cm W: 30cm

Using the motion of lenticular printing technique to hide and reveal the words 'advent' and 'adventure'. Their root meaning is 'something is about to happen'. Whether we are caught by surprise or looking intentionally, those words fluctuate in front of us, unsettling our gaze. What will we see – an advent, a wonder?

ELCIN PERSSON

Mesmerizing

Oil on canvas

H: 140cm W: 110cm

The captivating energy and spellbinding quality of a wave. I want the realism to pull the viewer into the water, allowing them to look and wonder. Nature awes us, enveloping us with its magic and power.

through
t

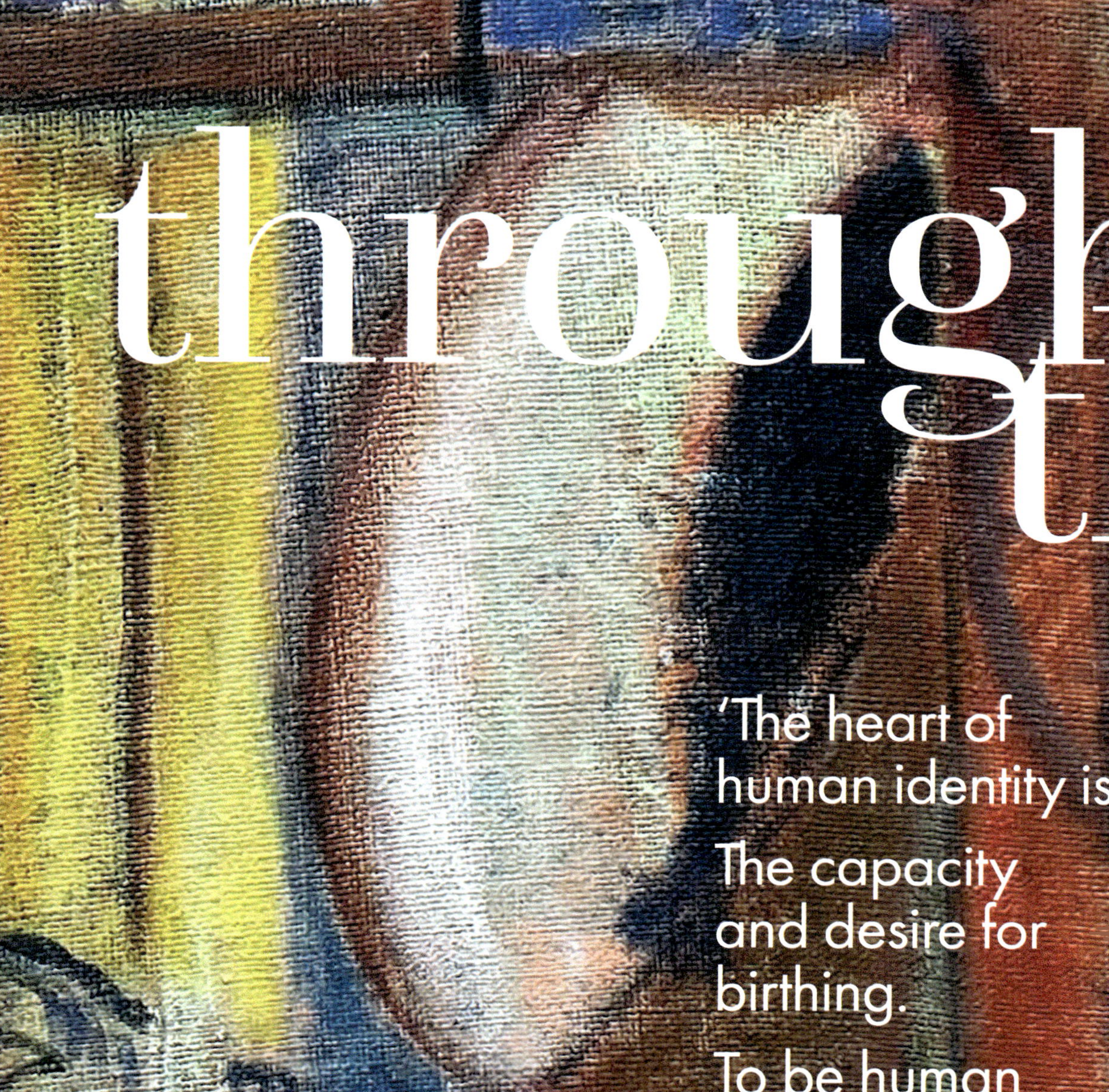

'The heart of
human identity is
The capacity
and desire for
birthing.
To be human
is to become
creative
And bring forth
the beautiful.'

JOHN O'DONOHUE[57]

newardrobe

THE MAGICIAN'S COAT

I SEE YOU,
but you do not see yourself.
The storm raged.
The oppression crushed.
Pain made you vulnerable,
earthbound,
courage disappeared.
Oppressed by all your yesterdays.
You thought yourself alone,
bereft of the kindness of consolation.

I, the magician, had scooped you,
because of love,
into my magic coat,
a sanctuary against all elements,
because of love.

Weren't you born to somersault, to
leap and dive,
to ride upon the wind?

The time is now –
The coat is open wide –
Will you dare?
Will you risk?

Emerge, disturb,
allow change to prise open
the aroma of
your dreams?
Embrace the space you were born for,
expel fear and
live what you love.

'Each of us is more than the worst thing we've ever done.'

BRYAN STEVENSON[58]

« **Detail** — See page 62

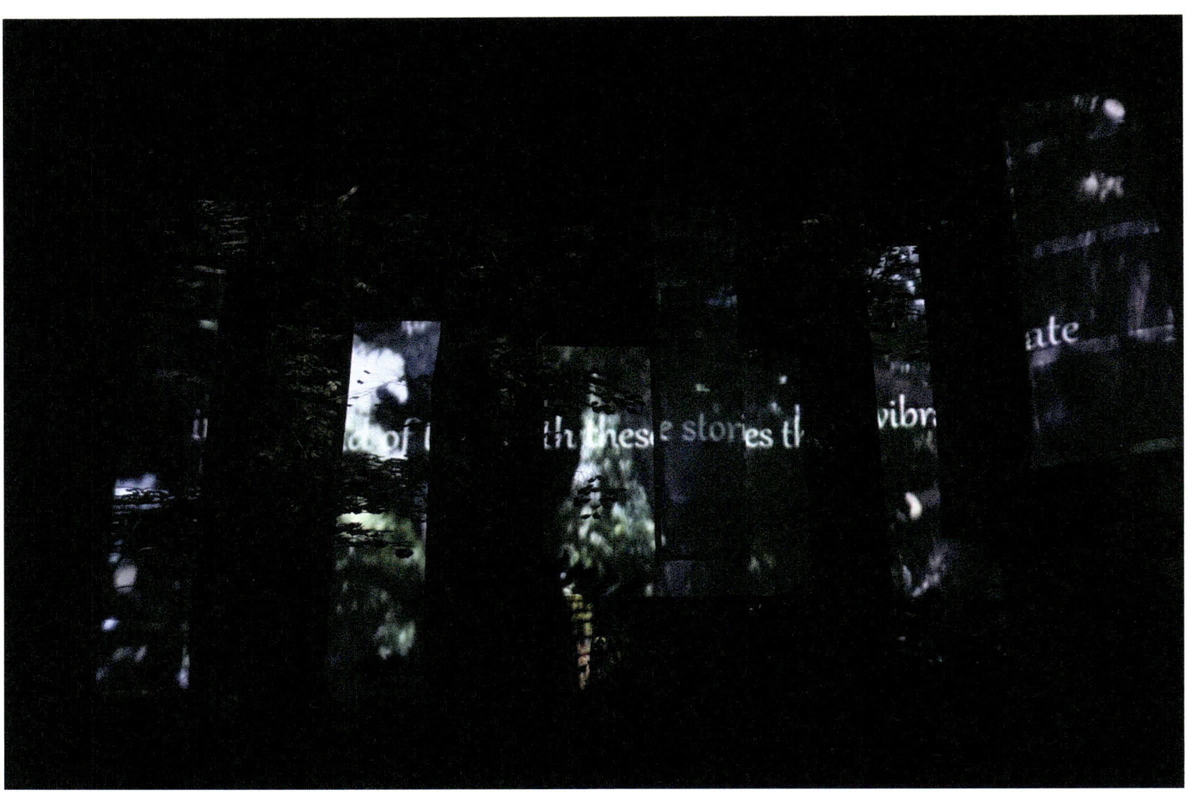

JANE HOUSTON GREEN

Beyond the Routes 1

Film installation

Video: 7 mins

A conversation with a forest, organised through the Moving Image Makers Collective in the Scottish Borders. The installation explores what we feel and hear versus what we see. Images of protected world trees are projected onto witch elm. Themes of belonging, acceptance, feeling rooted, with qualities of quietness and peace.

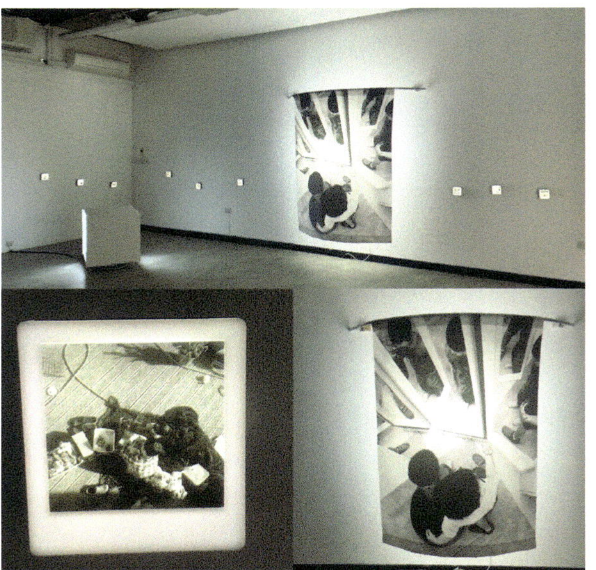

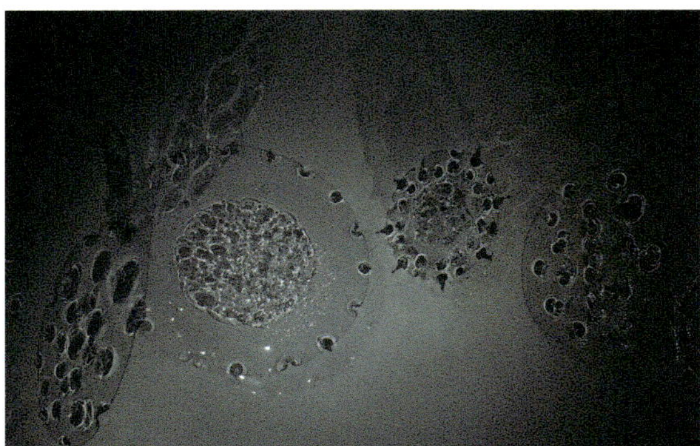

LI ANN LEE

Mother's Gaze

Double-sided infinity box, with photos

H: 65cm W: 65cm D: 65cm

There is a strand of educational theory that claims nurturing awe is the way to cultivate creativity, curiosity and reasoning. The photographs used in the artwork capture moments of childhood awe, wonder, fascination and discovery. All these elements work to use the physicality of the viewer to play and interrogate the work.

JILL WOODS

Bathed in the Same Light

Perspex, nylon thread, LED lights

H: 250cm W: 350cm D: 200cm

An installation piece of heat-sculpted Perspex cells, exploring the oxymoron of 'simple complexity' to evoke a sense of wonder about creation. Cells are the simple building blocks of all, yet the 37.2 trillion cells in our bodies create humanity.

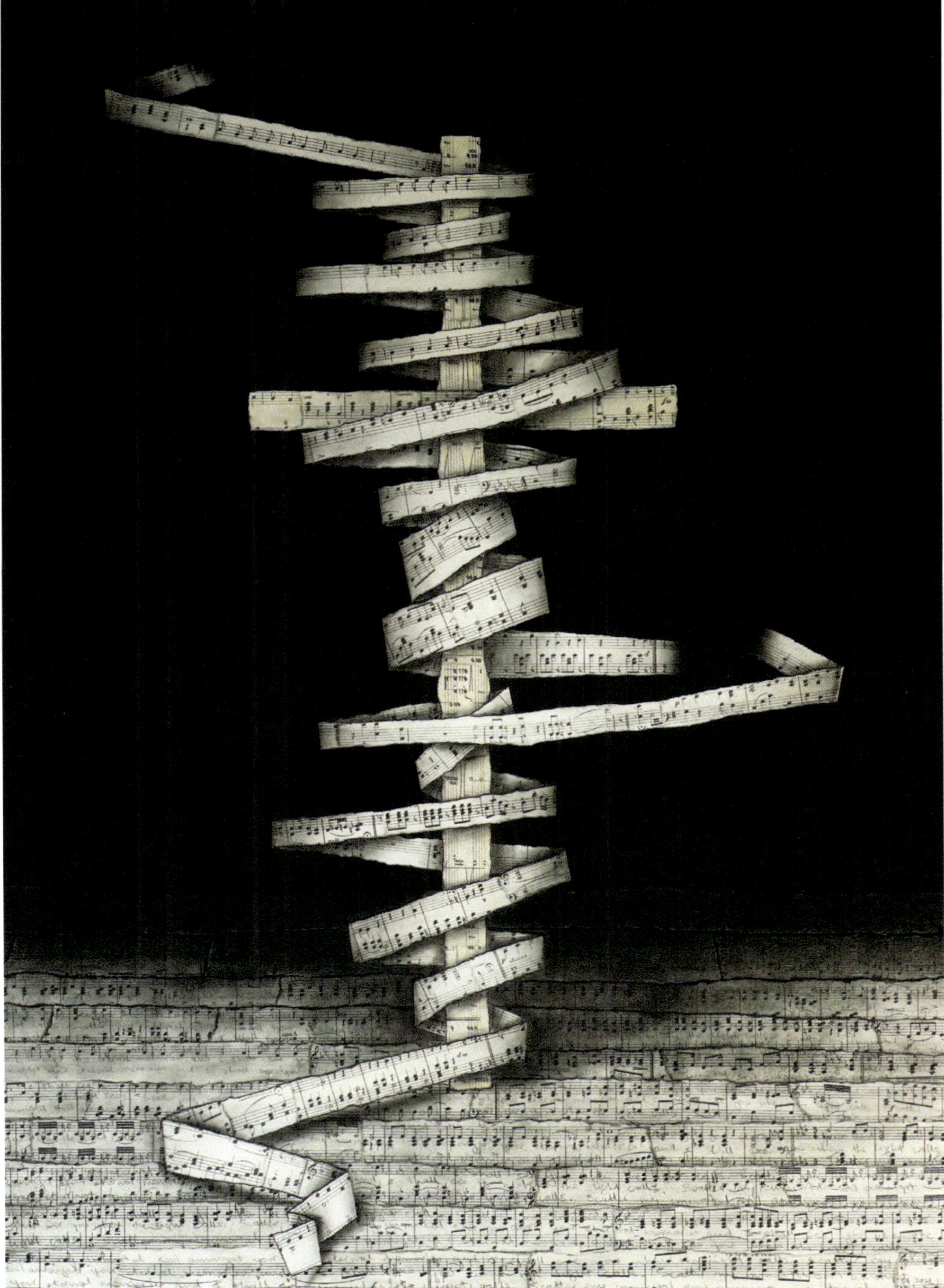

STANLEY GREENING

Inattentional Blindness and the Absence of a Song

Mixed media – collage, pastel, pencil, Musou paint on board

H: 59cm W: 42cm

'Scatter my immortal soul amongst your eternal memories and I shall see you when the light calls.' In 2020, my life shifted dramatically and traumatically when I lost my son. Now on a visual search for meaning; exploring the human compulsion to believe in 'other', the metaphysical and ethereal, as a concept of transformation. I was drawn to the music sheet, not as a musician, but by its beauty and complexity.

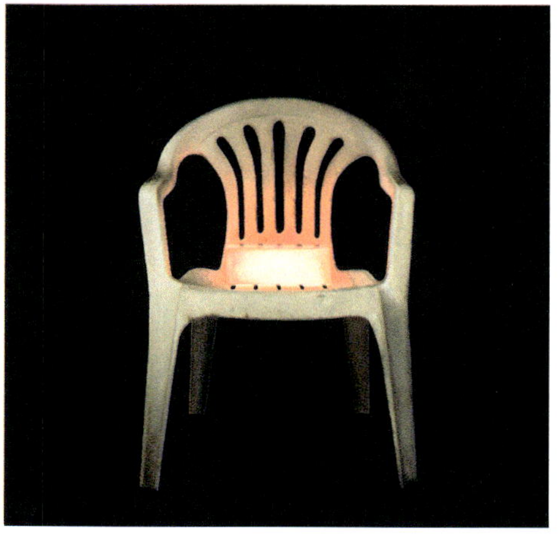

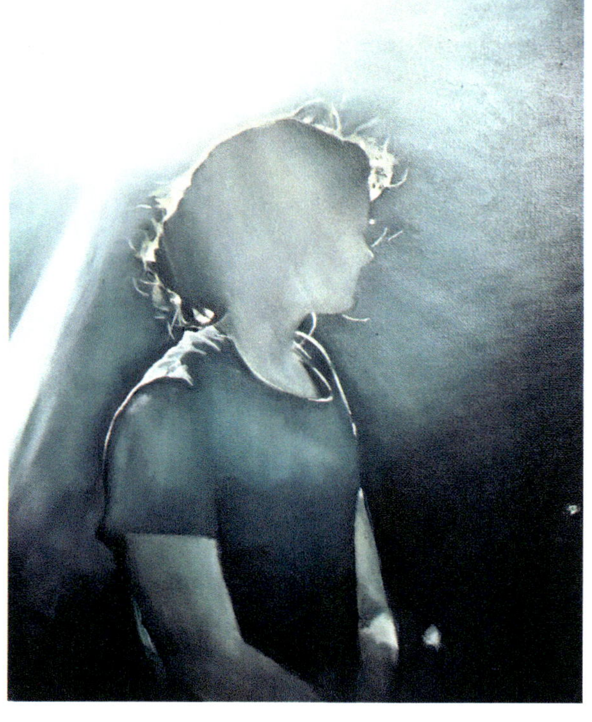

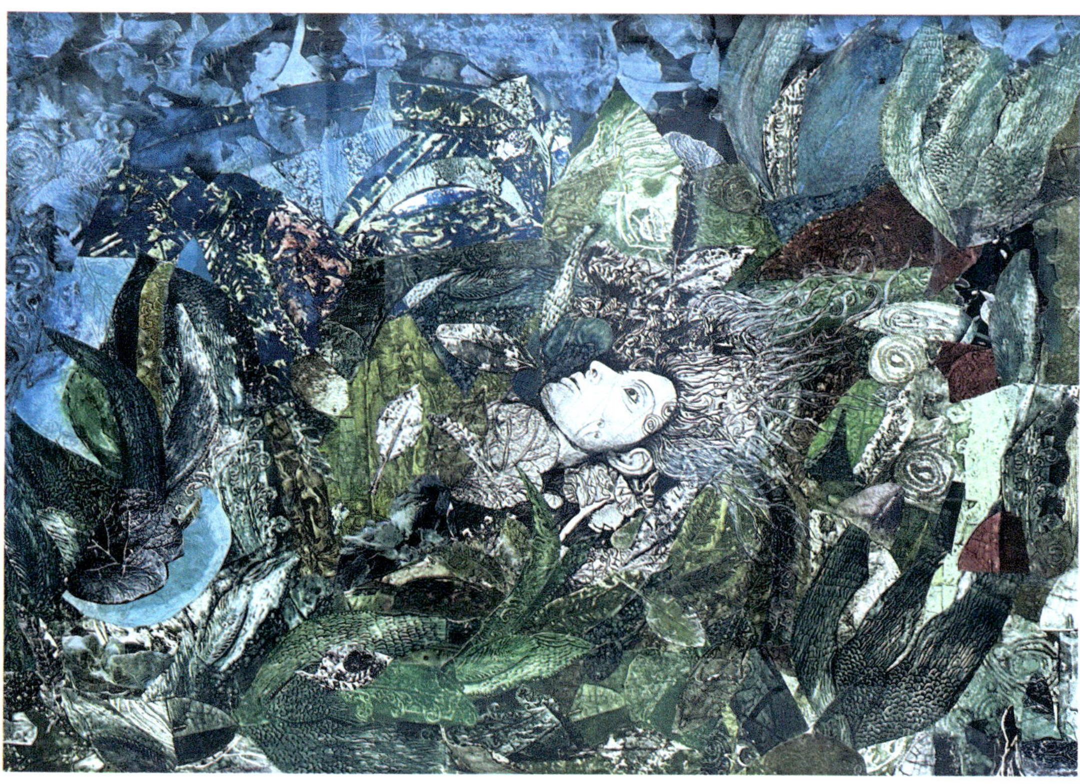

STEPHEN JOHNSTON

Portrait of a Red Chair

Oil on canvas

H: 76cm W: 76cm

The burden of negativity. In a rare moment of stillness and clarity when driving home early one morning, I stopped at a red traffic light. Alone in the red glow, I sensed I had arrived at something. I switched off the engine and waited. I watched the red light appear and disappear several times. Stilled, I found contentment. I invite the viewer to.

ALI MULROY

Still

Oil on canvas

H: 40cm W: 30cm

The power of stillness within spirituality. Being in stillness is an act of surrender. To open oneself up to peace and wonder. The transformation that light brings and the feeling of peace. An air of mystery and majesty.

ELISABETTA PANCUCCI

From Inside The Garden My Mother Could See The Whole Universe

Monotype, collagraph, gouache and pencil

H: 81cm W: 108cm

I and my mother have always believed in God. She unfolded to me the extraordinary minutiae of the natural world. Transformation is not found in material matters, but in connection with God, through the beauty, wisdom and riches in nature.

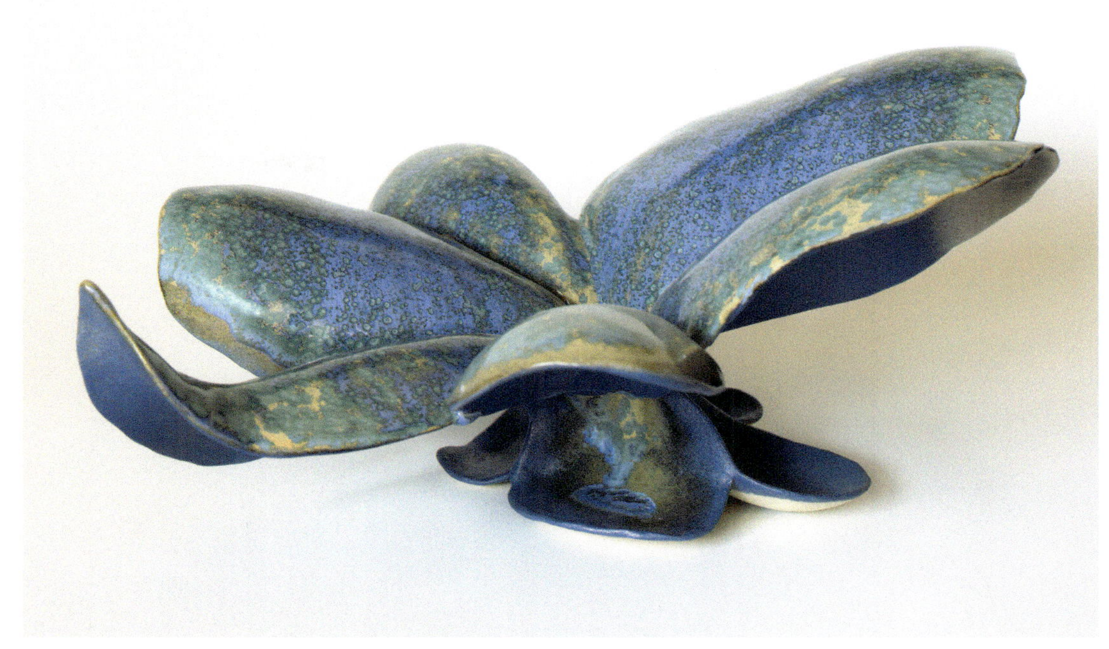

UNU SOHN

Welcome

Ceramic (glazed stoneware)

H: 16cm W: 42cm D: 34cm

An invitation. I am interested in the vulnerability involved in opening a door, implying my desire for you to enter, to connect and relinquish control. There is an electric sense of awe in having such an invitation extended or received. Appreciation for the gravity of that moment, followed by a fear of its consequence.

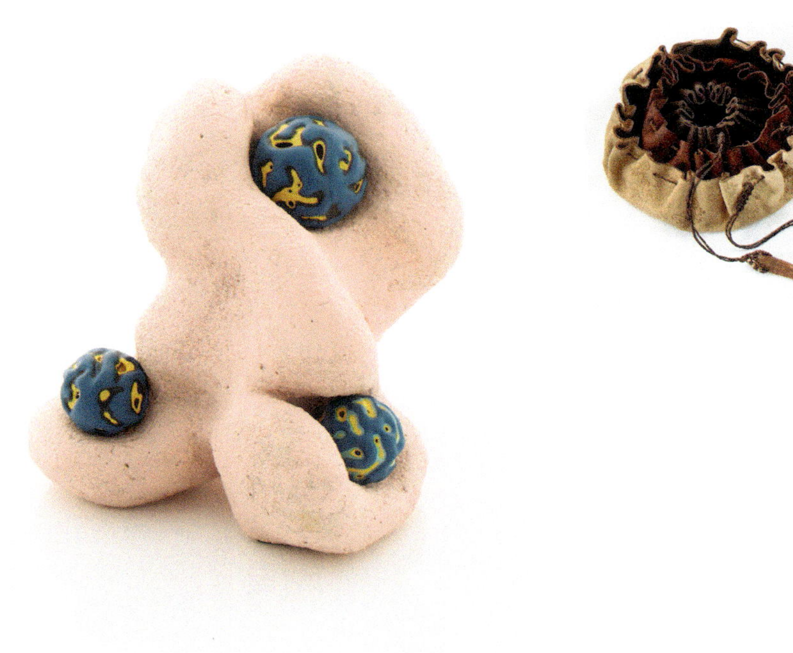

GAYI SOORI

Sentry Epidermidis

Stoneware ceramic with sandblasted coloured porcelain inclusions

H: 30cm W: 28cm D: 28cm

(photo credit Sylvain Deleu)

My Sentry sculptures were inspired by the immune process, where white blood cells engulf and ingest invading microbes. Without our knowledge or conscious control, these miniature battles are constantly fought. Perhaps we should direct our wonder to within ourselves.

MIA LEIJONSTEDT

Portals Into Being

Mixed media installation

H: 6cm W: 33cm D: 22cm

A tale of a spiritual journey. The nested soft vessels on show may contain all that we carry with us internally; things we hold dear, or experiences that hold us back. It asks questions: who placed it there, are you free to choose what is in your vessel? A portal to connect with the ethereal and with the earthly.

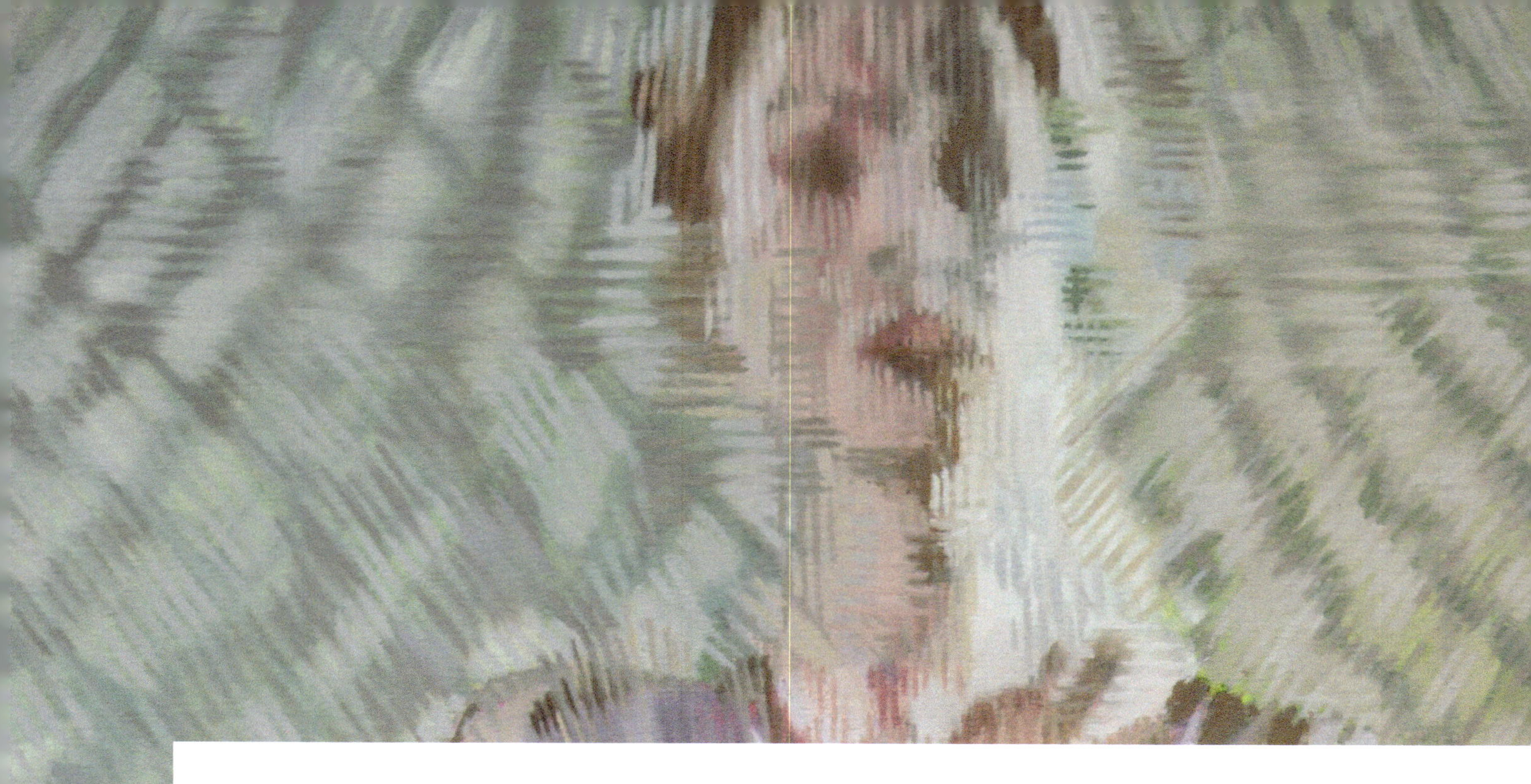

EARTHRISE

KARA, a young woman, just sixteen years old, vibrant, joyous, with many plans for her future, contracted cancer and died. As her spirit left her body, she watched her parents' grief. It was a pain that broke them, each differently. Her brother, older, wasted with emotion he could not express, held on to them tightly. It was a cavernous hurt that led them into separate spaces of lonely anguish.

God loved Kara. Recognising Him and the love pouring out of Him towards her, she felt her whole self dance with joy as He embraced her. It was an enfolding she never wanted to end but, remembering, she asked if He might grant her a choice – to stay with Him or to return to her beloved family. His eyes, so tender and loving, held hers, and He gave her one earth hour to decide.

The angel Delvina, appointed as her guide, took her hand.

'Blink,' she said.

They stood by a waterhole, fed from a waterfall dropping from a high stone outcrop sprouting with orchids, daisies, all manner of rockface plants. Kara nestled on lush grass underneath a huge, vibrant, spreading tree. The sounds of animals and insects filled her ears. Monkeys chattered, birds sang or tapped on bark, the drone of bees – everything sang with its own sound and its whole heart. Creatures, angels and other beings, some lapping at the water – no predator, no prey – harmony. And God walked among it all.

Before her beckoned life without fear. Fear of anything in the past, any mistreatment, aggression, oppression. No outworking of

power and its relentless pressing. No dislike, envy, comparison, hatred. To journey with no fear of attack or any kind of vulnerability.

She blinked again. Darkness. Absolute darkness. She lifted her hand to her face but could see nothing. She expected an overpowering, debilitating fear. Afraid of what might come to meet her, grab her, overpower her, kill her! But... there was none. She had never known such an experience of safety. How was that possible?

She extended her palm and it was grasped. 'Delvina,' she breathed.

'Of course,' said the angel.

'Where am I?' she asked, curious as she hung suspended.

'Watch,' said Delvina.

Her eyes adjusted as the angel positioned them to the rear of the dark-grey, pitted, uneven surface of the moon. They waited as a light emerged, and then Kara's breath caught in her throat, and she held it. Unbelievably, before her eyes, the earth was rising, a blue marble emerging from behind the moon. So blue, so beautiful, so stately, and her heart longed for home.

A moment, her eyes readjusted. Now she beheld a large spiral galaxy.

'The sense of being enough, alongside being nothing in the Presence of Fullness.'

'That's your galaxy,' said Delvina. 'The Milky Way.'

'How is this possible?' thought Kara. 'Why can I breathe, move, exist?' She looked at Delvina, identifying her form as comparable, but also transparently distinct from her own.

'Will I become like you?' she asked.

'Different and more,' said Delvina. 'Blink.'

She did so and became suddenly overwhelmed by her mistakes, her lies, her jealousy of her brother, her fearfulness, her determination to win, to be the best, to succeed, and tears fell. She sat down, finding herself unexpectedly on verdant grass, and put her head in her hands.

'I don't want this me,' she said.

'I want you, all of you, always,' came another voice, one she knew – God's.

And love's potion infused her as exquisite perfume permeated the space, filling her nose, her very being, its potency creating a circle of light around her.

The sense of being enough, alongside being nothing in the Presence of Fullness.

... of joy within a suffusion of unparalleled ecstasy.

... of completion in the manifestation of wholeness.

'We have much to do,' He laughed.

And consummate bliss embraced and in-filled her. It brimmed into swirls of euphoric movement, as if together they had begun an intimate dance of immeasurable happiness. Unable to contain it, she opened her mouth and sounds of joyous glory joined the glorious song of creation.

'Blink and you may return,' said God.

'Tell them I love them,' said Kara.

'They know,' replied God.

« **Detail** – See page 17

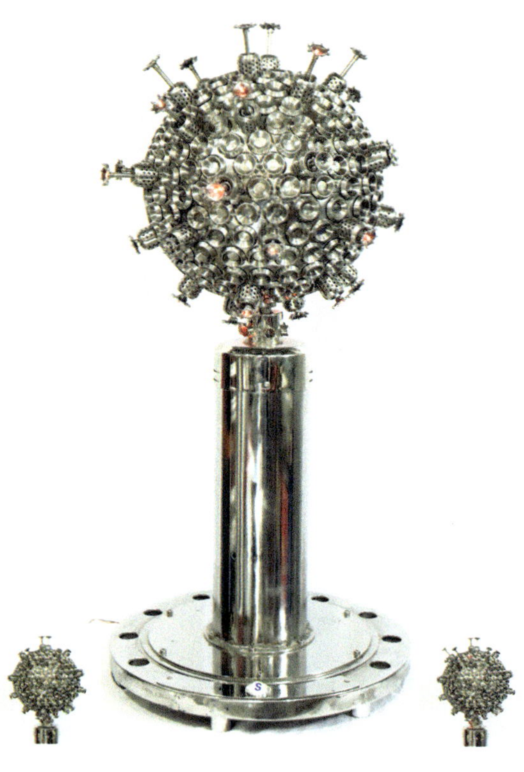

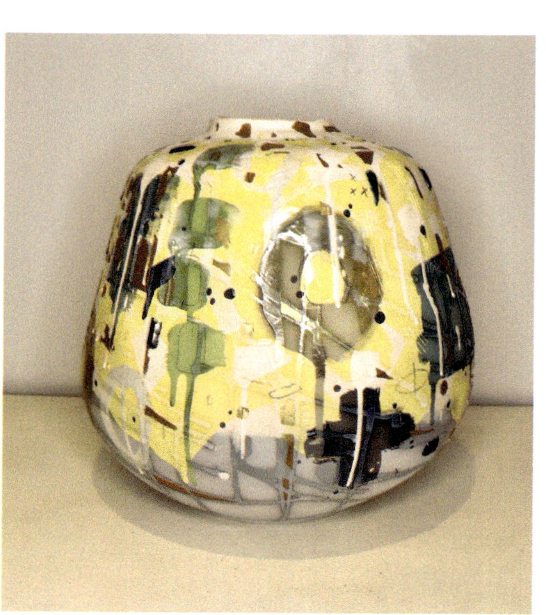

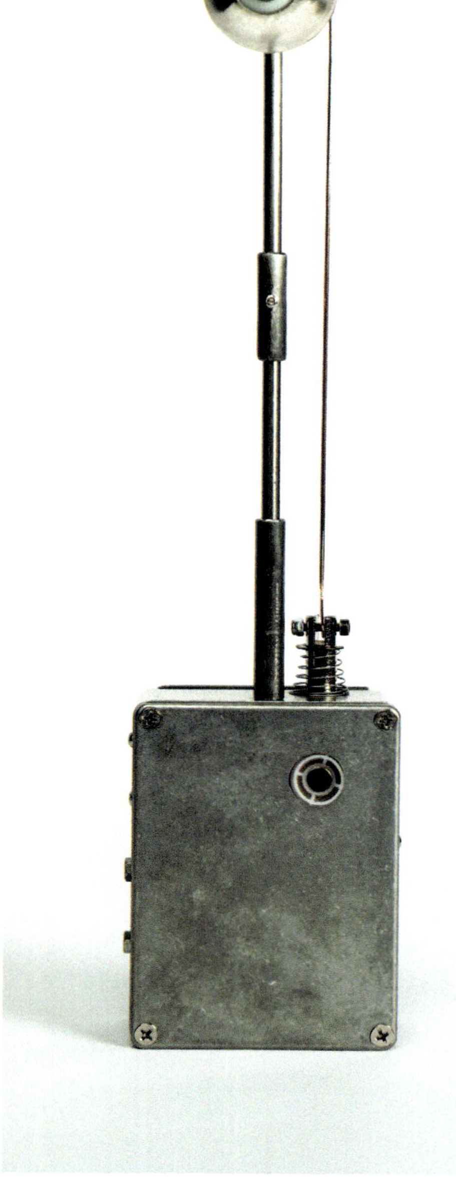

TONY TANNER

Going Viral – Covid-19 – a Most Resilient Virus

Metal sculpture with sensors

H: 82cm W: 40cm D: 40cm

Inspired by the Covid-19 pandemic, the work incorporates a map of the globe, demonstrating both vaccine application and virus mutation. A sensor triggered by an approaching viewer causes the sphere to revolve and morph into the spreading virus. This infinitesimal virus has controlled our lives, claimed many in death, confounded leaders and disrupted our world.

JIM BOND

Silver Blink

Interactive kinetic silver and glass eye sculpture

H: 29cm W: 8cm D: 9cm

In 1914 my grandfather, the only survivor of a frontline explosion at Passchendaele, lost his eye. As a child I was fascinated by his lifelike but vacant glass eye. Blink attempts to breathe life into a glass eye. To make it responsive. When you look, it looks back, it has a soul.

DAWN HAJITTOFI

Then There Was Light

Large coiled earthenware vessel decorated with coloured slips, underglazes and pencil, partially glazed with additional gilt

H: 41cm W: 42cm D: 42 cm

On the first day of God's creation story He said, '"Let there be light," and there was light' (Genesis 1:3). For me, that first demonstration exhibits God's eternal creative power, majesty and glory. A piece to tell the unfolding story of creation and the beginning of life.

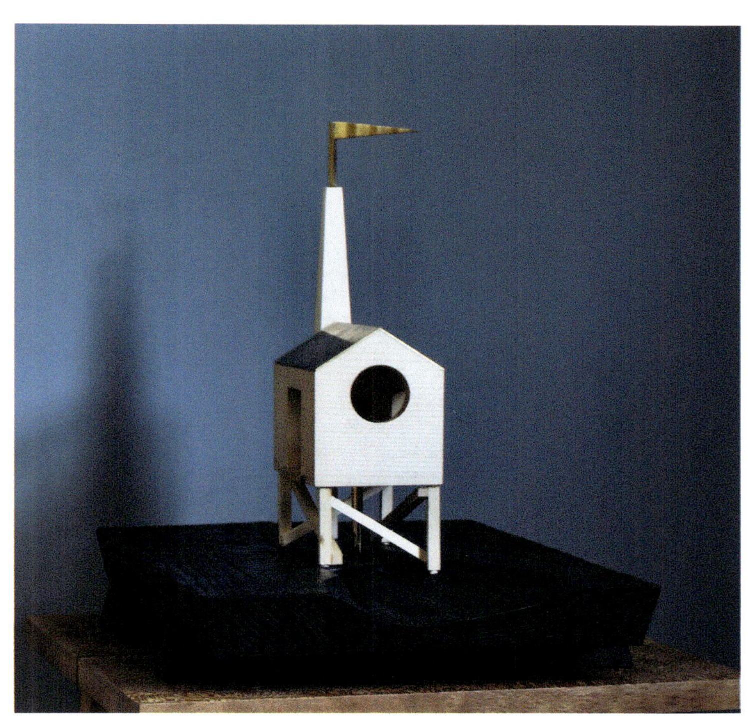

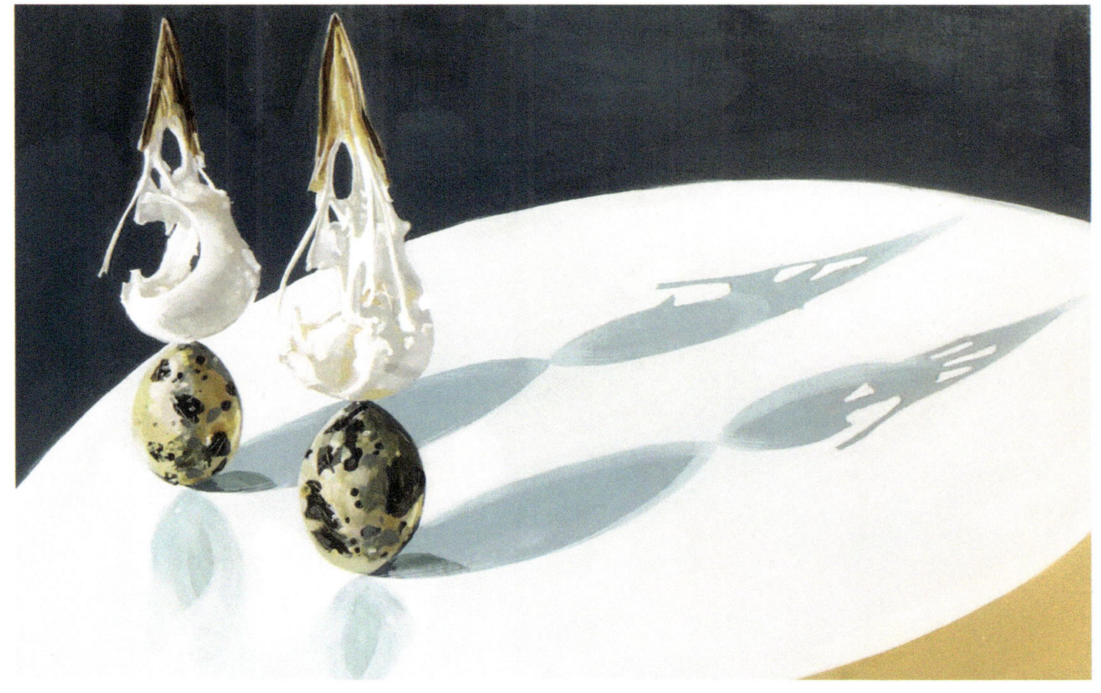

SANDY BUCHANAN

Dreams & Nightmares

Sculpture – offcuts, metal and wood

H: 30cm W: 33cm D: 23cm

The piece is a continued exploration into my relationship with depression, often awestruck how the human mind creates incredible highs and devastating lows. Unease, anxiety manifest, but the moon inside the piece is where hopes and dreams rest cocooned. A brass flag flies for mental health awareness.

JENNY BLOUNT

Balance

Waterbased ink on board

H: 20cm W: 39cm

The shock of watching Ukrainian refugees under bombardment left me with a sense of privilege for my life. A contemporary *memento mori* recognising the fragility of life; the speed of passing time; catching joy when it comes. As an adult, awe and wonder now coexist alongside bittersweetness.

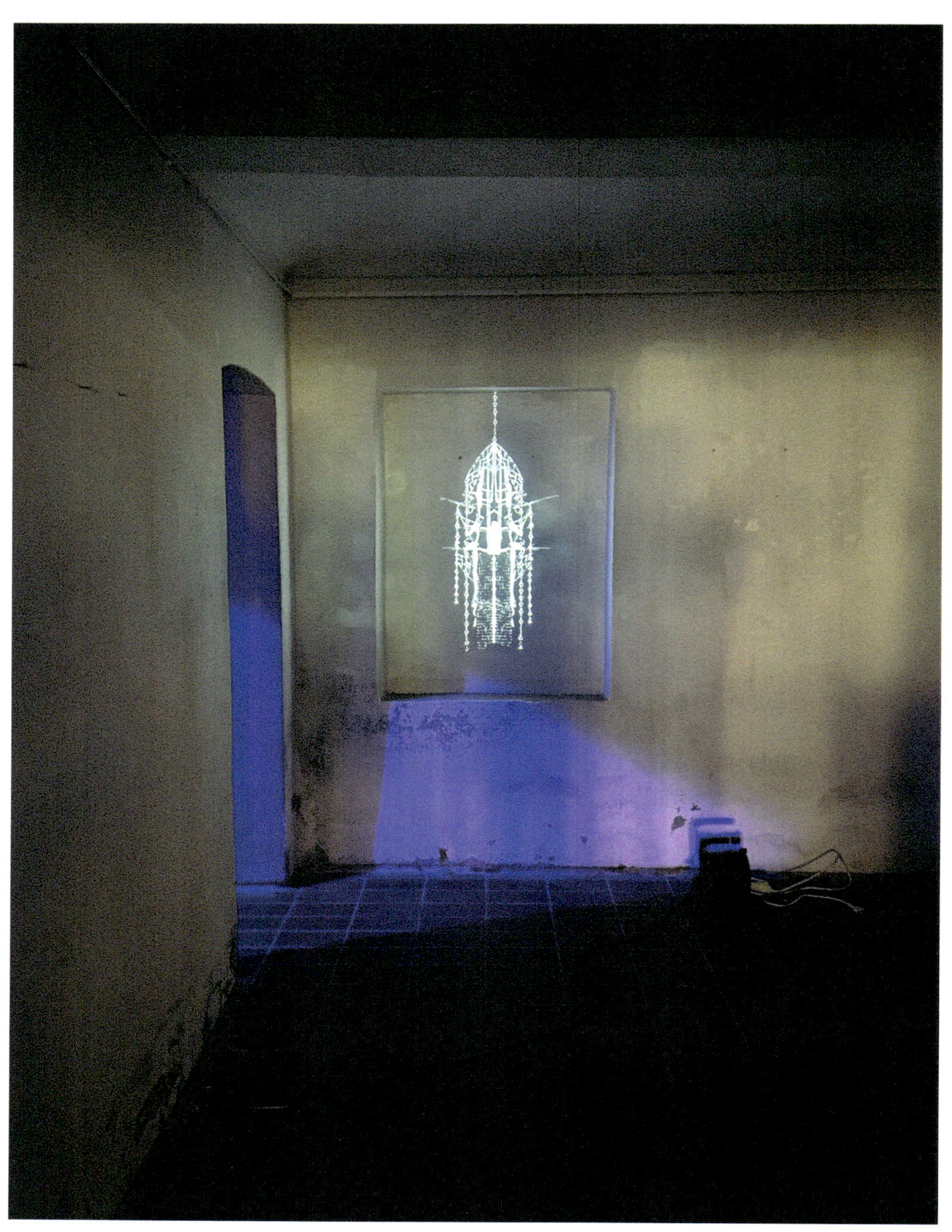

WILLIAM LOWRY

The Moth, the Madonna

Digital composition of original biro drawings, photographs, prints and paintings projected onto stone, with original sound piece written and produced by the artist

H: 82cm W: 62cm

With images from the sanctuary of the Black Madonna of Oropa, Italy, interleaved with an allusive moth-like figure, and accompanied by a musical composition, the piece offers an immersive experience. With themes of memory, childhood, the maternal, nature, it underscores our yearning for the sacred in everyday life.

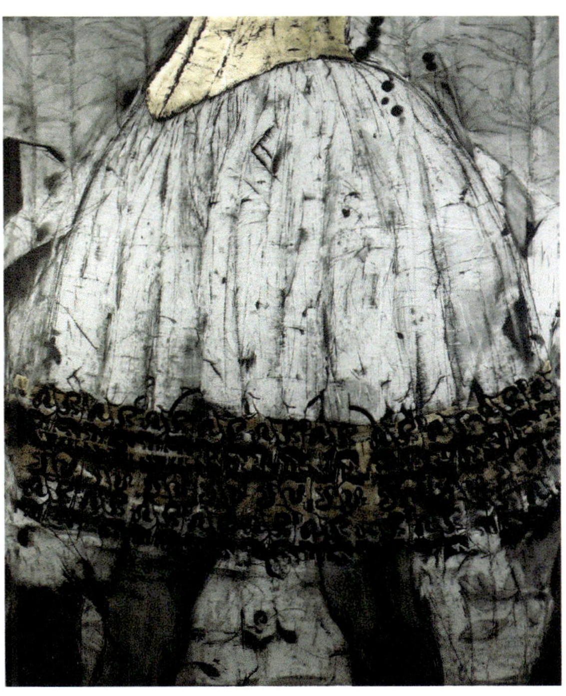

JOY WOLFENDEN-BROWN

Ochre Light

Oil paint on paper (framed)

H: 128cm W: 38cm

At times in life, the veil between ourselves and the core of our being becomes almost transparent. There are moments of spaciousness and of restriction. Both states offer fruitfulness but also fragility and risk. Fragile, awkward, expectant, still, there is awkwardness in presence. A quest. Her hope of a sanctum.

JULIA POLONSKI

Hemmed

Charcoal and pencil on paper with gold finish

H: 156cm W: 129cm

Drawn after a close examination of Degas' sculpture, the 'Little Dancer'. Looking at fabric and potential narratives led to an exploration of patterning, and the marks of damaged, stained material. Worn cloth is a document that holds the body's narrative, a map of physical occupation, human experience and personal history.

I heard a voice
thunder from the Throne:

'Look! Look! God has moved
into the neighbourhood,
making his home with men
and women! They're his
people, he's their God.
He'll wipe every tear
from their eyes.

'Death is gone for good –
tears gone, crying gone, pain
gone – all the first order of
things gone.'

The Enthroned continued,
'Look! I'm making...

» **Detail** — See page 19

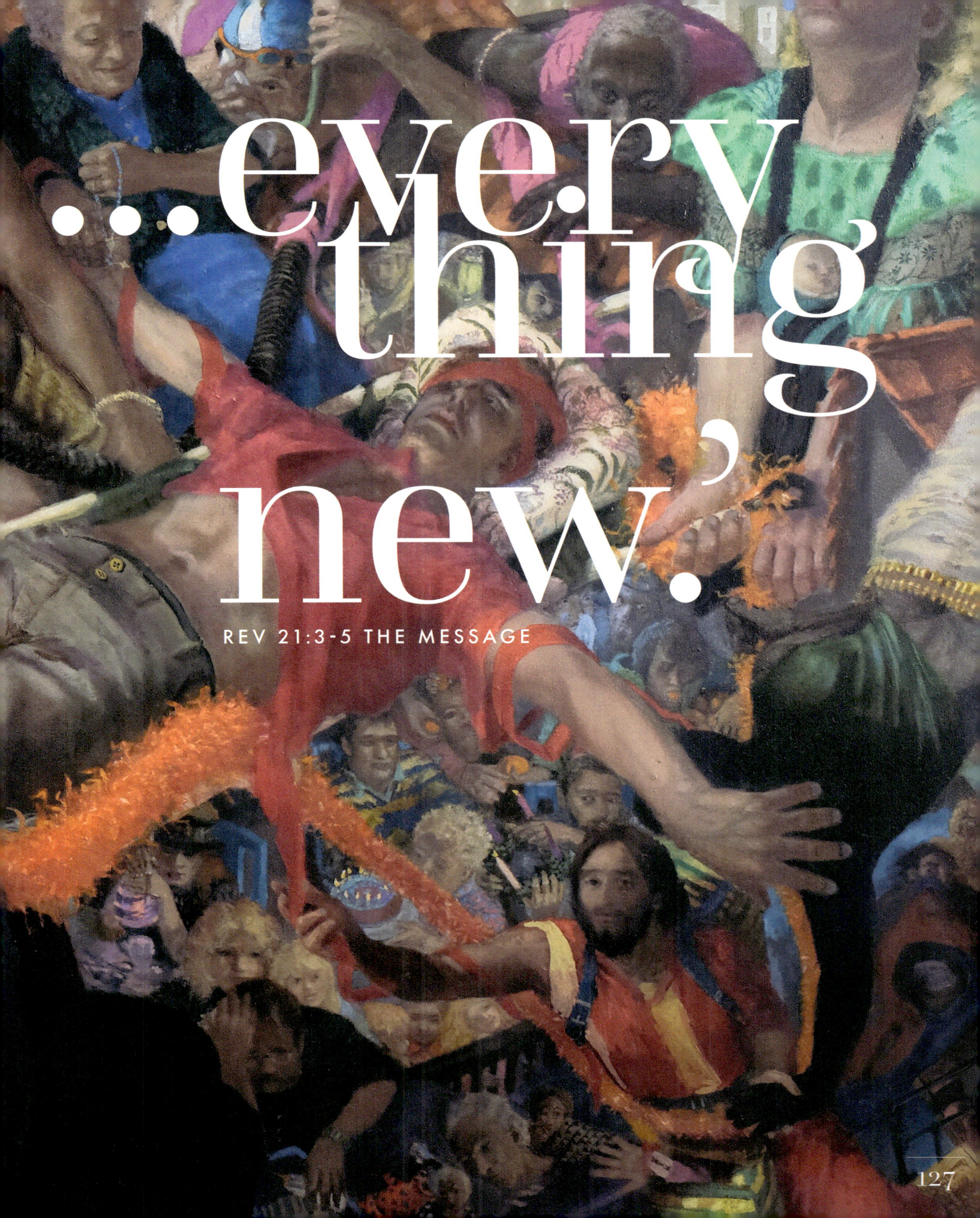
...every
thing
new.'
REV 21:3-5 THE MESSAGE

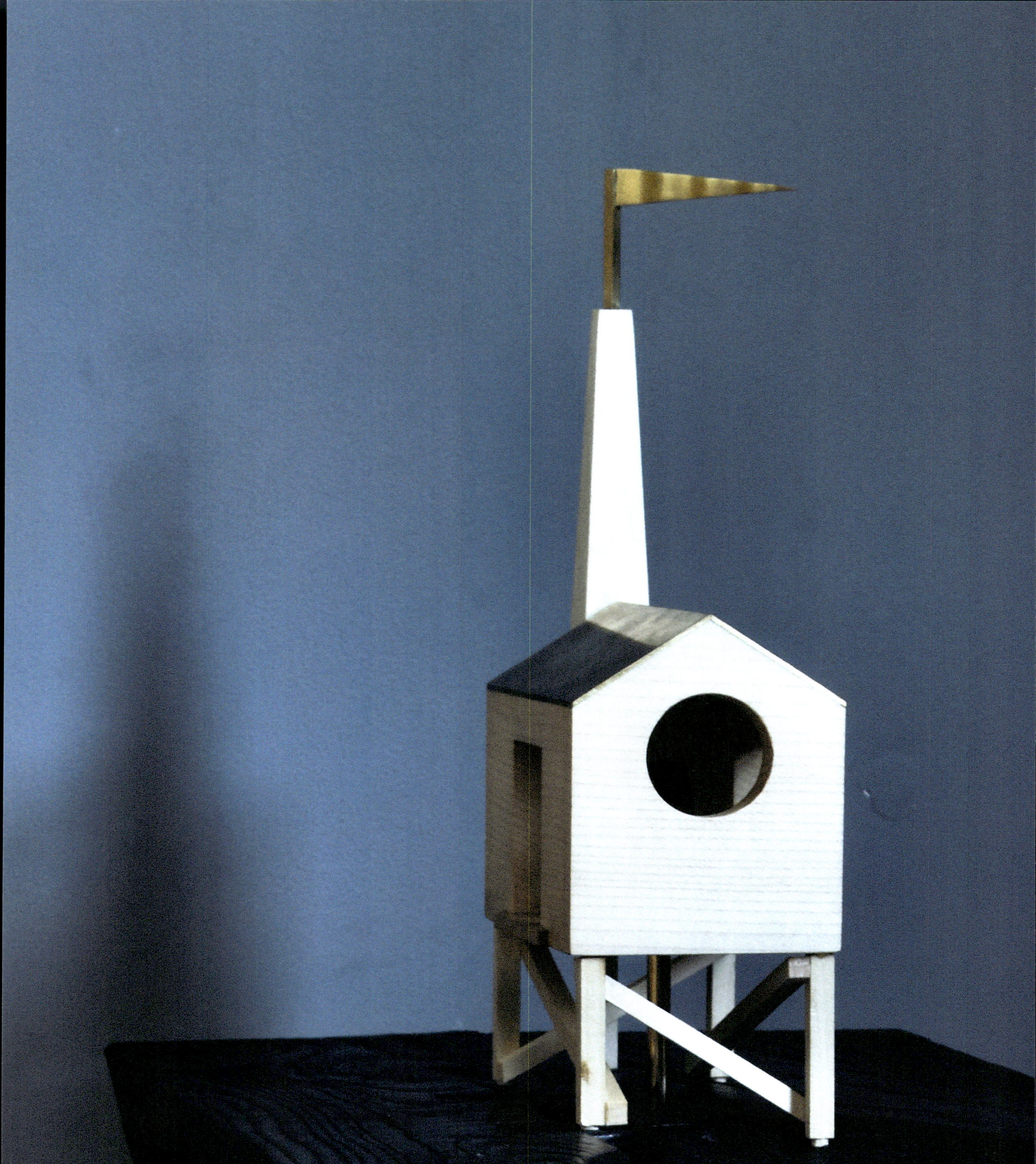

curator

THE INVISIBLE IN TERMS OF THE VISIBLE

Alastair Gordon, artist and co-curator Chaiya Awards 2023

WRITING IN THE 1940S, Scottish poet Nan Shepherd described her native Cairngorms in terms of both their awesome grandeur and intimate beauty. *The Living Mountain* evoked such a personal encounter of the Highlands we might equally imagine she was writing about a lover or favourite book as much as the Scottish mountains. Often she hiked with no specific destination in mind, reaching nowhere in particular, but having gone out merely to be with the mountain as one visits an old friend.

In curating *Awe+Wonder* I was struck by similar glorious contradictions. This year's artists find moments of awe and wonder in the most antipodal of places. In terms of both the intimate and remote, personal and universal, familial and feral, visions of sublime grandeur in the dregs of a teacup. You may encounter the divine in domestic rituals, transcendence in bodily fluids, a shared meal that builds community, digital realities and portals to other worlds, scientific enquiry, lament in the loss of loved ones, rivers deep and an ocean of astonishment in a darling's eye, and *axis mundi* on the tip of a biro. Even the word 'awe' seems wracked with paradoxical intent. From the Old English, *ege*, meaning 'terror' or 'dread', with possible origins in the Greek for 'pain', we might equally consider the awe of awful as well as the awesome.

It's such familial and contradictory encounters with the sublime I found most intriguing. How to render the invisible in terms of the visible? How to apprehend the indefinite? For my part, I stand in awe of the artists in our exhibition who have achieved this very thing. To take the ruddy stuff of paint, film, clay, plastic, pixels and wood, and then turn them into something that transcends material parts... Wandering the entries was as much to ascend the sheep trails of the Cairngorms.

My heartiest congratulations to all our artists. To borrow from another great wanderer of the mountains, John Muir, who suggested, 'for going out, I found, was really going in',[59] I hope you enjoy roving the pages of this book and find unexpected moments of wonder as you wander. Whether you find yourself in a landscape of nature as void, city, body, digital realm or kitchen table, I trust your journey out will also bring you home.

« **Detail** – See page 123

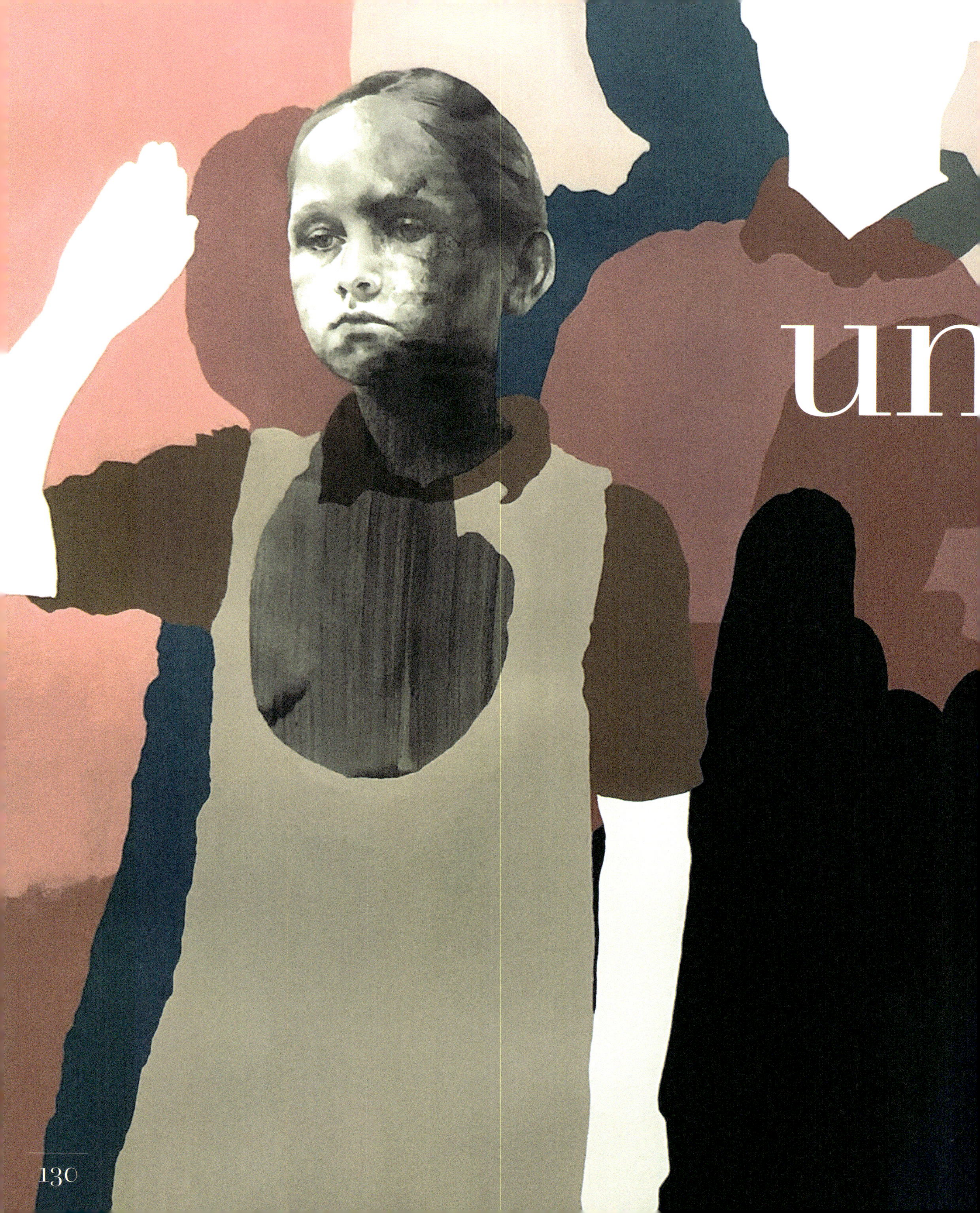
un

seen

Creative therapies are a lifeline for many of the modern slavery survivors we support at Unseen.

Exploring creativity through arts and crafts provides a safe space, away from traumatic memories and the day-to-day struggle to recover.

Our safehouses contain a range of art and craft materials for use at any time, and the resulting photographs, paintings and drawings are displayed on the walls, where they act as a reminder that creativity is deeply important to the process of healing.

Survivors report a sense of pride and a boost to their confidence from having their work on show. There's also a sense of community from seeing the output of past residents. Such interactions give our support staff a new way to communicate with survivors, to help them process their moods, thoughts and feelings.

'I like to see the pictures,' says one of the survivors Unseen works with. '[It] gives me good memories... happy memories...it's home.'

Unseen is proud to partner once again with Chaiya Art Awards in celebrating the empowerment and positivity that art can bring to everyone.

Thank you for your support.

Andrew Wallis OBE
CEO, Unseen UK

Our charity partner Unseen is working towards a world without slavery. It provides safehouses and support in the community for survivors of human trafficking and modern slavery. Unseen also runs the Modern Slavery & Exploitation Helpline and works with individuals, communities, businesses, governments, other charities and statutory agencies such as the police to end slavery forever.

Unseen also uses art as therapy to aid the recovery of survivors.

Chaiya Art Awards helps fund this vital work by donating a percentage of all artwork sales from its exhibitions.

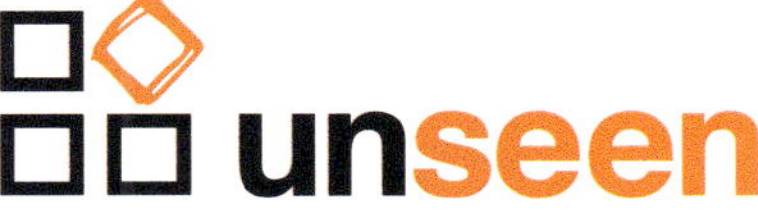

www.unseenuk.org

Registered charity no. 1127620.
Registered company no. 06754171

« Detail — See page 78

endnotes

1. Alastair Gordon, *Why Art Matters* (London: IVP, 2021). Page 6
2. Dacher Keltner, *Awe: The Transformative Power of Everyday Wonder* (London: Allen Lane, 2023). Page 11
3. Jean Arp, artist, sculptor, poet, www.brainyquote.com/quotes/jean_arp_105012. Page 12
4. 1 Kings 19:12, KJV. Page 13
5. Gordon Hempton, acoustic ecologist, www.goodreads.com/quotes/7267419-silence-is-not-the-absence-of-something-but-the-presence. Page 13
6. Monty Python, The Life of Brian (1979). Page 27
7. Franklin D Roosevelt, www.brainyquote.com/quotes/franklin_d_roosevelt_101840. Page 29
8. T S Eliot, *The Waste Land and Other Poems*, www.goodreads.com/quotes/9769127-all-our-knowledge-brings-us-nearer-to-our-ignorance-all. Page 30
9. Martin Heidegger, www.goodreads.com/author/quotes/6191.Martin_Heidegger. Page 31
10. www.brainyquote.com/quotes/dia_mirza_1098199?src=t_oneness. Page 38
11. www.brainyquote.com/authors/pericles-quotes. Page 39
12. www.quozio.com/quote/fa900503/1025/hope-is-like-a-bird-that-senses-dawn-and-carefully-starts. Page 40
13. With thanks to John F Schumaker, whose work inspired me to write this piece. www.newint.org/columns/essays/2016/04/01/psycho-spiritual-crisis. Page 40
14. www.goodnewsnetwork.org/maya-angelou-quote-on-joy-and-love. Page 40
15. www.encyclopedia.com/literature-and-arts/language-linguistics-and-literary-terms/english-vocabulary-d/demoralize. Page 41
16. www.generositymonk.com/2020/07/12/henri-nouwen-and-vincent-van-gogh. Page 41
17. www.brainyquote.com/quotes/freya_stark_124546. Page 48
18. www.brainyquote.com/quotes/mother_teresa_107032. Page 48
19. www.brainyquote.com/quotes/wayne_dyer_384143. Page 49
20. www.geneva-academy.ch/galleries/today-s-armed-conflicts. Page 49
21. www.statista.com/statistics/1293492/ukraine-war-casualties. Page 49
22. Dacher Keltner, *Awe: The Transformative Power of Everyday Wonder*. Page 50
23. www.goodreads.com/quotes/38640-earth-s-crammed-with-heaven-and-every-common-bush-afire-with.. Page 50
24. www.brainyquote.com/quotes/oprah_winfrey_163087. Page 56

25. www.goodreads.com/quotes/67563-gratitude-unlocks-the-fullness-of-life-it-turns-what-we. Page 57
26. www.theguardian.com/books/2023/jan/05/awe-by-dacher-keltner-review-the-transformative-power-of-wonder. Page 59
27. C S Lewis, *The Joyful Christian* © copyright 1977 CS Lewis Pte Ltd. Extracts used with permission. Page 61
28. www.theguardian.com/books/2023/jan/05/awe-by-dacher-keltner-review-the-transformative-power-of-wonder. Page 66
29. Adapted from Luke 1:28-38. Page 69
30. www.goodreads.com/quotes/501115-lie-still-lie-still-my-breaking-heart-my-silent-heart. Page 72
31. Leo Tolstoy, *War and Peace*, www.goodreads.com/quotes/7496646-there-is-something-so-enchanting-in-the-smile-of-melancholy. Page 72
32. www.goodreads.com/quotes/228308-you-may-not-control-all-the-events-that-happen-to-you. Page 73
33. www.quotefancy.com/muhammad-yunus-quotes. Page 74
34. www.brainyquote.com/quotes/desmond_tutu_383784. Page 75
35. www.goodgoodgood.co/articles/humanity-quotes. Page 75
36. www.goodreads.com/quotes/tag/art-quotes?page=3. Page 81
37. www.nasa.gov/content/ultra-high-definition-video-gallery. Page 82
38. www.maiawalczak.com/products/cosmic-art-print-maia-walczak-the-overview-effect. Page 83
39. www.abeautiful.world/stories/the-overview-effect/. Page 83
40. www.abeautiful.world/stories/the-overview-effect/. Page 83
41. *Back to Earth*, www.sealpress.com/titles/nicole-stott/back-to-earth/9781541675049/. Page 83
42. www.geographyrealm.com/overview-effect-quotes-from-astronauts/. Page 83
43. www.brainyquote.com/quotes/neil_armstrong_101138. Page 83
44. www.goodreads.com/quotes/9648808-i-find-it-curious-that-i-never-heard-any-astronaut. Page 83
45. www.goodreads.com/quotes/8094696-to-look-out-at-this-kind-of-creation-out-here. Page 83
46. www.goodreads.com/quotes/101712-i-looked-and-looked-but-i-didn-t-see-god-speaking. Page 83
47. www.goodreads.com/quotes/22847-the-creation-of-something-new-is-not-accomplished-by-the Page 90
48. www.teacherswithapps.com/67552-2 Page 90
49. A reference to the poem 'Solitude' by Ella Wheeler Wilcox. Page 91
50. www.teacherswithapps.com/67552-2. Page 91
51. Auguries of Innocence, www.poetryfoundation.org/poems/43650/auguries-of-innocence. Page 93
52. www.goodreads.com/quotes/8524438. Page 93
53. www.brainyquote.com/topics/hope-quotes. Page 95
54. www.brainyquote.com/quotes/chanda_kochhar_848186. Page 99
55. www.bookroo.com/quotes/erwin-raphael-mcmanus. Page 102
56. www.annclifford.co.uk/blog/you-cant-be-brave-if-youre-not-scared. Page 107
57. John O'Donohue, *Divine Beauty: The Invisible Embrace* (New York: HarperCollins, 2004). Page 114
58. Bryan Stevenson, *Just Mercy* (New York: Spiegel & Grau, 2014). Page 115
59. www.goodreads.com/quotes/32946-i-only-went-out-for-a-walk-and-finally-concluded. Page 129

thanks

Book text written by:
Ann Clifford

Art compiled by:
Alastair Gordon, Ann Clifford, Katrina Moss

Judges:
Marcus Lyon, Kaffe Fassett, Alastair Adams, Dr Christo Kefalas, Favour Jonathan, Alastair Gordon, Ann Clifford, Katrina Moss

Exhibition curators:
Alastair Gordon, Julia Lucero

Social Media and Promotional Video:
Katie Carter, Kate Burke

Book design:
David Salmon

Website, Branding & Marketing:
Josh Morley, Richard Ward

Administration:
Anna Stellardi, Jordan Martindale, Katrina Moss

Sponsors:
Souter Charitable Trust
The Anchor Foundation

With thanks from Ann

This project, despite all difficulties, is a joy. Its spiritual inspiration encapsulates a legacy that will live long in peoples' hearts. Thank you, artists all – I salute you.

Many thanks to Instant Apostle, David Salmon the designer, and the vibrant and encouraging team.

Thank you, Katrina, for your vision, inspiration, the journey of our Really Big Adventure, and for being my friend for decades.

Friends and family and wider family, thank you for your constant support, particularly my husband, Steve.

Thank You, Trinity Three, from whom I receive constant, needful, refilling.

With thanks from Katrina

To all the many artists who engaged with these awards, and shared with us how you interpreted Awe and Wonder. We thoroughly enjoyed seeing your creativity, imagination and skills; it is always difficult that we can only select a fraction of the wonderful work submitted.

To every individual, company or trust who has had any input into the Chaiya Art Awards, your contribution large or small is so, so appreciated.

To my friends, my family and my church, thank you for your continued encouragement and prayers, which sustain me throughout this challenging journey.

To Ann, I could not and would not want to do this without you.

Lastly and most importantly to God who birthed this project, who I pray directs and guides it and allows me to share in the adventure: Your continued kindness and love fill me with Awe and Wonder.

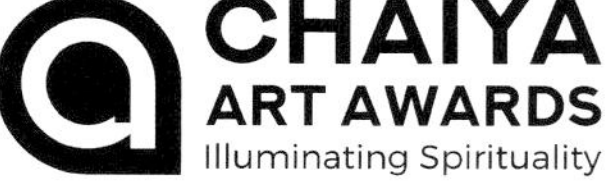